A Commercial Republic

American Political Thought

Wilson Carey McWilliams and Lance Banning
Founding Editors

A Commercial Republic

America's Enduring Debate over
Democratic Capitalism

Mike O'Connor

 UNIVERSITY PRESS OF KANSAS

Published by the University Press of Kansas (Lawrence, Kansas 66045), which was
organized by the Kansas Board of Regents and is operated and funded by Emporia State
University, Fort Hays State University, Kansas State University, Pittsburg State
University, the University of Kansas, and Wichita State University

Library of Congress Cataloging-in-Publication Data is available.

Library of Congress Control Number: 2014938665
ISBN 978-0-7006-1971-9 (cloth)

British Library Cataloguing in Publication Data is available.

Printed in the United States of America

10 9 8 7 6 5 4 3 2 1

The paper used in this publication is recycled and contains 30 percent postconsumer waste.
It is acid free and meets the minimum requirements of the American National Standard for
Permanence of Paper for Printed Library Materials Z39.48-1992.

To Rebecca, with appreciation and great love

Contents

Acknowledgments

I first began to consider the issues that motivated this book as a graduate student in the American studies program at the University of Texas at Austin. In my first semester there, I and my fellow entering students took a required course from Dr. Robert Crunden. Giving shape to my poorly articulated interests, he suggested that I write that semester's paper on Friedrich Hayek. His direction was instrumental in helping me to focus my research area. Soon after that semester ended, the fifty-eight-year-old Crunden died suddenly of a heart attack. My experience with him, though quite brief, greatly affected the intellectual development that led to this book, and I do not know if it could have been written without him.

Among faculty at Texas, Bill Stott was crucial in helping me to find my voice as a writer. Though I never worked directly with Steve Hoelscher, he consistently expressed an enthusiasm for my scholarly interests. I only met Harry Cleaver once, but a twenty-minute office visit with him forever changed the way I thought about scholarly writing. After I enrolled in Daniel Slesnick's undergraduate microeconomics course, he allowed me to pester him incessantly about economic theory even as I made few attempts to bone up on my rusty calculus. Jeff Meikle and Janet Davis led me through comprehensive exams, helping me to obtain the background necessary for a project as wide ranging as this one. Committee members Gretchen Ritter, Julia Mickenberg, and Bill Brands all gave valuable input on the dissertation as it lumbered toward completion. Dan Bonevac was a thoughtful and engaged philosopher who was consistently generous with his time. Mark Smith introduced me to the field of American intellectual history, indulged my overly ambitious dissertation, and eventually agreed to chair my committee. Acquiring him as a mentor and friend is among the most valuable achievements of my graduate years.

In my time at the University of Texas, I was particularly fortunate to have met fellow students Kyle Barnett, Chris Jennings, and Amy Ware, who became my good friends. John Balz, Alicia Barber, Andrew Busch, Bill Bush, Russ Cobb, Jonathan Davis, Joel Dinerstein, Bill Fagelson, Tony Fassi, Adam Golub, John Haddad, Matt Hedstrom, Elinore Longobardi, and Siva Vaidhyanathan provided valuable feedback and advice on all manner of subjects. Alan Blake was one of the few friends I made during this period who was not a graduate student. He nonetheless exhibited more excitement about this project than just about anyone else, and I appreciated it. Finally, it was in 1998 that I first met Allison Perlman, who soon became my roommate, sounding board, adviser, proofreader, and closest of friends. My relationship with her defined my time in Austin, and I could not be more appreciative of her emotional and intellectual support.

After graduate school, I became an itinerant lecturer, moving across the country three times in as many years. Such transience did not nurture the focus required for a long-term research and writing project, and I was desperately in need of colleagues. I found them on the Internet, living all over the country. United by a desire to build a space to pursue a mutual interest in American intellectual history, these historians came to constitute my primary professional community. We founded first a blog, then a conference, and ultimately the Society for U.S. Intellectual History (S-USIH). It was within this scholarly and institutional environment that I worked out the ideas that define this book. Whatever contributions I have to offer would not have seen the light of day were it not for the camaraderie, insight, knowledge, and hard work of these early bloggers: Julian Nemeth, Lauren Kientz Anderson, Joe Petrulionis, Sylwester Ratowt, Ben Alpers, James Levy, Paul Murphy, and Tim Lacy. Through the annual conference, I was able to meet David Steigerwald, Jennifer Burns, and Jennifer Ratner-Rosenhagen, each of whom has helped me to think through my ideas more clearly. Three other members of the S-USIH community have played a particularly prominent role in the development of this book. Ray Haberski has been especially generous with his time and good humor. The society's first president, Andrew Hartman, has been invaluable in sharing his knowledge of twentieth-century US history, belief in the value of the project, and great friendship. More than anyone save me, my good friend David Sehat has left an imprint on this book. His pointed criticism and sage counsel have made its writing clearer and its arguments sharper.

At the University Press of Kansas, Fred Woodward deserves great thanks for not only seeing the potential in my original proposal but also shepherding the manuscript through a process of completion to which I brought interminable delays. The supportive criticism of readers James

Morone and Joyce Appleby inspired me to produce a book worthy of their time and attention, and I am grateful to Peter Onuf for his helpful critique. Joan Sherman's copyediting improved my writing immeasurably, and I very much appreciate the patience and professionalism shown by Larisa Martin in producing the book itself.

Nicholas Dagen Bloom helped me to navigate my first year as a full-time faculty member at the New York Institute of Technology, and Mike Gorman did the same for me at Penn State–Erie. I was lucky to teach for three years at Georgia State University and am grateful for the feedback and support of faculty members I knew there, particularly Brian Ingrassia, Larry Youngs, Rob Baker, Alex Cummings, Karen Phoenix, Larry Grubbs, Tom Bobal, and John McMillian.

Years ago, when I was an inexperienced graduate student, I wrote to David Hollinger and asked if I could talk to him about my project during an upcoming visit to the Bay Area. He agreed to meet, and he offered some encouraging counsel. His willingness to do that made a big impression on me, and it speaks well of his generosity and commitment to the discipline. Since then, I have frequently prevailed upon others whom I do not know for help with my work, and the presumption of a mutually supportive academic enterprise has seldom let me down. Those who have responded to my requests to read parts of this book by sharing their time and insight include Daniel Horowitz, Kevin Mattson, Brian Domitrovic, and Angus Burgin.

My abiding interest in politics and history I owe to my father, Jack. It is no doubt because of him that my earliest memories include the words *Vietnam* and *Watergate*. My mother, Susan Hoppe, encouraged me to do what I love while exemplifying the commitment to meeting one's responsibilities. My brother Brian has always inspired me with his work ethic and commitment to improving himself. I could not have gotten to this point without the love and support of my family.

Over a decade ago, I took home a three-month-old puppy from the Austin pound. I cannot claim that Sophie has refined my thinking or improved my writing, but she is the only one who has been with me every day and in every city that I was writing this book. That makes it hers as much as anyone's. In writing this book, I relied heavily on her affection and enthusiasm, which never wavered.

Finally, one of the few positive things that I can say about the life of the nomadic and marginally employed scholar is that it allowed me to meet Rebecca, the woman who is now my wife. She has said that this book "took away my husband," and no doubt she is right. Yet she never questioned my belief in its value, nor did she express anything less than complete confidence in my abilities and total support for my ambitions. The facts did not necessarily offer support for her faith in me, but I never saw it waver. For that I will always be grateful.

A Commercial Republic

The Idea of Government Economic Intervention

In 2008, the federal government of the United States began a program of intervention in the private economy unlike any the nation had seen since World War II. The immediate cause of this new direction was a financial crash so great that it unceasingly evoked comparisons to 1929. As is the case with most bursting economic bubbles, the years immediately preceding the crisis had been very good ones for banks and other financial institutions. Opportunities had seemed so lucrative and investors had held so much cash that these businesses had felt the need to find increasingly exotic vehicles in which to invest their holdings.

One of the major destinations for these funds became home mortgages. The popularity of these investments had much to do with the "securitized" form in which Wall Street brokers began selling them. When investors buy housing loans from the original lender, they are purchasing the right to collect the monthly payments owed on the loan. If the borrower should default, however, the loan's owner would lose his or her entire investment. Thus, the purchase of such a loan carries a certain element of exposure. Financial houses mitigated this risk for their customers by combining a large number of mortgages and then splitting the resulting mass into smaller pieces, which were sold one by one. The resulting securities would carry less risk than an ordinary home loan. If, for instance, a potential investor is considering the purchase of one home mortgage, the success or failure of this venture will be entirely determined by the behavior of the original borrower, who might or might not, for any number of reasons, continue making payments. Alternatively, an investor who buys 1 percent of 100 aggregated loans has purchased an equivalent amount of debt as has the person in the previous scenario. But the long-term worth of the latter investment will turn on the behavior of a hundred separate borrowers, rather than that of one particular person. This innovation rendered home mortgages a much more attractive investment than they had been previously.

The increased demand for these loans set in motion a series of events that ended in financial catastrophe. Many companies that initiated home loans, in the face of this lucrative opportunity, came to view selling mortgages to investment houses as their primary business, rather than evaluating and servicing borrowers. Wanting as many customers as possible and not planning to hold the mortgages for too long, these firms steadily dropped their standards for creditworthiness and offered low introductory interest rates and minimal early payments. These policies seduced borrowers into signing up but often left the new homeowners unable to keep up with their mortgages. Americans, facing great encouragement to borrow money, sought more and bigger homes, and the construction industry was happy to meet this demand. Housing became one of the biggest industries of the first decade of the twenty-first century.

It was, in retrospect, an unsustainable state of affairs. Both the financial and the housing industries, two of the nation's largest in this period, based their growth on credit. The economy was producing very little in the way of tangible goods and services, but investors saw no problems as long as the prices of securities continued to climb. After the fact, commentators often compared the American economy of the century's opening decade to a Ponzi scheme, in which earlier investors were paid off with the money of later ones in order to hide the fact that the underlying asset has not grown in value. In his book on the financial crisis, former *Wall Street Journal* reporter Roger Lowenstein invoked a similar idea to explain this behavior. "Mortgage bankers and investment bankers believed that there would always be another lender, another loan, to relieve them of the bad coin," he wrote. "Economics alone cannot explain such dizzying speculation. The lenders, whether on Main Street or Wall Street, were swept up in a gale of mass hallucination."[1] Meanwhile, the federal government performed little oversight of the financial industry, kept taxes low (by historical standards), and financed its operations by the sale of low-interest bonds to foreigners. Paul Krugman, the Princeton economist and *New York Times* columnist, characterized the nation's economy throughout much of this period as one in which "Americans made a living by selling each other houses, which they paid for with money borrowed from China."[2]

Inevitably, the housing market softened. By the end of 2007, new homeowners were defaulting in large numbers, and as a result, the value of

mortgage-backed securities declined significantly. Those who had been purchasing these instruments stopped doing so, seeking instead to sell the ones
they had. This pushed the value of the assets down even further. Nearly all
of the major Wall Street players held these securities as a substantial part of
their portfolios; as the worth of the paper declined, so did the firms' access
to cash. Many companies were perilously close to defaulting on their obligations, and one by one, they began to collapse. The resulting atmosphere
on Wall Street resembled a fire sale, as once-venerable companies closed
their doors or agreed to be purchased by still-solvent institutions.

Though this catastrophic state of financial affairs represented the culmination of a pattern of private decisions, government officials nonetheless
felt the responsibility of mitigating the possible damage. The intertwined
financial firms owned so much of each other's debt that the collapse of any
one company would have real effects on the balance sheets of many others.
Such failures would consequently threaten the demise of the entire financial
system, an event whose reverberations would certainly be felt by ordinary
citizens—read voters—as they affected consumer credit, banking, and ultimately employment.

Most often, federal assistance came in the form of the promise of cash or
of the use of the government's good name in borrowing money. In March
2008, Bear Stearns—founded in 1923 and a survivor of the Great Depression—required a guarantee of $30 billion from the Federal Reserve to
remain in business. Such a promise turned out to be insufficient, and Treasury Secretary Hank Paulson pressured the company to sell itself, in the face
of near-certain insolvency, to JP Morgan Chase.

The government remained heavily involved in the crisis. In September,
a series of frantic actions prevented what easily could have become a complete meltdown of the global financial system. First came Fannie Mae and
Freddy Mac. Initially formed by the government to help Americans purchase homes, both had, by the time of the crisis, been private entities for
decades. Though the two collectively controlled 55 percent of the nation's
mortgages, they had been plagued by corruption, mismanagement, and debt.
In response to the deteriorating financial condition of these firms, on September 7 Paulson announced that the federal government was placing the
two mortgage giants in conservatorship and replacing their leadership teams.
Federal agencies pledged up to $100 million in support of each company,
taking in return 79.9 percent of its common stock.

Next, Paulson again interjected the government into the market by *refusing* to offer Lehman Brothers a bailout similar to the one earlier granted to

Bear Stearns. The secretary of the Treasury had instead encouraged Bank of America to purchase the company; however, its chief executive officer (CEO), Ken Lewis, demurred and opted to commit the bank's money to acquiring the venerable yet ailing Merrill Lynch. Lehman, the fourth-largest investment bank in the United States, had no choice but to file for bankruptcy. Shortly thereafter, the Federal Reserve granted a line of credit to insurance giant AIG only minutes before the company would have run out of cash. In exchange, the government took a 79.9 percent stake in the company and installed a new CEO. On September 25, regulators from the Federal Deposit Insurance Corporation (FDIC) seized tottering Washington Mutual in the biggest bank failure in US history. They placed it into receivership and quickly sold its assets to JP Morgan Chase. Finally, after the FDIC brokered a deal in which Citigroup would buy most of the assets of the Wachovia Corporation for only $1 a share, Wells Fargo tendered a better offer at the last minute and bought the entire company (for a still-low $7 a share) without government assistance.[3]

This one-month period marked only the beginning of government involvement in this economic crisis. No matter who owned them, the securitized mortgages were still a problem. Few wished to purchase, at any price, those commodities that were increasingly being referred to as "toxic assets." Without purchasers, no market existed to properly assess their value. The companies that held them had great difficulty making sense of their own balance sheets or moving forward with new plans, and this posture was locking up the nation's credit system. To deal with this problem, the government stepped in again, this time with the Troubled Asset Relief Program (TARP). Proposed by Paulson, supported by President George W. Bush, and reluctantly approved by Congress, the plan was signed into law (as part of the Emergency Economic Stabilization Act) on October 3, 2008. The program allotted up to $700 billion for two purposes: directly purchasing assets from financial institutions and investing directly in these corporations through the purchase of nonvoting stock. TARP was authorized for two years; in that time, the United States invested nearly $500 billion in hundreds of financial institutions, even as hundreds of others failed.

TARP had been proposed and championed by a Republican presidential administration and passed by a Congress controlled by Democrats. Though neither of the two major parties offered overwhelming or unwavering support for the program (the House initially voted it down), the legislation that authorized TARP passed on the strength of a more-or-less bipartisan conviction that the severity of the crisis demanded emergency government economic intervention. Indeed, Barack Obama, a sitting Democratic member of the Senate who was running for president, not only supported the bill as a candidate but also voted for it as a senator. After winning the presidency, he assertively used the powers that the new law granted him. He pushed hard for continued payments to banks, and most notably, he used TARP funds as leverage to sack the CEO of General Motors (GM), force the company into bankruptcy, and assume government ownership of the corporation that emerged.

Outside of Washington, however, the muscular government response to the financial crisis did not enjoy even the muted support accorded it by professional politicians. Some saw a significant break with American free-market traditions. In February 2009, for example, the reliably centrist *Newsweek* magazine published a cover article by veteran journalists Jon Meacham and Evan Thomas. In their opinion piece, titled "We Are All Socialists Now," the two writers suggested the recent government actions had demonstrated that the United States had completed its drift toward European-style social democracy. Noting that the "U.S. government has already—under a conservative Republican administration—effectively nationalized the banking and mortgage industries," they warned against a "fail[ure] to acknowledge the reality of the growing role of government in the economy." This reality, they claimed, represented the end to an ongoing creative tension that characterized American political economy in the past. The nation now needed to develop the tools to guide this new socialist economy through the twenty-first century. "For the foreseeable future," the writers concluded, "Americans will be more engaged with questions about how to manage a mixed economy than about whether we should have one."

Meacham and Thomas were not the only observers who saw the September bailouts and the TARP as an economic Rubicon that the United States had already crossed. Others who noted these developments, however, did not view them with the same equanimity. They looked upon these policies less as a new reality to which Americans had to adjust than as a tide that had to be beaten back. Two weeks after the appearance of the *Newsweek* article, Rick Santelli, an editor and reporter for the financial network CNBC, captured the nation's attention with an on-air tirade. Reporting from the floor of the Chicago Board of Trade, Santelli was asked by the network anchor about a $75 billion plan, announced the previous day by President Obama, that would help homeowners who had difficulty paying their mortgages. He responded by proposing that the administration should instead initiate an online referendum allowing Americans to vote on whether the government should "subsidize the losers' mortgages" or, alternatively, set up a system whereby foreclosed cars and houses might go to "people who might actually prosper down the road . . . people that could carry the water, instead of drink the water." After many of the traders working near Santelli loudly expressed their enthusiasm for his ideas, he concluded by saying that he was "thinking of having a Chicago Tea Party in July. All you capitalists that want to show up to Lake Michigan, I'm going to start organizing."[4] Santelli's perception of a threat to American capitalism and his attendant outrage immediately touched a nerve: within two weeks, dozens of "tea party" protests had sprung up all over the country. The Tea Party movement soon became a major voice within the Republican Party, spawning caucuses in the House and the Senate and fueling the political ambitions of several presidential candidates.

Though they took different attitudes toward this economic intervention, both the mainstream journalists and the conservative activists articulated a belief that the government's actions represented a significant break with American traditions. In so doing, they implicitly invoked the idea of a national past in which the federal government played a minimal or nonexistent role in the national economy. This notion of a prelapsarian period in which the government refrained from influencing economic affairs plays a prominent role in contemporary conservatism. The website of one of the more influential Tea Party groups, for instance, advances as one of the organization's three "core values" the principle that "the founders believed that personal and economic freedom were indivisible, as do we. . . . Therefore, we support a return to the free market principles on which this nation was founded and oppose government intervention into the operations of private business."[5] The most prominent version of this narrative places the responsibility for ending this long Edenic idyll with the New Deal programs of the 1930s. Indeed, in the inaugural issue of the movement's flagship journal, *National Review*, the magazine's founder, William F. Buckley, Jr., went so far as to identify conservatives with "those who have not made their peace with the New Deal." In 1989, near the end of his presidency, the conservative icon Ronald Reagan clearly had the New Deal in mind when he claimed, in delivering his annual economic report to Congress, that his administration had "reversed a 50-year trend of turning to the government for solutions." Americans under Reagan had "relearned what our Founding Fathers knew long ago—it is the people, not the government, who provide the vitality and creativity that make a nation." More recently, conservative journalist Amity Shlaes has argued the New Dealers "forced . . . collectivism on their own country."[6]

Certainly, no one would deny that the New Deal played a significant role in defining the economic practices and policies of the federal government. But that fact alone does not justify the implied conclusion of the traditional conservative narrative—that before the Great Depression, the US government exerted little or no influence on the economy. This is not a justified interpretation of American history but a utopian conservative political ideal read backward into the past. The actions of the federal government have always influenced the character of the nation's economy, as one might expect given the many roles that this institution has been asked to perform: regulator, legislator, tax assessor, purchaser, law enforcer, employer, military protector, provider of infrastructure, and many others. For as long as there has been a United States, its federal government has exerted considerable influence on the nature and shape of the national economy.

That the American experiment has consistently admitted of government economic intervention, however, does not mean that this practice has gone unchallenged. Politicians, activists, and scholars have continually sought to justify and decry particular visions of federal economic stewardship and regulation. As a result, the history of the United States is characterized by a long-standing and contentious exchange about the desirability, scope, attributes, and limitations of such plans. The ongoing debate over the proper role of the federal government in the American economy is the subject of this book.

This volume is a work of intellectual history that employs a case study approach, concentrating at any one time on a specific policy, text, personality, or decision. This method allows for a deep excavation of the assumptions and insights that motivated politicians and thinkers as they articulated the principles that shaped the debate over the desirability and character of federal economic intervention in different periods. It is further based on the presumption that, in the realm of political economy, specific historical eras are defined by characteristic preoccupations, questions, and problems. Though the particular subjects of the case studies might be idiosyncratic, the wider points that emerge from studying them are broader and more applicable than the given topic. Beginning with the early national debate over the economic plans proposed by Alexander Hamilton, continuing through the legal construction of the corporation in the Gilded Age and the New Deal commitment to full employment, and concluding with the contemporary concerns over lowering taxes and limiting government intervention in the market, the book seeks to demonstrate that the modern-day libertarian conception of US political economy has served as only one perspective among many.[7]

To consider the shifting perspectives on the subject of government economic intervention, however, is inevitably to investigate two particularly significant American intellectual motifs: democracy and capitalism. The democratic character of the nation's politics has often served as the primary justification for groups of citizens to demand from the government policies that have unmistakable economic impact. At the same time, the widespread American consensus in support of private property and market mechanisms has frequently motivated those who strongly oppose exactly the same programs. The intellectual and political cultures of the United States, for the most part, have been reluctant to cast aside their commitments to either of these ideals. Thus, the competing commitments and insights that have shaped the debate over government intervention in the economy have served as proxies for positions on the meaning and compatibility of two constitutive American values. The ever-shifting contours of this debate illuminate the possibilities and limits of American democratic capitalism.

Of course, the nation's founders did not see themselves as creating either a democratic polity or a capitalist economy. Instead, they frequently referred to the type of nation that they hoped to construct (or, in the case of some of them, to avoid constructing) as a "commercial republic." The employment of contemporary terms to describe older ideas is anachronistic and ahistorical. The use of these words here is intended only to provide a certain continuity throughout the text, not to suggest that earlier generations were progenitors of some more modern understanding. To that end, the terms *democracy* and *capitalism* are intended here in broad, nontechnical senses. Though the idea of democracy raises many central historical, political, and philosophical questions, in this context it should be understood in its most basic sense, as a theory of legitimacy. A government is democratic when its rulers depend for their power on the continued support of the people (however defined), when popular approval plays a significant (but not necessarily definitive) role in the formation of policy objectives, and when the people in turn feel justified in using their voice (however expressed) to shape public policy. Capitalism should be understood here in an equally broad fashion, as an economic system that presumes the institution of private property and that distributes goods through the aggregated decisions of individuals in the market.

Ever since the very founding of the United States, Americans have struggled to reconcile their commitment to the political sovereignty of the people with their equally fervent desire to ensure the integrity of markets and to protect private property. The ongoing attempt to honor these conflicting impulses has led to a variety of innovations and insights for which the simplistic conservative narrative can offer no room. A proper understanding of the story of American democratic capitalism allows for an appreciation of the facts that the nation's highest ideals have consistently faced significant challenges to their realization and that these values have demonstrated a great capacity to surmount those obstacles. This insight will remain relevant for as long as Americans continue to be motivated by urges toward democracy and capitalism.

Chapter One

Stewardship

President Ronald Reagan, the most popular political figure of his day, left office in 1989. Five years later, he announced that he had been diagnosed with Alzheimer's disease. Though this condition imposed a low profile on the man once dubbed the "Great Communicator," the nation did not forget its beloved former president. Eight years after Reagan left office, antitax activist Grover Norquist founded the Ronald Reagan Legacy Project, with the purpose of placing the Gipper's name on at least one landmark or public building in each of the fifty states. Within a year, the group celebrated a major achievement when the Washington, D.C., airport was rechristened in Reagan's honor. Perhaps buoyed by this success, Norquist's group unveiled an even more ambitious goal: the placement of the former president's face on the $10 bill.

But the sawbuck was already spoken for, being graced by the visage of one Alexander Hamilton. As aide-de-camp to General George Washington in the Revolutionary War, delegate to the Constitutional Convention, one of the primary authors of the *Federalist Papers,* first secretary of the Treasury, and architect of the banking and monetary systems that played a substantial role in the emergence of the United States as an economic power, Hamilton had certainly paid his dues. Yet his credentials failed to impress at least one representative of the Legacy Project, who dispatched this founder rather quickly with a damning sobriquet. Hamilton, it would seem, was "a big-government guy."[1]

The application of this present-day label to an eighteenth-century figure exemplifies a regrettably typical phenomenon in contemporary American thinking, one by which historical figures are presented as paradigms of contemporary political categories. None suffer greater damage at the hands of this trend's propagators than those who, like Hamilton, played a role in the founding of the nation itself. In the realm of political economy, the decisions of the nation's founders exerted a tremendous influence on later developments. But the choices that they faced were not the same as those that challenge us today, and there is no meaningful sense in which the policies they instituted revealed some sort of essential American attitude toward the subject.

During the founding era, the nation's policy makers conducted America's first and most basic debate about whether the federal government would be involved in the country's economy at all. Hamilton's eloquent and forceful arguments in favor of federal economic stewardship emerged victorious, though the same cannot be said of Hamilton himself. The debate that he won, however, is not one that modern-day Americans can easily recognize. Hamilton's vision of economic intervention did not include the welfare state, the mitigation of economic inequalities, the regulation of business, or any of the other positions that frequently animate today's advocates of government action. Moreover, his opponents, led by Thomas Jefferson and James Madison, grounded their opposition to Hamilton's program on their hostility to commerce, industrialism, and the market itself. They would never have embraced what would later be called laissez-faire, even had they known what it was. The constellation of positions that characterized the early national debate over political economy simply offers no parallel or analogue to the modern-day political or intellectual framework.

Hamilton believed that the nation's political survival depended on the American economy's ability to develop a strong manufacturing sector. Industry would diversify the nation's agricultural economy and provide useful goods. Equally important, it would allow for a more self-sufficient military. Such autonomy would make the United States less dependent on other nations, any of which, in the volatile world of eighteenth-century geopolitics, could quickly become an enemy. Hamilton believed firmly in the desirability of an industrial economy, but he did not think that one could arise in the United States without government help. His implementation of federal economic intervention reflected not the philosophy of a "big-government guy" but that of an economic nationalist, and it was this perspective that guided early national policy toward government intervention in the economy.

Hamilton's Financial "System"

Among political figures in the late eighteenth-century United States, Alexander Hamilton was arguably the most influential and unquestionably the most controversial. George Washington's cabinet had only four positions, so each member wielded a great deal of power. No minister loomed larger in the eighteenth-century mind, however, than the secretary of the Treasury, and Hamilton's activist policies did little to quell the fears of a political class whose primary concern was the usurpation of power by a newly established federal government. Nor were these fears necessarily ill founded. Hamilton was heavily influenced by the thought of philosopher David Hume, who believed that human beings are motivated by their passions and self-interest rather than their reason or virtue. James Madison's defense of the Constitution in Federalist 51 had famously articulated the basic strategy that animated the government then only proposed. "Ambition," he argued, "must be made to counteract ambition."[2] By separating powers in the government, the selfish elements of human nature could act as the best check on those elements themselves. Hamilton's economic plans, however, did not call for reining in such self-interested motivations. Instead, Hamilton wished to channel these passions into directions that would benefit the fledgling government. His willingness to engage rather than suppress these impulses led his opponents to charge that he was abusing his government position by playing favorites with the citizens affected by his policies.

Moreover, Hamilton's financial and economic plans allotted great powers to the federal government and to the Treasury itself. Thus, many of Hamilton's opponents elided their opposition to his ideas and politics with personal accusations. Generally unfounded, such charges usually took the form of suggesting that the secretary of the Treasury was seeking to enrich or empower himself or his friends. For example, a 1792 letter from Jefferson, then serving as secretary of state, to President Washington alleged that certain members of Congress had fallen under Hamilton's sway. Jefferson complained that these individuals had "swallowed his bait" and set themselves up "to profit by his plans." These (unnamed) people, Jefferson argued, should have recused themselves from the votes that applied to Hamilton's scheme. "These were no longer the votes then of the representatives of the people, but of deserters from the rights & interests of the people," he claimed; their votes "had nothing in view but to enrich themselves," and they did not represent the view of "the fair majority, which ought always to be respected."[3] Though Jefferson clearly disliked Hamilton's policies, he took a further step in attacking the motives of those who supported them. In the partisan 1790s, however, such rancor was quite typical.

What was often conspiratorially referred to by Hamilton's opponents as the secretary's financial "system" was primarily explicated in three reports that he submitted to Congress: the *Report on the Public Credit* and the *Report on a National Bank* in 1790 and the *Report on the Subject of Manufactures* the next year.[4] The first two reports dealt with pressing national problems and were consequently approved by Congress despite the misgivings of many of its members. The third, however, which described Hamilton's most comprehensive vision for a national economy, created the greatest controversy.

The *Report on the Public Credit* tackled the serious issue of government debt. States still owed a great deal of money from the Revolutionary War, and the previous national government—the Articles of Confederation, which had labored under what Hamilton called the "embarrassments of a defective constitution"[5]—ran in the red as a matter of course. Fearful of replacing the distant monarchy in Britain with a similar institution in the New World and jealous of the prerogatives of their individual states, the victorious revolutionaries had created an exceedingly weak confederation rather than a true national government. As pointed out by historians Cathy Matson and Peter Onuf, many early American economic actors initially welcomed a weak regulatory regime, but they soon became aware that such an arrangement created economic problems of its own. State laws were often aimed merely at improving competitive positions with other states, and the consequent patchwork of conflicting regulations fostered an unstable business climate. Meanwhile, Congress, intentionally endowed with few economic powers, was unable to negotiate favorable economic conditions with other nations.[6] The framers of the US Constitution, including Hamilton and Madison, met in Philadelphia in 1787 to construct a new government structure that would address these and other difficulties. The new national charter was ratified the next year, and Washington took office as the first president in 1789. Hamilton's primary charge as secretary of the Treasury was to put the American financial house in order, and he intended to make good use of the added powers and stronger central government that the Constitution afforded. But the impulses that had given rise to the Articles of Confederation—intrastate rivalries and the fear of despotism—were still very much in play. It was under these circumstances that Hamilton submitted to Congress the *Report on the Public Credit*.

He began this report by arguing that the United States should issue government securities in order to raise money to pay off its outstanding debt. This arrangement would entail a long-term commitment to the holders of these bonds and would require the nation to pay its financial obligations in specific amounts at specific intervals. Against the conventional wisdom,

Hamilton argued that "funding" the debt, as such a commitment was known, would constitute a positive good for a society in the position of the United States. Establishing a regular schedule of payments, he explained, would increase public trust in the government, stabilize the price of shares in the debt certificates, and consequently decrease the tendency toward speculation in these government securities. Besides the obvious "advantage to the public creditors" that such a policy would entail, benefits would ensue even for citizens who did not hold any certificates of debt because "in countries in which the national debt is properly funded . . . it answers most of the purposes of money."[7] In other words, shares in the national debt, once their trading value (which might approach but would never exceed their issued value) had stabilized, could function as both a store of value and a medium of exchange. This arrangement would benefit merchants, whose cyclically unused funds could earn interest if invested in the national debt; farmers and manufacturers, who would find it easier to raise capital when more currency was in circulation; and "the public and individuals," who could "borrow on cheaper terms."[8]

The first few pages of the *Report on the Public Credit* established Hamilton's great support of the funded debt. His view, however, was not widely shared. Those who opposed Hamilton's plan believed that the government should be devoted to paying off the debt as quickly as possible. In their eyes, his refusal to reduce government functions to a negligible level in order to get the nation's accounts in order expressed an unfathomable preference for seeing the country in debt. James Madison, for example, wrote in a private letter at this time, "I go on the principle that a public debt is a public curse."[9] Nonetheless, the source of the controversy that attached to the *Report on the Public Credit* was less the funded debt itself—for which Hamilton argued so eloquently and forcefully that many reluctantly granted its efficacy—than two attendant recommendations: that the United States pay current holders, rather than the original recipients, of government certificates of debt and that the federal government take responsibility for state Revolutionary War debts.

Much of the outstanding domestic debt dated to the Revolutionary War, during which the cash-strapped Continental Congress had issued notes payable at a later date. Many of those who had been granted such securities, in turn, had been soldiers in General Washington's army. A great number of these veterans had since fallen upon hard times financially; this fact, combined with the precarious state of the nation's accounts, had prompted many to sell their certificates for a fraction of their face value. When Hamilton proposed to make good on the nation's debts, the value of these certificates began to rise. Under his plan, those who had bought such securities from their original holders would come in to a significant windfall, whereas the sellers, of course, would gain nothing beyond the payment already received from the private buyers. This scenario struck many as unfair, but Hamilton saw no way to rectify the perceived injustice. Tracking down the earliest holders would have been a logistical nightmare, and furthermore, there was no way to know who had sold his or her shares out of necessity and who had merely lacked faith in the longevity of the United States. Hamilton's primary concern, however, was with the negative effect that "discrimination" between original and subsequent holders would have upon the nation's credit. In rewriting the terms of its notes after they were issued, the country would be sending the message to potential creditors that its word in financial matters was unreliable. "The impolicy of discrimination," wrote Hamilton in the *Report on the Public Credit*, "rests on two considerations." The first was that it would destroy "the *quality* of the public debt" through rendering unreliable the "*security of transfer.*" The other was that it would initiate a "breach of faith" on the part of the United States, which would lead "lenders to demand a higher premium for what they lend."[10] In the end, this would cost the United States money.

Evidently not persuaded by this argument, Madison was adamantly opposed to this particular recommendation, and much to Hamilton's surprise, he proposed in the House a scheme for discrimination. Madison's fellow representatives rejected his bill by a vote of thirty-six to thirteen, but the dispute over discrimination marked the beginning of a break between the two statesmen, whose collaborative relationship, so evident not long before in the mammoth undertaking of writing *The Federalist Papers,* was quickly receding into the past.

The second major controversy prompted by the *Report on the Public Credit* concerned Hamilton's recommendation that the federal government take on all the debts that states had accumulated during the Revolutionary War. He argued that leaving the responsibility for those debts to the states would lead to "interfering regulations, and thence collision and confusion"[11] as each one separately levied taxes to pay off its obligations. Moreover, Hamilton wanted to use the debt to consolidate support for the still new and somewhat precarious union of the states. "If all the public creditors receive their dues from one source, distributed with an equal hand," he explained, "their interest will be the same. And having the same interests, they will unite in the support of the fiscal arrangements of the government."[12]

This provision for "assumption" of the various debts was met, if any-thing, with greater resistance than Hamilton's earlier refusal to sanction dis-crimination. Thomas Jefferson would later write of assumption that the "measure produced the most bitter & angry contests ever known in Con-gress, before or since the union of the states." Having recently returned from France, he was somewhat of a player in the controversy, quickly mak-ing common cause with Madison against Hamilton's plan to consolidate the national debt. Jefferson, Madison, and their fellow administration opponents were concerned that those states that had exercised great caution in running up smaller debts, as well as those that had taken some care in repaying their obligations, would essentially be punished when the federal government assumed all state debts indiscriminately. On the floor of the House, Madi-son expressed concern that assumption would compel the more fiscally responsible states "after having done their duty, to contribute to those states who have not equally done their duty."[13] Madison's congressional leadership and Jefferson's backroom maneuvering dealt the assumption plan a crush-ing blow, and it was narrowly defeated in the House in April 1790. Yet Hamilton, convinced that assumption was necessary to the survival of the union, refused to allow the plan to die there. In June, he dined with Madi-son and Jefferson at the latter's home. There, according to lore, the plan was saved with some political horse trading. Hamilton agreed to secure enough congressional votes to place the national capital at a site on the Potomac River (rather than in his adopted hometown of New York City) in exchange for the passage of the assumption bill.[14] Both proposals—for the location of the capital and for the assumption of state debts—were finally approved in the House in July, having been previously passed in the Senate.

Though much of the controversy surrounding the *Report on the Public Credit* turned on state and regional rivalries, the concerns that it generated touched on deeper issues as well. Hamilton's commitment of the nation to a costly funding scheme suggested that an invasive government taxing mechanism would soon be encroaching upon republican liberty; his unwill-ingness to support discrimination struck many as favoring the concerns of speculators over those of military veterans; and his assumption plan stoked fears that the federal government would soon envelop the states. The con-cerns of Madison, Jefferson, and the opponents of the administration would harden into full-fledged ideological resistance by the time the *Report on Man-ufactures* appeared. In the interim, Hamilton fueled opposition suspicions even further by proposing that the United States charter a national bank.

Hamilton's worry about the nation's unstable financial infrastructure predated his tenure as Treasury secretary and even the Constitution itself. As aide-de-camp to General Washington during the Revolutionary War, he was continually frustrated with the inability of the Continental Congress to support the value of its own currency, procure adequate supplies for the army, and impose order on the competing impulses of the various states. Thus it was that some eleven years before officially proposing a national bank, Hamilton had been hatching plans for such an institution. In a letter to New York congressman James Duane, the twenty-five-year-old Hamilton articulated a vision of the bank that would prove to be remarkably similar to the one adopted much later. Equally important, however, was the underlying philosophy that supported Hamilton's intricate financial structure. The only way to establish the nation's good credit, he wrote, was to "engage the monied interest[s]" by "making them contribute the whole or part of the stock" in exchange for "the whole or part of the profits." The United States, he argued, did not lack for "monied men" who were "enlightened" and "enterprising" enough to take this opportunity. He saw the problem, instead, as being with the government, "which does not exert itself to engage them in such a scheme."[15]

This same philosophy would continue to animate Hamilton's thinking years later, as evidenced in the *Report on the Public Credit* and the *Report on a National Bank*. Hamilton believed that the financial health of the nascent United States—indeed, the country's prospects for long-term stability more broadly—depended to a large degree on the extent to which the wealthy were willing to invest in the new nation. In a cash-poor country, their capital was utterly necessary if the economy was to grow and diversify; in a country suffering from shaky credit, their purchase of government securities implied confidence. But the "monied interests" would not part with their assets unless the government could give them a reason to think that the value of these investments was likely to grow. Therefore, Hamiltonian political economy began with the assumption that the government bore a responsibility to provide conditions under which the elite classes could safely invest their money.

This premise would be an embattled one. To those who opposed the administration's plans, enticing the wealthy to invest in the federal government looked suspiciously like using political power to benefit this elite class; clearly, such a policy would have violated the country's emerging democratic opposition to hierarchy of any form. Opponents also tended to hold to a notion of the American social class system that characterized the elites as disproportionately urban and northern, occupied with making a living in financial and commercial pursuits. According to this schema, the more ordinary Americans were typically rural, frequently southern, and necessarily involved in agriculture.[16] Jefferson expressed his concerns to fellow Virginian George Mason shortly after Hamilton issued the *Report on a National Bank.*: "The only corrective of what is corrupt in our present form of government will be the augmentation of the numbers in the lower house so as to get a more agricultural representation, which may put that interest above that of the stock-jobbers."[17] Moreover, the motives that Hamilton attributed to himself—the diversification and growth of the national economy—were, in the eyes of administration opponents, not things that anyone should want. To them, Hamilton was at best misguided, at worst dangerously corrupt.

Administration opponents also found much to dislike about another pillar of Hamilton's "system": the establishment of a national bank. Two main objections motivated this animosity. First, they feared that the bank's potentially lucrative financial mechanisms, which decoupled monetary rewards from both land and labor, would promote self-interest and undermine a concern with the public good. Second, they saw in the national bank a perfect example of the kind of hierarchy that the American experiment was designed to avoid, for it would use the power of the state to reward the urban, wealthy, and commercially minded elite to the detriment of the nation's agrarian class.

Hamilton, for his part, made it all too easy for opponents of the administration to see his complicated, interlocking financial schemes as conspiratorial and dangerous. The institutions that he was building were each dependent upon one another, so that every time one more was added to the mix, it further strengthened those already in place. Hamilton's bank report, for instance, required that investors buy into the bank with a combination of funds, three-quarters of which had to take the form of shares in the public debt. Because Hamilton hoped that these shares would come to function as currency, this practice aided the bank by providing capital that would be far more liquid than precious metals or land. But it also served the purposes of the funded debt, as the requirement would necessitate an increase in the demand for its shares. Moreover, the government interest payments on the shares of the debt accrued to the bank, which further intertwined those two institutions.

The *Report on a National Bank* was submitted to Congress in December 1790, nearly a year after the *Report on the Public Credit*. The debate over the bank would be perhaps the most partisan event in what was to become a particularly partisan age. Surprisingly, however, the proposal for a central bank, chartered by the United States, would eventually meet with less resistance legislatively than the recommendations of the earlier report. The nation had little in the way of financial infrastructure and quite simply needed, in the words of Hamilton biographer Ron Chernow, "an institution that could expand the money supply, extend credit to government and business, collect revenues, make debt payments, handle foreign exchange, and provide a depository for government funds."[18]

Hamilton began his *Report on a National Bank* by energetically attempting to convince his readers of the benefits of having a bank in the first place, concentrating his arguments on the now-commonplace financial axiom that banks can actually multiply the amount of money that is available in a given economy. To make the point perfectly clear, in addition to his usual recital of facts and figures Hamilton added a more homespun argument. No one benefits from the money held by a merchant who lacks an appropriate opportunity to spend it, he argued. But if a person in that position were to put that money in a bank, it would serve as "a fund, upon which himself and others can borrow to a much larger amount. It is a well established fact, that [b]anks in good credit can circulate a far greater sum than the actual quantum of their capital in [g]old & [s]ilver." [19]

After presenting his argument for the bank's ability to increase capital flows, Hamilton contented himself with stating that further benefits of the bank could "readily be inferred as consequences from those, which have been enumerated."[20] Claiming a desire not to try the patience of his House readership, he quickly turned to a much lengthier consideration of the bank's many "disadvantages, real or supposed." He acknowledged that a people concerned with equality and the rejection of elitism and hierarchy would find particular fault with some of the bank's negatives, among them a tendency toward usury, a monopolization of the nation's capital, and a temptation for the abuse of credit as a component of fraudulent schemes.[21] Yet these concerns held up very poorly in the face of Hamilton's arguments: that the bank itself would gain little from charging usurious rates, that its capitalization would be determined by the legislature, and that possible abuses of credit should not be considered in isolation but rather be balanced against the good that a central bank could do. "If the abuses of a beneficial thing are to determine its condemnation," Hamilton argued, "there is scarcely a source of public prosperity, which will not speedily be closed. In every case, the evil is to be compared with the good." And banks, he maintained, clearly met this standard: "The new and increased energies derived to commercial enterprise, from the aid of banks, are a source of general profit and advantage; which greatly outweigh the partial ills of the overtrading of a few individuals, at particular times."[22]

The last point is the most telling in illuminating the difference between Hamilton and his critics. The subsequent debate in Congress and within the Washington cabinet was concerned less with technical details, such as the appropriate interest rate or the "compound ratio" of circulating notes to gold stock, than with the wisdom and desirability of banks themselves. Hamilton saw these institutions as boons to society with a few potentially pernicious effects, whereas his opponents viewed them as corrupting influences that might nonetheless—and unfortunately—turn out to be necessary.

Seeing that even the skeptics appeared to be leaning toward supporting the bank, Madison and Jefferson concentrated all their objections not on the character or desirability of a central bank but on the question of whether establishing one was something the government was allowed to do under the Constitution. The Constitution said nothing about chartering a bank; it only granted the federal government the power to "regulate [c]ommerce . . . among the several [s]tates." Both men saw in the establishment of a national bank nothing short of a constitutional crisis, a violent abuse of the so-called elastic clause that gave Congress the "power to make all laws which shall be necessary and proper for carrying into execution the foregoing powers." To them, the success of Hamilton's proposal would signify the creeping encroachment of the government into the sphere of liberty, using its power to abet avaricious speculators at the expense of the independent farmer. On the floor of the House, Madison objected to the bank because its authorization would imply an excessively lenient reading of the Constitution. The words *necessary and proper*, he explained, were not a license to interpret the national charter. In fact, they were just the opposite, terms so restrictive as to be "merely declaratory of what would have resulted by unavoidable implication."[23] The appropriate interpretation of the Constitution, argued Madison, could not be more at odds with the broad allocation of power that characterized the bank bill, whose language would authorize anything that "might be conceived to be conducive to the successful conducting of the finances; or might be *conceived* to *tend* to give *facility* to the obtaining of loans."[24]

Madison's exhortations were for naught; the House passed the bank bill by a wide margin, as the Senate had already done. The final hope for the opponents was that the president would veto the bill. Not quite two weeks after Madison's speech in Congress, Jefferson submitted to Washington, at the president's request, his "Opinion on the Constitutionality of a National

Bank." Like Madison, the secretary of state saw a threat to the Constitution in the precedent set by the establishment of a national bank. In a strained reading of the wording that began Section 8 of Article I, Jefferson argued that the power of Congress to tax was limited to situations in which the raised revenue would "pay the debts or provide for the welfare of the Union." Thus, Congress was not authorized "*to do anything they please* to provide for the general welfare, but only to *lay taxes* for that purpose." To interpret the document otherwise was to "reduce the whole instrument to a single phrase, that of instituting a Congress with power to do whatever would be for the good of the United States; and, as they would be the sole judges of the good or evil, it would be also a power to do whatever evil they please."[25]

Madison's speech on the House floor had questioned the meaning of the words *necessary and proper* themselves, but Jefferson attacked the issue from the other end, by asserting that the existence of a bank could not be construed as "necessary" to the performance of constitutionally sanctioned functions. No enumerated constitutional power existed, he argued, whose execution was impossible without the existence of a bank. The sought-after bank was not, therefore, "necessary" but only "convenient"; as such, the price to pay for it was too high. Could the Constitution have intended, Jefferson asked, "that for a shade or two of *convenience,* more or less, Congress should be authorized to break down the most ancient and fundamental laws of the several [s]tates[?]"[26] For him, as for Madison, the establishment of a national bank was more than a policy or direction he opposed: it was a full-fledged national threat. Articulating the earliest vision of a characterization that would come to define the landscape of opposition politics, Madison and Jefferson characterized Hamilton's system not as an alternative view of the public good but as a subversion of it.

It was against this backdrop that the secretary of the Treasury submitted his "Opinion on the Constitutionality of a National Bank" to the president. Before making his decision as to whether to sign the bank bill, Washington had given Hamilton the opportunity to respond to the reports filed by Jefferson and Attorney General Edmund Randolph (who also believed the bank to be unconstitutional). Hamilton's original report on the bank had not even considered the argument that the federal government lacked the constitutional authority to establish such an institution. In addressing that possibility in his response to these criticisms, Hamilton submitted what is widely considered to be among the most articulate and influential defenses of the so-called loose school of constitutional interpretation.

"Opinion on the Constitutionality of a National Bank" made it clear that Hamilton was more concerned with the business of governing than with advocating a specific theory on the true meaning of the Constitution. "In all questions of this nature," he wrote near the end of his submitted opinion, "the practice of mankind ought to have great weight against the theories of [i]ndividuals."[27] And it is evident that Hamilton's experience as the most active and influential member of the executive branch had led him to believe that the objections of Jefferson and Randolph (and, by extension, Madison), if allowed to carry the day, would cripple the new government. The interpretation of the Constitution advanced by the opponents of Hamilton's plan would not only have denied new powers to the federal government but also have restricted it from taking on responsibilities whose prior assumption had raised no objections in the past.

Hamilton viewed the abilities of the government through the lens of sovereignty. As he saw it, if a nation was to be sovereign within its own territory, then denying its government a specific ability in that space was tantamount to claiming that such power was by its very nature illegitimate. "Every power vested in a [g]overnment," he wrote in his bank opinion, "is in its nature *sovereign*." From that observation followed "a right to employ all the *means* requisite, and fairly *applicable[,]* to the attainment of the *ends* of such power." If not "precluded by restrictions & exceptions specified in the [C]onstitution," if not "immoral," or if not "contrary to the essential ends of political society," government prerogatives should be assumed to be an appropriate exercise of government sovereignty.[28]

The fulcrum upon which this argument balanced was, of course, the claim that sovereignty by its nature implicitly entailed the assumption of certain powers, whether or not they were specifically granted. Broadly speaking, Hamilton presented two arguments to this effect: one, empirical in nature, claimed that the United States had been executing these sorts of authorities all along; the other, more theoretical, asserted that since the concept of "necessity" itself described the contingent and variable difficulty in accomplishing a given task, it could not be a category of legal or moral analysis.

Hamilton advanced his first argument by noting that the federal government had already used means not specifically enumerated in the Constitution in order to accomplish that document's sanctioned ends. Using the example of a previously enacted law allowing for the construction of lighthouses and other navigation aids, he contested Madison's claim (implicitly supported by Jefferson in his memo) that, under the prevailing understanding of the Constitution, a means was "necessary" only if without it the ends at hand were unattainable. No one could plausibly maintain that the United States could not regulate commerce without lighthouses. Thus, argued Hamilton, according to Jefferson's reasoning the construction of these beacons would be beyond the government's authority.

Other common understandings, Hamilton asserted, demonstrated that the United States did possess certain powers by the very nature of its sovereignty. If the nation uncontroversially retained such authorities in lands that were not incorporated as states (such as the Northwest Territory and the yet-to-be-named Washington, D.C.), then it would be difficult to argue that the Constitution forbade them to the federal government outright. Furthermore, Hamilton acknowledged that Jefferson's objection might seem reasonable enough when offered as a criticism, but he also noted that it would beg an important question were it to be admitted as an actual principle of government: how clearly do political ends need to be specified before they can fairly be considered constitutional? "Accurately speaking," he reasoned, "no *particular power* is more than *implied* in a *general one*. Thus the power to lay a duty on a *gallon of rum,* is only a particular *implied* in the general power to lay and collect taxes, duties, imposts and excises."[29]

The "Opinion on the Constitutionality of a National Bank" found Hamilton, despite his concern for the business of governing, offering primarily philosophical criticisms of his opponents' positions. In his view, the question of whether a specific action is necessary to achieving a particular goal could be answered only by reference to the contingent state of affairs in a given place and time. To cite one example, Jefferson had argued that many of the state banks could serve whatever functions the national bank was intended to execute. But what if, asked Hamilton, no state banks happened to exist? Would the establishment of a national bank be "necessary" in one case but not the other? If so, the Constitution would not serve to delineate which powers the various governments were justly given and denied; it would only mediate the difficulty of achieving particular tasks. Since Americans did not take such a view of their Constitution, Hamilton concluded that necessity was not—and could not be—a viable constitutional category. "The *degree* in which a measure is necessary," he wrote, "can never be a test of the *legal* right to adopt it. That must ever be a matter of opinion; and can only be a test of expediency."[30] Washington evidently found Hamilton's arguments compelling, as he signed the bank bill two days after receiving the opinion. Chartered in 1791, the Bank of the United States began operations that same year.

The building that housed the first Bank of the United States from 1797 to 1811 still stands in Philadelphia. (Courtesy Library of Congress)

Though Hamilton spent the latter half of his opinion arguing the specifics of the national bank and answering, point by point, the charges of Jefferson and Randolph, it is his overall philosophical, administrative, and constitutional vision that make the most lasting impression. In his "Opinion on the Constitutionality of a National Bank," he revealed himself to be less the naked ideologue or Machiavellian schemer of legend than a statesman who was far more comfortable with the give-and-take of republican political life than his two most prominent opponents. Differences of opinion on such vital matters, he wrote, "are inherent in the nature of the federal constitution." Because of the "division of the legislative power," some activities would "clearly [be] within the power of the [n]ational [g]overnment," and others would be forbidden to it; there would also be "a third class, which [would] leave room for controversy & difference of opinion, & concerning which a reasonable latitude of judgment must be allowed."[31]

In the 1790s, however, within that realm of "reasonable latitude of judgment" there was serious disagreement about the most fundamental goals of the American experiment. Americans of the time drew their political battle lines right through the issue of political economy, and placing the United

States on a secure financial footing was Hamilton's most urgent goal. Having established a mutually supporting system of funded debt and national bank, he next turned to the relationship between the government and the private economy, an arena where he would encounter the fiercest resistance.

Liberalism and Republicanism

Though Hamilton's system answered many of the nation's financial needs, it met with a violent opposition expressed in the most vitriolic of registers. The network of supporters organized by Hamilton, as well as the growing resistance to his ideas—most prominently represented by Jefferson inside the administration and Madison in Congress—had by then formalized into the nation's first political parties, called, respectively, the Federalists and the Republicans.[32]

Those who opposed Hamilton's growing influence saw in it the destruction of the principles of the revolution. To the modern mind-set, such a reaction might seem hyperbolic. Within the context of the early national period, however, this position—at least to the Republicans—manifested a reasonable concern over the perceived intentions of Hamilton and his party. The difficulty in making sense of the Republicans' reaction stems from the fact that the categories of political thought in play during the period immediately after the American Revolution were quite different from our own.

To see the founders as early versions of ourselves is to view them as adherents of the political outlook known as Liberalism. This political orientation is the dominant one in the United States today. In this sense of the term, nearly all Americans—Democrats and Republicans, liberals and conservatives—are essentially arguing about the proper and appropriate meaning of Liberalism. This philosophy is so prevalent in the modern era that its distinctive intellectual commitments often get lost, appearing to many Americans as little more than common sense. "Liberalism," in the words of historian Joyce Appleby, "entered the history of America as a set of powerful ideas; it remained to dominate as a loose association of unexamined assumptions."[33]

Liberalism originally developed as a response to local political conditions in seventeenth-century England. It received its most influential early exposition in the writings of John Locke, whose 1690 *Second Treatise on Civil Government* is still Liberalism's foundational text. Based on the assertions of that work and distilled over the succeeding centuries, the central tenets of Liberalism are three.

- *Human beings are by nature free and equal.* Given its most powerful statement in the American context in Jefferson's Declaration of Independence, this idea contrasts directly with the hierarchal understanding that characterized the then-dominant feudalism. Within a Liberal framework, state sovereignty does not by itself justify the impingement of the liberty of citizens or the elevation of some over others.
- *Inviolable rights inhere in each and every human being.* Also a rejection of the hierarchy of medieval Christianity, this idea explicitly rejects the religiously sanctioned "Great Chain of Being" concept in favor of the equally Judeo-Christian idea that each person is made in the image and likeness of God. What makes this claim more than merely a restatement of the first one is the specific nature of these rights. Locke's consistent position that "no one ought to harm another in his [l]ife, [h]ealth, [l]iberty, or [p]ossessions"[34] elevated the right to own property to a status equal to that of other rights.
- *Governments are constituted from the voluntary alienation of rights by individual human beings.* States come to exist only when individuals decide that they have more to gain by founding such institutions than they do by reaping the benefits—and bearing the attendant costs—of their own freedom. Thus, Liberals view the individual as logically and politically prior to the state, which itself exists, philosophically, only as an abstraction. More communitarian political philosophies (such as socialism) frequently take off from precisely the opposite point. Noting that one seldom finds a human being who is unconnected to some community, they claim that it is the idea of the self-sufficient individual that is ungrounded in political reality. The Liberal view of the origin of governments imposes significant limitations on political power, as the state can only usurp the specific rights that individuals have agreed to give up. This consequence of Liberalism placed it at odds with monarchy in the eighteenth century and totalitarianism in the twentieth.

(It is an unfortunate accident of history that in the United States, the word *Liberal* refers both to the philosophical tradition under discussion here and to a specific political application and interpretation of this ideology, that is, the contemporary outlook normally contrasted with *conservative* and generally associated with the post–New Deal Democratic Party. There is, in fact, a distinct difference between the applications of this word, and one should not assume that the meaning of the word *Liberal* in reference to, say, John Locke is the same as that of the word when used to describe, for example, Franklin Delano Roosevelt (FDR). In this work, the word will be capitalized when intended in its original, philosophic form; its specifically political application will be lowercased.)

Since the Civil War, no political ideology has been as influential in the United States as Liberalism. The doctrine's long-standing primacy had led many historians to believe that it has been the only important philosophical orientation in the nation's history. This position was most influentially argued by political scientist Louis Hartz in his 1955 classic, *The Liberal Tradition in America*. Hartz pointed out that Liberalism was so widespread in the United States that its influence had been distilled into the oft-quoted Latin slogan *Locke et praeterea nihil* (Locke and nothing else).[35]

In recent decades, however, many historians, most prominent among them Bernard Bailyn, J. G. A. Pocock, and Gordon Wood,[36] have offered a more complicated picture of the political thinking of the revolutionary era and early republic. Some have argued that many American colonists and, later, revolutionaries were motivated by an ideology known as republicanism. (In the interest of clarity, throughout this chapter the Republican political organization will be capitalized, whereas the republican philosophy will be lowercased.) Unlike Liberalism, republicanism is no longer relevant to contemporary categories of political thought, so the extent of its influence on the debate over early American government economic interaction is less comprehensible to modern understanding.

Republicanism traced its origins back not to the ideas of John Locke but to a tradition of resistance to the English monarchy that grew up around the events of the English Civil War (1642–1651) and the Glorious Revolution (1688); its adherents were known as country party thinkers or commonwealthmen. The precise meaning of the term *republicanism*, however, is more elusive. Even in the eighteenth century, it was vaguely defined. In many cases, it served as an honorific that both sides of a given debate would claim as their own. Historian Linda Kerber wrote that "usually republicanism was simply what monarchism was not."[37] Early American republicanism began with a conclusion based upon historical observation, rather than with a moral or political principle. "Most conspicuous in the writings of the [r]evolutionary period," stated Bailyn, "was the heritage of classical antiquity."[38] Despite the fact that the very name *republicanism* reflected a fundamental preoccupation with the Greeks and Romans, these early Americans were less concerned with the glories and triumphs of Athens, Sparta, and Rome than with their eventual declines. Aiming to diagnose the ills that they found in contemporary English politics, eighteenth-century republicans were in the market for a cautionary tale rather than an exemplary model. "The history of antiquity," in the words of Wood, "thus became a kind of laboratory in which autopsies of the dead republics would lead to a science of social sickness and health matching the science of the natural world."[39]

And Americans found a consistent explanation, according to Wood, for the success and failure of the classical civilizations: "It was not the force of arms which made the ancient republics great or which ultimately destroyed them. It was rather the character and spirit of the people." What ensured the strength and survival of a polity was "frugality, industry, temperance and simplicity—the rustic traits of the sturdy yeoman." The revolutionaries referred to these positive attributes collectively as *virtue*. This term's opposite was *luxury*, a word that at the time, unlike today, connoted naught but perniciousness in its effects. "Luxury," explained Wood, "was what corrupted a society: the love of refinement, the desire for distinction and elegance eventually weakened a people and left them soft and effeminate, dissipated cowards, unfit and undesiring to serve the state."[40]

In broad strokes, then, republicanism represented three ideas: the rejection of monarchy, aristocracy, and other hierarchal forms; the assumption that liberty was quite fragile in the face of the corrupting influence of power; and the attendant centrality of virtue as a necessary bulwark against such untoward influences. Virtue predisposed a person to act for the benefit of the society at large, whereas luxury, by definition, prompted a person to consider his or her own welfare above that of others. When understood this way, the proposition that a stable and healthy republic was filled with virtuous people was axiomatic or tautological: such people, by definition, were those who only acted to improve the position of the polity itself. From the republican standpoint, therefore, the purpose of social organizations was not to set up conditions under which each person could most effectively pursue his or her own vision of the good life. Instead, republican ideology suggested two major courses: set up government so as to avoid any major concentration of power, and allow it only to engage in activities that would increase the likelihood of producing a virtuous citizenry.

Such an attitude is broadly incompatible with the Liberal emphasis on the rights of the individual, but these traditions appeared to coexist, jostling

Thomas Cole's *The Course of Empire* (1834–1836), a series of five paintings depicting the same civilization at different moments in time, vividly illustrated the republican view of the inevitable rise and decline of societies. The first two works showcased the taming of a hostile natural environment, and the third, *The Consummation of Empire* (pictured above), characterized the later, prosperous stage as one awash in luxury. The fourth painting presented violence and decay as the inevitable result of such opulence, before the series finale, *Desolation* (pictured below), demonstrated nature reclaiming the territory that once hosted this fantastic civilization. (Collection of New-York Historical Society, accession numbers 1858.3 and 1858.5)

for primacy in the thinking of the politically minded early American. "None of the Founding Fathers," wrote Wood, "ever had any sense that he had to choose or was choosing" between these two traditions.[41] The American revolutionaries, Appleby concluded, "had at their disposal not one social theory, but two: the ornate concept of constitutional balances and civic virtue of classical republicanism, and the simple—simplistic even—affirmations about human nature" that characterized a Liberal approach.[42]

In the 1790s, then, the intellectual currents that ran through American political society carved different channels, with Liberal and republican ideas competing for the greater influence. And the powerful resistance to the *Report on Manufactures* was heavily influenced by the tenets of republicanism.

Republican Economics

Three months after Hamilton submitted to Congress his *Report on Manufactures,* the *National Gazette,* a consistent vehicle for Republican positions and ideas, published a piece titled "Fashion." Written by James Madison, the article began by noting that the buckle manufacturers of Birmingham had thrown themselves on the mercy of the Prince of Wales for relief because the recent vogue for shoestrings and slippers had put them out of work. This development left the future president incensed. Observing that occupations that depended upon fashion to sell their products were "the most precarious of all," Madison asserted that a system that distributed the ability to gain one's livelihood on the basis of the arbitrary desires of others offered only "the most servile dependence of one class of citizens on another class."

> *Twenty thousand* persons are to get or go without their bread, as a
> wanton youth . . . may fancy to wear his shoes with or without straps,
> or to fasten his straps with strings or with buckles. Can any despotism
> be more cruel than a situation, in which the existence of thousands
> depends on one will, and that will on the most slight and fickle of all
> moves, a mere whim of the imagination[?][43]

Madison's concern about the vagaries of fashion prefigured what would become a persistent criticism of capitalism: that treating human beings as a "labor market" can lead to great suffering when that market undergoes a correction. Thus, his position was, in some sense, anticapitalist. But it is important to be precise as to what aspect of capitalism failed to meet with

Madison's favor. He did not specifically criticize, for example, its potential to generate inequality or poverty. Instead, his quote suggests that it was the condition of *dependence* that concerned Madison. The nature of this particular criticism marked his objections as particularly republican in nature: the mutual dependence foisted by capitalism upon employers, customers, suppliers, and owners was unlikely to promote the ability to ignore one's self-interest and virtuously pursue only the common good.

Central to this line of thinking was the primacy of agriculture and the conviction that the person who produced his or her own food was truly self-sufficient, no matter what might be happening in the rest of the economy. The contemporary of Madison's who has become most strongly associated with that position is, of course, his fellow Republican Thomas Jefferson. "Cultivators of the earth," wrote Jefferson in a 1785 letter to John Jay, "are the most valuable citizens. They are the most vigorous, the most independent, the most virtuous, & they are tied to their country & wedded to it's [*sic*] liberty & interests by the most lasting bonds."[44]

Appleby, though affirming Jefferson's commitment to agriculture, has strongly contested the claim that Jefferson's thought exhibited a republican character. Arguing that, from a young age, he "saw in rising food prices the promise of flourishing American trade in grains," she described Jefferson as believing that the "prosperity of ordinary farmers . . . would form the economic base for a democratic progressive America."[45] Jefferson's well-known interest in scientific progress and, as president, his embrace of American nationalism, she asserted, were difficult to square with the notion of a backward-looking republican. Moreover, his attachment to agriculture was not antithetical to a belief in progress, modernity, or capitalism. "Agriculture did not figure in his plans as a venerable form of production giving shelter to a traditional way of life," Appleby claimed; "rather, he was responsive to every possible change in cultivation, processing, and marketing that would enhance its profitability."[46]

"Jefferson's story," in the words of Peter Onuf, "cannot be reduced to lifelong advocacy of a single principle,"[47] and Herbert E. Sloan has suggested that "the [r]epublican and country party Jefferson . . . does not automatically exclude the [L]iberal Jefferson."[48] Appleby's criticism of the tendency among historians to paint Jefferson with such broad republican strokes might be well placed. But the horrified reaction of Jefferson and Madison to the *Report on Manufactures* does appear to be best understood from within a republican framework—a framework that only favored market mechanisms to the extent that they would benefit agriculture.

The republican denunciation of market tendencies was not a blanket one: the aspects of this economic system that might support agrarianism—such as the tendency to provide far-flung markets for surplus crops—were most welcome. At the same time, different manifestations of capitalism's increasing prominence, such as its propensity to promote and reward financial speculation, were decried in no uncertain terms. Madison's solution to the problem of the workers at the buckle factory provides a perfect illustration of this republican outlook. Rather than arguing that manufacturing should be taken over by the government or invoking some sort of redistributive scheme, Madison suggested that the roots of the problem lay in the fact that the workers were engaged in manufacturing in the first place. As long as one was producing goods for which the demand would fluctuate, there was no hope of economic independence. He observed that "American citizens," by contrast with Europeans, "live on their own soil" where their "labour [*sic*] is necessary to its cultivation." And those who did engage in commercial pursuits supplied "wants . . . founded in solid utility, in comfortable accommodation, or in settled habits," rather than in fashionable whims. The result was a "reciprocity of dependence, at once ensuring subsistence and inspiring a dignified sense of social rights."[49]

Madison accorded legitimacy to those who engaged in the manufacture and selling of goods for which demand was solid and steady, but this endorsement occurred only against the backdrop of his broader condemnation of the impulse to make money through the satisfaction of consumer demand—the motivation that is at the heart of capitalism. Madison's objections to the system that put laborers to work in the buckle factory were primarily republican in nature, and they showcased his ambivalence about a system of production for the market. Thus, his strong reaction against Hamilton's several plans to use the government to stimulate the American economy should not be understood as an early version of laissez-faire. Madison did not want to protect the market from the intrusions of government as much as he hoped to minimize commercial and industrial activity itself.

At the heart of the republican economic program was the same agenda that motivated this ideology's political project: the support and protection of the virtue of the average citizen. Although republicans saw the main political threat to moral uprightness in the temptations of power, they viewed the primary economic danger as financial dependence, which could tempt citizens to yield to the will of others rather than to virtuously consider the needs of the nation itself. Jefferson echoed this point in the most famous passage of *Notes on the State of Virginia* (1787). Like Madison in his "Fashion" piece, Jefferson offered a contrast between Europe and the United States, and also like Madison, he argued in a vein that echoed the republican theme of independence being the best guarantor of virtue. Jefferson contrasted the United States with Europe, where "lands are either cultivated, or locked up against the cultivator." On the Continent, in other words, people turned away from agriculture only because they were forced to do so. But in the United States, he asserted, "we have an immensity of land courting the industry of the husbandman," and the country would be better off if as many people as possible joined in "improving" that land. "Those who labour [sic] in the earth," he wrote, "are the chosen people of God." Their "breasts he had made his peculiar deposit for substantial and genuine virtue. . . . Corruption of morals in the mass of cultivators is a phænomenon of which no age nor nation has furnished an example." Moral depravity was instead "the mark set on those, who not looking up . . . to their own soil and industry . . . for their subsistence, depend for it on the casualties and caprice of customers."[50]

Republican political economy was based upon two main premises. The first was that Americans could maintain their independence only through engaging in agriculture. The second was that this independence was the only guarantor against the corruption of virtue that characterized, in the republican view, the more "advanced" industrial societies. Consequently, those who subscribed to a republican way of thinking saw no reason for the United States, having been blessed with ample amounts of fertile land, to engage itself in any other sort of economic activity. Manufacturing and industry, in particular, should be kept in Europe, as Americans could trade their surplus agricultural produce for the rarely needed manufactured articles.

Yet the emphasis on farming as the only source of virtue and independence cannot fully explain the attitude of early national republicans toward capitalism itself. The heavy reliance on slavery among the "independent" and "virtuous" Virginia republicans (and Jefferson's well-known taste for European finery) would render the agrarian ideal little more than a hypocritical caricature were it the entire story. But the republican extolling of agriculture was underwritten by a series of key assumptions that defined late eighteenth- and early nineteenth-century political economy. Historian Drew McCoy articulated and explained these more fundamental ideas in his 1982 book *The Elusive Republic: Political Economy in Jeffersonian America*. There, McCoy asserted that republicanism was not merely a political ideology but also an economic one; the concern for virtue that animated republicanism carried implications for the nation's business as well as its politics. The American revolutionaries "assumed that a healthy [r]epublican government demanded an economic and social order that would encourage the shaping of a virtuous citizenry." To found a new republic according to these principles, they had to do much more than erect an appropriate governmental structure: "They had to define, and then attempt to secure, a form of economy and society that would be capable of sustaining the virtuous character of a republican citizenry. They had to establish, in short, a republican system of political economy for America."[51]

McCoy explained that this system was based upon a set of assumptions about the nature of society itself. Human social arrangements, it was widely believed, were subject to a progression of growth and decay that was as inexorable as any physical law. These "several phases of organization" proceeded inevitably "from 'rude' simplicity to 'civilized' complexity." In order of ascending sophistication, the stages of development consisted of "hunting, pasturage, agriculture, and commerce."[52] Since this progression was an inexorable feature of human social organization, it could not be halted or reversed. "The 'republican revolution' in political economy," argued McCoy, "was based on the assumption that America would remain at a 'middle stage' of social development." The overall goal of this way of thinking was therefore to significantly slow this process so that American society could remain, for a very long time, arrested somewhere between the agriculture and commerce phases. This would allow Americans to "adapt the moral and social imperatives of classical republicanism" to its attractive antithesis, "modern commercial society." This vision would allow the United States "to grow prosperous and civilized without succumbing to luxury."[53]

Thus, as the new government began operation in the late 1780s, partisans did not specifically debate whether the United States would embrace capitalism or retain its barter-oriented, "subsistence-plus" character. Though they did see these issues, they viewed them through a different lens than we might today. In terms of political economy, the major issue of the day was whether the nation should embrace manufacturing or do everything in its power to remain a primarily agricultural society.

In the Washington administration, Jefferson's was the loudest voice for the latter position. Hamilton chafed at the fact that the country's lack of a manufacturing sector rendered it entirely dependent on other countries for many economic and military necessities, but Jefferson was just as adamant that manufacturing would speed the decline of the personal independence upon which the citizenry's virtue depended. The philosophical elegance of the Jeffersonian vision, however, was complicated by the empirical reality that the vestiges of commerce had already taken hold in the United States. McCoy noted "an uneasy suspicion (and sometimes recognition) among the [r]evolutionaries that even predominantly agricultural America was already a relatively advanced commercial society, that Americans were already to a great extent an ambitious commercial people with refined tastes and manners, and that under such conditions inflated expectations of classical public virtue might be unrealistic." In seeking to "permit liberty, commerce, and prosperity and, at the same time, to deny their potentially corrupting effects," American republicanism was characterized by an unsustainable tension.[54]

Jeffersonians believed that they could massage this seemingly daunting theoretical contradiction by manipulating the conditions under which it would play out. In particular, they advocated American territorial expansion—which would provide land for farmers to work—and international trade—which would supply an outlet for the excess capacity generated by increasingly efficient American agriculture. In a letter to Madison written before the Constitution was ratified, Jefferson stated, "Our governments will remain virtuous for many centuries; as long as they are chiefly agricultural; and this will be as long as there shall be vacant lands in any part of America. When they get piled upon one another in large cities, as in Europe, they will become corrupt as in Europe."[55] Thus, since the population of the United States would grow, the nation had to acquire new lands so that the people could farm. Trading agricultural surpluses to Europe for manufactured goods would enable Americans to have these products without having to locate any dreaded industry on their side of the Atlantic.

This emerging republican vision of a sort of mildly commercialized agrarianism ultimately failed to provide a solution to a fairly serious republican dilemma: if self-sufficiency and industriousness were equally virtuous and if avarice and covetousness undermined republican institutions, then it was not clear what a yeoman agrarian was supposed to do with his or her time once basic subsistence needs had been met. Raising extra crops for the purpose of selling them would be dangerously commercial, whereas refusing to do so was just plain lazy. Despite themselves, McCoy argued, Jeffersonians "almost unthinkingly absorbed into their republican outlook this logic of the importance of foreign markets and free trade to American agriculture." Yet this set them up for nothing less than a tragic intellectual failure. Their "grand quest" was to create "a society that would somehow reconcile their commitment to the cultivation of an active, industrious, enterprising, virtuous people with their commitment to the maintenance of a predominantly simple and agricultural social order." In marrying commercial expansion to its geographic counterpart, they hoped to "defy the seemingly inexorable logic of social progress through time and remain at a middle stage of development, somewhere between the undesirable extremes of a rude and barbarous simplicity, on the one hand, and an overrefined and corrupt decadence, on the other."[56]

The plan of pursuing a policy of international trade and territorial annexation in order to maintain a virtuous and agricultural order put a great deal of strain on republican doctrines. Since commerce and industry were ideologically linked with social decline, any policy that might suggest support for market-oriented enterprise automatically threatened the very stability of the still-fragile young republic. But the strong contradictions in republican political economy made such a proposal almost inevitable. The desire for autonomous agrarianism was on a collision course with the conditions that would have to hold in order to obtain it; the two elements met in the person of Alexander Hamilton and his *Report on Manufactures*.

The *Report on Manufactures* and Its Implications

"In many respects," wrote McCoy, "Hamilton was an anomaly; perhaps more than any of his countrymen, he had succeeded in discarding the traditional republican heritage that heavily influenced the [r]evolutionary mind."[57] Against the background of his opponents' insistence that agriculture represented a moral and political bulwark against the forces of luxury that threatened the American experiment, as well as the growing sense that he was usurping the power of the government for his own nefarious ends, the secretary of the Treasury audaciously presented a plan whose purpose was to increase the role of industry in the economic life of the United States. Though Hamilton was always a practical politician rather than a grand theorist, his *Report on the Subject of Manufactures* stands alongside his work on *The Federalist* as among the most significant intellectual achievements of the founding period.

The *Report on Manufactures* arose in response to a request from Congress, which was concerned primarily about the military and strategic vulnerability that would arise from an inability to produce needed supplies and weapons. Hamilton spent nearly two years gathering information and writing his other reports before finally complying with the request in December 1791, not quite a year after the *Report on a National Bank* and almost two since the initial *Report on the Public Credit*. In this period, opposition to Hamilton had begun to harden, for the success of his earlier reports had alarmed Republicans, who were determined to prevent his newest recommendations from establishing new institutions and policies. Since the dominant opinion of the day viewed manufacturing and agriculture as polar opposites, the greater prominence of one necessarily eating into the influence of the other, prevailing Republican sentiment was aligned against Hamilton before anyone had even read the report. Indeed, only a few months later, the secretary himself would write in a personal letter that he had become "unequivocally convinced" of the fact that "Mr. Madison cooperating with Mr. Jefferson is at the head of a faction decidedly hostile to me and my administration."[58]

The two main points of the *Report on Manufactures,* which Hamilton prepared with the help of his assistant Tench Coxe, were that the United States was greatly in need of more industry and that this need justified government support. Hamilton made clear in the report that he was swimming against the tide of conventional wisdom. Noting early on, with great understatement, that "there still are . . . respectable patrons of opinions, unfriendly to the encouragement of manufactures,"[59] he structured much of the writing around refuting these commonly held views. He listed the major arguments against manufacturing and then used the *Report on Manufactures* to dismiss them one by one. Though acknowledging that "the cultivation of the earth . . . has *intrinsically a strong claim to pre-eminence over every other kind of industry,*" he denied "that it has a title to any thing like an exclusive predilection" to the nation's economic attention. Supporting the commonly held view of agriculture's preeminence would require "more evidence . . . than has yet been given in support of the position."[60] Hamilton had spent the better part of two years collecting empirical data, and he clearly believed that the preference for agriculture to the exclusion of manufacturing was a function of a dangerous ideological fixation rather than a concern for the best interests of the United States. Still, he did not claim to be able to prove that industry was more productive than farming; instead, he argued only that the preference for farming was not grounded on solid evidence.

On this point, Hamilton engaged in a bit of disingenuousness. The central issue of the day was not whether manufacturing could be more productive than agriculture; few claimed that a diverse economy and stronger commercial sector would have no value for the United States. Instead, the debate was a more philosophical one, about the nature of the society that the new Americans were trying to create. Republicans argued that manufacturing brought with it pernicious moral consequences that would ultimately spell the decline of the republic. In phrasing the question as one of productivity, Hamilton not only pushed aside the emotional and philosophical force of the most damaging objections of his opponents but also constructed the battle on terrain in which he had an advantage: few, if any, people in the young nation knew as much as he did about the state of the country's economy.

The major points that Hamilton offered in support of increased American industry were that diversifying the economy would boost overall economic output and that a prominent manufacturing base would make for greater national independence. The Republicans were not well disposed toward this reasoning, believing that both of Hamilton's concerns could be addressed with a program of European trade. Since the United States had no shortage of arable land, whereas Europe was having difficulty feeding its populations, Hamilton's adversaries were generally content to follow the assessment of the situation that Jefferson had made over a decade before in *Notes on the State of Virginia.* "While we have land to labour [*sic*] then," he wrote, "let us never wish to see our citizens occupied at a workbench, or twirling a distaff. . . . [F]or the general operations of manufacture, let our workshops remain in Europe." Since it was the "manners, and spirit of a people which preserve[d] a republic in vigour [*sic*]," Jefferson feared that the "manners and principles" of "workmen" would detract from the "happiness and permanence of government" to be found in America. "The mobs of great cities," wrote the sage of Monticello, "add just so much to the support of pure government, as sores do to the strength of the human body."[61]

Jefferson's skepticism about the economic prospects of industry in the United States was intimately related to his distaste for manufacturing itself. The *Report on Manufactures,* however, ignored the perceived moral damage resulting from the presence of manufacturing firms and instead concentrated on refuting the notion that a greater manufacturing presence in the country would have only negative economic results. Hamilton provided seven reasons why opinions along the lines of Jefferson's were mistaken, varying from the practical (factory workers would have to buy produce from farmers in order to eat) to the idealistic (new industries would furnish "greater scope for the diversity of talents"). The type of logic employed in many of his arguments was captured in a thought experiment in which Hamilton imagined two hypothetical two-person economies: one with two farmers and another that featured both a farmer and an "artificer." In the former

case, the need for manufactured goods—"cloathing [*sic*] and other articles"—would still exist, and the husbandman would have to spend part of
his time producing them. Since he would presumably be less efficient at
manufacturing such goods than someone who did this all day and was able
to employ the economies of scale, the "whole quantity of production . . . in
provisions, raw materials and manufactures, would certainly not exceed in
value the amount of what would be produced in provisions and raw materials only, if there were an artificer as well as a farmer."[62] From the perspective of the entire country, the scenario involving one of these two laborers
going into manufacturing created the greatest amount of goods overall. The
benefits flowing from the division of labor, in other words, would enable
the same two workers to produce more total goods. If, in addition to maximizing what we would today call gross domestic product, the provisions created by the new industry were also ones needed in the county, then there
could be only advantages in encouraging the economy to produce them.

Moreover, one implicit assumption of the Republican alternative—that
the young, weak United States could procure favorable terms of trade with
its more powerful and established European partners—had *not* been borne
out by the American experience up to that time. In fact, the protectionist tariffs that had previously been put in place by the United States, argued
Hamilton, had already limited the American ability to engage in international trade, placing the nation "to a certain extent in the situation of a country precluded from foreign [c]ommerce."[63] Due to the effect of retaliatory
tariffs from other nations, the United States could effectively buy but not
sell. In this situation, American agricultural producers were unable to get
good prices for their crops, and consequently, they encountered difficulty
in acquiring the cash needed to purchase foreign goods.

Under such conditions, Hamilton implicitly argued, Jefferson's prescription to "let our workshops remain in Europe" was unworkable. "In
such a position of things," Hamilton wrote, "the United States cannot
exchange with Europe on equal terms; and the want of reciprocity would
render them the victim of a system, which should induce them to confine
their views to [a]griculture and refrain from [m]anufactures." If the economy was devoted solely to farming, American demands for European manufactured goods would constantly increase, and the European interest in
American products would stagnate. Refusing to embrace the potential benefits of industrial development would "expose" the United States to "a state
of impoverishment, compared with the opulence to which their political and
natural advantages authorise [*sic*] them to aspire."[64] Thus, the strategy of

depending on European imports to meet the American demand for manufactured goods would be disadvantageous to the point of unviability: "If
Europe will not take from us the products of our soil, upon terms consistent
with our interest, the natural remedy is to contract as fast as possible our
wants of her."[65] Under these circumstances, argued Hamilton, the only
remaining options were to develop a domestic manufacturing sector or to
simply do without manufactured goods entirely.

The second major point of Hamilton's *Report on Manufactures* was that
the United States lacked some of the necessary features that would allow it to
realize its potential in the manufacturing arena and that, consequently, the
federal government should step in to develop this economic sector. His
arguments to this effect revealed Hamilton's limited faith in the market itself,
even as his nationalist tendencies provided strong support for the development of commerce and industry in the United States. Following a point originally made by David Hume (and implicitly contradicting Adam Smith's
famous notion of the "invisible hand"), Hamilton argued that people were
unduly influenced by their previously developed habits, following market
signals only reluctantly or, often, not at all. The success of the emerging
industrial sector required that "the confidence of cautious sagacious capitalists . . . be excited," but new projects tended to be "precarious." As a
result, concluded Hamilton, potential entrepreneurs and investors "should
be made to see . . . the prospect of such a degree of countenance and support from government, as may be capable of overcoming the obstacles,
inseparable from first experiments."[66] Without federal support, the private
manufacturing sector would not be able to get off the ground.

Hamilton mentioned two impediments to his vision of long-term manufacturing success for the United States: the scarcity and expense of labor,
on the one hand, and the lack of capital, on the other. Over time, he
believed, population growth and machinery, respectively, would solve both
aspects of the first problem. With regard to the second, however, Hamilton
must have raised Republican hackles when he pointed out how well the previously installed federal financial architecture could provide funds and col-
lateral for industrial ventures. He recycled the argument from his *Report on
the Public Credit* that shares in the public debt could perform the function of
currency, noting, "Public [f]unds answer the purpose of [c]apital, from the
estimation in which they are usually held by [m]onied men; and consequently . . . can be turned into money."[67] But Hamilton's system did more
than create a medium of value: it actually increased the amount of capital,
systemwide, that could be invested. This was because the denominated

amount of debt in circulation in any given year (which would theoretically equal the amount of the entire outstanding debt) would always be significantly greater than the amount being removed from circulation through taxes levied to service the outstanding obligation (which would only total the amount needed to pay the annual installment on the debt). For example, imagine that in a given year the federal government paid 6 percent interest and retired 2 percent of the outstanding principal. The outstanding obligation would total 8 percent of the debt, and the only way to get this money would be to tax the citizenry, that is, to remove the money from circulation. But for this cost of 8 percent of the outstanding debt, the nation would be allowed to circulate the other 92 percent. Because shares of the debt functioned as money, the funded debt essentially created sorely needed circulating capital from thin air. As long as the debt remained outstanding, Hamilton explained, "*at every instant of time* during the whole period" in nationwide circulation would be an amount of shares "corresponding *with so much of the principal* . . . as remains *unredeemed[,]* . . . employed, or ready to be employed[,] in some profitable undertaking. There will therefore constantly be more capital, in capacity to be employed, than capital taken from employment."[68] In this way, Hamilton's "system" perpetuated itself: the funded debt, detested by the Republican opposition, created capital that could be used to create equally despised industrial plants.

To the opposition, this maneuver in particular posed the most basic threat to the future of the American republican political system. Among the fundamental tenets of revolutionary ideology was the rejection of the use of power to draw distinctions between people. Yet Hamilton, as the Republicans saw it, was proposing to have the government create money in order to reward those who sought to enrich themselves without working. Of course, Hamilton viewed things differently. He believed that without a significant infusion of funds, the economy of the United States could not support vital industries, some of which were necessary for national security. Given this need, the nation's government had to take some action to provide this capital. Since sources that might have generated revenue to fund manufacturing ventures, such as an income tax, were beyond the realm of contemporary economic orthodoxy, Hamilton had few available tools for such a task. His only real option was to encourage those with available funds to invest them in the American economy rather than putting them elsewhere. Without any authority to compel such behavior, he had to make those investments as attractive as possible. Thus, economic inequality, in Hamilton's view, was far from a scourge on society: the money of the wealthy was absolutely *necessary* to the continued survival and health of the nation's economy.

Hamilton's concern for those playing the markets in government securities appeared to Republicans as nothing more sophisticated than elitist cronyism. His proposals, they feared, would put the government in service to the personal interests of the secretary of state and similarly situated individuals—Jefferson's feared "stock-jobbers." Though historians have cleared Hamilton of most of these charges and generally found his opponents' personal attacks somewhat paranoid and conspiratorial, his series of reports did pose a serious referendum on the future direction of American political economy. In their monumental work on the 1790s, *The Age of Federalism*, Stanley Elkins and Eric McKitrick resolved the many issues raised by Hamilton's intertwining financial programs. They found that despite the fact that Hamilton's policies were "impeccable" on "technical grounds," they nonetheless carried "broad ideological implications." Though his "principles may have accorded with the public interest . . . [n]othing he did was undertaken in a spirit basically hostile to . . . those men in whose hands he believed the nation's future prosperity rested." Thus, Republicans "were not wrong when they repeated in endless ways that Hamilton was using the financial power of the United States—as he had determined to do from the beginning—for the benefit of speculators."[69]

In his history of financial speculation, Edward Chancellor noted that the word *speculation* is difficult to characterize precisely. It is "conventionally defined as an attempt to profit from changes in market price," but such a description, Chancellor observed, renders the term difficult to separate from its more respectable sibling *investment* and from the family black sheep *gambling*.[70] Regardless of the definition, however, speculation was clearly outside the realm of virtuous behavior as it was generally understood in the last decade of the eighteenth century. From such a perspective, it should not have been tolerated, much less invited. Yet Hamilton's entire financial program was designed to encourage speculation in government securities.

Republicans saw speculation itself as inherently corrupting. They claimed that it rewarded those who produced no goods and performed no services and consequently discouraged work in favor of sloth. In a letter to George Washington a few months after the submission of the *Report on Manufactures*, Jefferson characterized "all the capital employed in paper speculation" as "barren & useless, producing, like that on a gaming table, no accession to itself." Such moneys had been "withdrawn from commerce & agriculture where it would have produced addition to the common mass" and had furthermore "nourished in our citizens habits of vice and idleness instead of industry & morality."[71] Viewing Hamilton's report as an expression of economic folly, political tyranny, and moral decline, Jefferson, Madison, and their followers were prepared to make sure that its recommendations were not enacted.

Reception and Significance of the Report

Hamilton was at heart a policy wonk. Despite the theoretical implications of the *Report on Manufactures*, about half its pages were taken up with specific recommendations, including a comprehensive list of materials and products that should be taxed. One proposal in particular stood out as both unprecedented and controversial. Besides more traditional practices such as protective tariffs, prohibition of rival foreign goods, and exemption from taxation of necessary raw materials, Hamilton also mentioned "pecuniary bounties," or cash payments to those engaged in the manufacture of goods in which the government had a specific interest. He had already argued that it was in the best interest of the country to have the government subsidize manufacturing, but he had left open the question of the most appropriate method of doing so. Bounties, he explained, were "a species of encouragement more positive and direct than any other." Differential taxes on input goods did not affect foreign competitors, he pointed out, and tariffs raised all prices indiscriminately. Finally, duties could "have no influence upon the advantageous sale of the article produced, in foreign markets."[72] Bounties, in contrast, directly aided the domestic manufacturer, who could sell goods more cheaply. As a result, bounties could increase foreign demand for American goods in a way that other subsidies could not.

Hamilton was aware of the fundamental philosophical objection to his recommendation—the "appearance of giving away the public money . . . to enrich particular classes, at the expense of the [c]ommunity." Dismissing this argument as a "prejudice," he fell back on his nationalism. "There is no purpose, to which public money can be more beneficially applied, than to the acquisition of a new and useful branch of industry; no [c]onsideration more valuable than a permanent addition to the general stock of productive labour [*sic*]."[73] Here, Hamilton's proposals in the *Report on Manufactures,* like those involved in chartering a national bank, all turned on the notion that they were good for the emerging United States. Administration opponents based most of their disagreements on exactly the opposite point. Their earlier constitutional objections to the bank had been rooted in the claim that Hamilton lacked the authority to charter that institution; whether the bank would be good for the country or even its citizens was entirely irrelevant. That argument did not carry the day, so administration opponents would argue differently against the provisions of the *Report on Manufactures*: these proposals were inherently threatening to the republican principles of governance and therefore *not* good for the American people.

Hamilton's proposals were forcefully presented in a sober fashion and supported with clear arguments. But to his Republican opponents, they were abhorrent. "By the close of the first session of the Second Congress in the spring of 1792," wrote Drew McCoy, the "ideological opposition to the emerging Hamiltonian system took on a bitter, at times hysterical, tone."[74] For instance, in a private letter Madison expressed great concern that the proposals would destroy the republican character of the United States. Describing previous "particular measures" of the Hamiltonian project as "extremely offensive," Madison predicted that if these odious policies "should be followed by the usurpation of power recommended in the [R]eport on [M]anufactures," he would "consider the fundamental & characteristic principle of the [g]ovt. [a]s subverted."[75]

In the span of about a year, Madison would publish, in the Republican organ *National Gazette*, eighteen unsigned essays, including "Fashion." All but two of them came out after Hamilton's report, and some of them dealt with it specifically. These articles demonstrated the nature of Madison's grave concern over the future of the republic should Hamilton's ideas carry the day. Some two and a half months after the release of the *Report on Manufactures*, Madison offered a list of different "species" of government. Here, he juxtaposed "republican governments which it is the glory of America to have invented" with a much less attractive and obviously Hamiltonian model—a "government operating by corrupt influence; substituting the motive of private interest in place of public duty; converting its pecuniary dispensations into bounties to favorites, or bribes to opponents; accommodating its measures to the avidity of a part of the nation instead of the benefit of the whole." Such a government would operate by "enlisting an army of interested partisans . . . whose intrigues, and whose active combinations . . . may support a real domination of the few, under an apparent liberty of the many."[76] Again, where Hamilton formed his system in accordance with what he saw as a national need for the increased civic participation of the wealthy, Madison could only perceive a corrupt giveaway that enabled the powerful few to dominate the virtuous many.

Another essay, revealingly titled "Republican Distribution of Citizens," found Madison arguing that manufacturing took a terrible toll on the health of the laborer.[77] By contrast, those who worked in agriculture enjoyed a more robust physical existence. But farmers were not merely healthier. They were also "the most truly independent and happy . . . the best basis of public liberty, and the strongest bulwark of public safety." Consequently, Madison concluded, "the greater the proportion of this class to the whole society, the more free, the more independent, and the more happy the society itself." Those things that brought about less favorable results "ought to be seen with regret," rather than "being forced or fostered by public authority."[78]

In another of these essays, Madison questioned the intrusive nature of Hamilton's plan with regard to property rights. He contended that an unjust government, by its very nature, was one in which "arbitrary restrictions, exemptions, and monopolies deny to part of its citizens that free use of their faculties, and free choice of their occupations, which not only constitute their property in the general sense of the word; but are the means of acquiring property strictly so called." In such states, "unequal taxes oppress one species of property and reward another species." Madison found that in societies of this type, human nature itself was warped, as "the keenness and competitions of want are deemed an insufficient spur to labor, and taxes are again applied, by an unfeeling policy, as another spur." He urged his nation, if it wished to earn "the full praise due to wise and just governments," to "equally respect the rights of property, and the property in rights."[79] Though Madison did not mention those who threatened these rights, the principles that he mentioned were obviously an exaggeration of those laid out in Hamilton's reports.

In April 1792, only four months after the submission of the *Report on Manufactures,* Madison published an essay called "The Union: Who Are Its Real Friends?" To this question, he provided an answer that was hardly surprising. The unnamed but unlucky few who failed to fit into the category of real friends included "those who favor measures, which [pamper] the spirit of speculation within and without the government," "those who promote unnecessary accumulations of the debt of the [u]nion," and "those who study, by arbitrary interpretations and insidious precedents, to pervert the limited government of the [u]nion." Those who rated as supporters of the nation, by contrast, were friends to "the authority of the people," "liberty," and "the limited and republican system of government" and enemies "to every public measure that might smooth the way to hereditary government." The answer to the essay's titular question, summarized Madison, was that the union counted among its allies those who were "friends to the republican policy throughout . . . in opposition to a spirit of usurpation and monarchy."[80]

Taking Madison's comments as representative, it is clear that the *Report on Manufactures* and the response to it had drawn distinct lines between Hamilton and his Republican adversaries. The report marked the culmination of Hamilton's financial system that the secretary's earlier efforts and their attendant legislation had set in motion. For Madison, Jefferson, and their allies, it harbored nothing less than a victory for tyranny and the abrogation of the nation's hard-won republican form of government.

Therefore, one might expect that a major conflict would have ensued when the *Report on Manufactures* was voted upon in Congress. But the showdown never occurred. Unlike Hamilton's previous recommendations, this report was never the subject of a systematic congressional debate or an up-or-down vote. Indeed, the conventional historical wisdom is that the report garnered little legislative attention and somehow just withered away and that the document is more important as a philosophical exercise than a political blueprint. Economist Douglas A. Irwin, however, somewhat modified this perception. Pointing out that the House approved a bounty for the fishing industry (though it had to be recast as a "rebate" before garnering sufficient support) only a few months after the filing of Hamilton's report, he argued that such actions were not anathema to that body. Moreover, when Congress asked for Hamilton's advice on raising money to fight Indians in the West, he recommended the same tariffs he had first suggested in the report. The resulting bill passed comfortably, even though some representatives objected that a bill originally intended as a security measure had turned into one to help manufacturing.[81]

Thus, the most direct legislative result of Hamilton's *Report on Manufactures* was the somewhat inauspicious imposition of several tariffs. On a somewhat longer view, however, nearly all of Hamilton's recommendations would eventually be implemented, in a supreme irony, during the presidencies of Jefferson and Madison. Indeed, as the Republicans gained political power in the nineteenth century, they increasingly came to champion the interests of manufacturers. Later in life and far removed from the presidency, Jefferson himself would admit his change of heart: "We have experienced what we did not then believe . . . that to be independent for the comforts of life we must fabricate them ourselves. We must now place the manufacturer by the side of the agriculturist."[82]

Though the *Report on Manufactures* generated little direct political legislation, it served as both an effective philosophical statement of Hamiltonian political economy and a harbinger of things to come. Hamilton's "system" would be modified and eventually replaced by other mechanisms. But its basic principles—that the nation has an interest in a diverse and healthy economy and that government has the right, if not the duty, to bring about such prosperity through economic intervention—have animated American democratic capitalism to the present day. But the debate over intervention did not end with Hamilton's premature death in 1804 at the hand of Aaron Burr or even with the reluctant Jeffersonian acceptance of many Hamiltonian positions. Within two generations, Jefferson's successors, by then known as the Democrats, had vanquished their political opponents and were able to shape the political landscape to their liking. As they did so, they faced an insurmountable tension between their embrace of popular liberty, as expressed in both the expansion of the franchise and the growth of the market, and their hostility to the mounting inequality brought about by these liberties themselves. Their failed attempt to resolve this contradiction by rolling back the Hamiltonian program constituted the next phase in the development of American democratic capitalism.

Chapter Two

Divorce

Though Andrew Jackson had served briefly in the House and the Senate, he rose to national prominence only after his military exploits in the War of 1812. Later gaining fame as an Indian fighter in the Seminole Wars, Jackson garnered even more attention as he effectively conquered Florida for the United States. "In the eyes of most Americans," declared biographer H. W. Brands, "he was the greatest hero since Washington."[1] "Old Hickory" was able to ride this wave of popularity to the White House, becoming the nation's seventh president in 1829.

Like many of his predecessors in the office, Jackson had practiced law. Also like them, he was white, male, and married. (He had become a widower by the time he took office, as had Jefferson before him.) As with George Washington, he derived much of his political influence from a prior military career. But in the eyes of many of his contemporaries, Jackson was defined by a trait that set him apart utterly from any of his predecessors: he was not a member of the eastern elite. His family origins were humble, and he had not attended college. He had grown up in North Carolina, one of the original thirteen colonies, but as a young man, he had made his way to the territory that would become Tennessee. Thus, Jackson appealed to voters who were western, self-made, and perhaps a bit coarse in their manners. And it was his great fortune to have come of political age at exactly the moment when this demographic began to exert significant power at the ballot box.

In today's terms, Andrew Jackson would be described as a populist. But such a designation fails to do justice to the changes that the Jacksonians— for that is what his supporters called themselves—wrought on the American political system. Jackson and his followers transformed the United States into what we would today recognize as a democracy. Though much of the

48

American political tradition to that point had centered on the resistance to tyranny and aristocracy, an equally important strand had taken it for granted that a true "rule by the people" could end only in anarchy. In defending what was then only the proposed constitution of the United States in Federalist 10, James Madison had praised the document for avoiding the problems that plagued democratic polities. Under such governments, he argued, "there is nothing to check the inducements to sacrifice the weaker party or an obnoxious individual. Hence it is that such democracies have ever been spectacles of turbulence and contention; have ever been found incompatible with personal security or the rights of property."[2] John Quincy Adams, Jackson's bitter enemy and the last person to serve as president before him, begged members of Congress not to become "palsied by the will of our constituents."[3] The paeans to the wisdom of the broad electorate that constitute a modern-day political shibboleth did not define the political culture of the early nineteenth century.

This situation changed markedly with the rise of what became known as Jacksonian democracy. After the passing of the founding generation and before slavery became the defining issue in American politics, the nation's dominant political movement was embodied by Jefferson's party, newly christened the Democrats and now led by Jackson. Like their Republican forebears, the Jacksonians spoke the language of populism, and they positioned themselves as enemies of hierarchy and elitism. But they went a step further in taking this commitment to entail support for the rights of common people (as they understood them) to determine the direction of government policies. In Jackson's first annual message to Congress, the president called for an elimination of the Electoral College on the grounds that "as few impediments as possible should exist to the free operation of the public will."[4] At the end of his presidency, he expressed his convictions in his farewell address. "Never for a moment believe," he told the nation, "that the great body of citizens . . . can deliberately intend to do wrong."[5]

Jacksonianism was confronted by a contradiction, however, in the realm of political economy. Carrying on in the Jeffersonian tradition, the Jacksonians expressed a suspicion of government economic intervention. But unlike the Jeffersonians, they unabashedly embraced modern commerce, nationalism, and industrialization. They could take these two positions consistently because they saw commerce and the market as an expression of the popular will rather than as a project of the elites. To them, government intervention was an attempt to rig the economy in favor of the wealthy and powerful. But cutting back on the nation's growing commercial and trading sector would be throwing the baby out with the bathwater. The Jacksonians' objectives could be achieved by merely removing government from the economic sector, in the name of populism.

With regard to government intervention in the economy, then, the fundamental Jacksonian project was still the attempt to roll back the Hamiltonian assumption of federal economic stewardship. The central issue of American democratic capitalism in the Jacksonian era remained the most basic one: did the federal government have the authority to intervene in the private economy? On this question, the orientation that defined the Jacksonian position was "divorce"—the complete separation of federal affairs from private economic ones. The limitations of this position, however, quickly became apparent. In championing both a greater political voice for the people and a reduced role for the government in the private economy, the Jacksonians were unable to respond coherently when the people themselves made it clear that they expected the government to manage and even boost that same economy. The tensions in the Jacksonian worldview became obvious in the aftermath of the financial crisis known as the Panic of 1837. In response to this economic calamity, President Martin Van Buren did not act to shore up the nation's banks and the country's money supply but instead aggressively emphasized the government's lack of responsibility for them. The controversy over this policy came to define his administration, and it served as the primary factor in his ignominious defeat in the next election. His rejection by the voters represented the last real challenge to the notion that the federal government should bear responsibility for the performance of the American economy.

The Franchise and the Market

Jacksonianism attempted to grapple with overwhelming political, economic, and social forces that it had itself done a great deal to unleash. Foremost among these was the practice of democracy. Members of the nation's founding generation did not see themselves as initiating a democracy, nor would they have been pleased to see their new nation so described. The prevailing view during that period was that democracy tended to replace the elegant machinations of the republican balance of political interests with an incessant appeal to the lowest common denominator. By the 1820s, however, this attitude had begun to change. The most significant development in this regard was a trend toward what became known as universal suffrage, which referred to the abolition of the property requirement for voting. Though modern readers might chafe at the pretense that the word *universal* could apply to a movement that excluded so many—among them women, African Americans, and Indians—the trend away from property ownership as a voting requirement nonetheless signified a tremendous conceptual shift. In his book on the expansion and restriction of the franchise in the United States, Alexander Keyssar has pointed out that the "lynchpin [*sic*] of both colonial and British suffrage regulations was the restriction of voting to adult men who owned property." Simple class prejudice played no small role in underwriting these restrictions, but such limits were not incompatible with the republican political ideas of the day, which offered two primary justifications for them. First was the prominent belief that those who held real property were dedicated to the success of their society in a way that others could never be; "freeholders" had a built-in motivation to take care of the polity in their desire to preserve the value of their land. The second reason cited by Keyssar would be familiar to any student of Thomas Jefferson: "Property owners alone possessed sufficient independence to warrant their having a voice in governance. . . . Conversely, the ballot was not to be entrusted to those who were economically dependent, because they could too easily be controlled or manipulated by others."[6] As late as 1838, foundational American novelist James Fenimore Cooper was still voicing this criticism in his work of political commentary titled, not insignificantly, *The American Democrat.* "When the pressure of society shall become so great," he wrote, "as to compel the man of small means to depend on the man of large for his comforts, or even for his bread . . . the power of money will probably be felt adversely under a suffrage that includes all, or as nearly so, as is practicable."[7] By this logic, expanding the franchise meant nothing less than an assault on democracy itself.

Notably, this expansion of voting rights took place at the state, rather than the federal, level. Unlike later advances in the access to the franchise, such as the constitutional amendments that guaranteed the vote to black men in 1870 and to women in 1920 or the Voting Rights Act of 1965, the march toward universal suffrage was a state-by-state affair. In the half century or so before 1855, all thirty-one states held at least one constitutional convention. At nearly every such meeting, the most significant issue concerned the distribution of power throughout the states' newly expanding and economically diverse populations. "The course of things in this country," exclaimed New York delegate Nathan Sanford in 1821, "is for the extension, and not the restriction of popular rights."[8] The facts seemed to support Sanford's claim: Delaware had eliminated its property requirement as early as 1792, and no newly admitted state ever required the possession of real property in order to vote. Though Virginia held on to such qualifications for all elections until 1850 and North Carolina restricted senatorial elections to the holders of real property until 1856, the overall trend was toward greater suffrage. By 1860, property requirements were virtually eliminated from the United States.[9]

The reasons for this development were not entirely noble or populist. Demographic change had produced a swelling in the number of people who could not meet property requirements, and to deny the vote to such large majorities was to risk social unrest. At the same time, newer states used an expanded franchise as an incentive to attract settlers. Inevitably, political parties hoped to benefit from extending the vote to this or that category of voters, on the assumption that the members of the newly included group would cast their ballots favorably. Racial components played a role as well, particularly in the South: abolishing property restrictions while retaining racial ones served to create a solidarity among whites that might not otherwise exist in a society exhibiting an increasing economic stratification. Finally, a tremendously important cause of extending the franchise was the ongoing need to satisfy the requirements of various military campaigns. Since armies were frequently made up of members of "the so-called lower orders of society," explained Keyssar, it had often been "rhetorically as well as practically difficult to compel men to bear arms while denying them the franchise." Additionally, he argued, the political and economic necessities of such engagements "meant mobilizing popular support, which gave political leverage to any social groups excluded from the polity." Though many historians have been attracted to the "romantic" notion that American egalitarianism grew organically from the conditions imposed by life on the frontier, "without doubt war played a greater role in the evolution of American democracy."[10]

For any number of reasons, then, the antebellum political situation was clearly and significantly changing. As a consequence, prevailing social philosophies had to be adapted to the new situation. This accommodation took the form of a growing acceptance and even celebration of "democracy" as a description of politics—both actual and ideal—in the United States. It was no coincidence, therefore, that the definitive commentary on the antebellum United States was titled *Democracy in America*. Written by Alexis de Tocqueville, the Liberal son of a French aristocrat, its two volumes were first published in 1835 and 1840, respectively. In his work, Tocqueville painted a picture of the United States in which democracy was so essential to the national way of life that it had to be understood as a phenomenon whose influence had spread beyond politics into the larger culture. "There are many important things to be said about the social conditions of the Anglo-Americans," argued Tocqueville, "but one feature dominates all the others. The social state of the Americans is eminently democratic."[11]

This was no empty claim, for Tocqueville saw the effects of democracy everywhere in American society. Democracy was the reason why public officials in the United States did not wear uniforms[12] and why taxes were higher in that country.[13] Because citizens of a democracy felt personally responsible for all the actions of their government, they viewed the criminal as "an enemy of the human race,"[14] and they exhibited an "annoying" and "irritable patriotism."[15] Democracy, by forcing upon each person a concern for the opinions of others, had removed from the United States "independence of mind and true freedom of discussion."[16] With regard to intellectual pursuits, Tocqueville stated that the "literature of a democracy will never exhibit the order, regularity, skill, and art characteristic of aristocratic literature; formal qualities will be neglected or actually despised."[17] At the same time, historians from democratic cultures were more likely to view sweeping social changes, rather than individual actions, as the causes of particular events.[18] Most of Tocqueville's observations revealed great insight; others—such as the claim that pantheism was the philosophical doctrine "most fitted to seduce the mind in democratic ages"[19]—were arguably less insightful.[20] Some were flattering to his hosts, and some were not. What is important here, though, is that Tocqueville did not think one could speak meaningfully about the United States without reference to a political orientation that would have been universally scorned in that country only a few decades before.

In addition to noting the rage for democracy in the antebellum United States, Tocqueville also observed that "the Americans put something heroic into their way of trading."[21] Here, he identified another central characteristic of the country during the Jacksonian era. Though most Americans still provided for themselves directly from the land, industrial production, commerce, and even market-oriented agriculture were all becoming more prominent. The lure of greater riches and the possibility of social advancement, which had been unattainable to most in the "subsistence-plus" agricultural markets of earlier generations, rendered the Liberal celebration of self-interest more and more attractive.

The integration of the market into American life was significantly abetted by large-scale national investments in transportation. In the colonial era, approximately 85 percent of Americans had provided their own subsistence through farming, and the underdeveloped economy could not provide the conditions necessary for this to change. The lack of a market for excess goods gave families little reason to produce more than they needed, and without this surplus production, farmers had nothing to exchange for other products. Thus, the society did not provide any incentive for individuals to provide goods or services that might diversify the economy. The primary reason for the inability of farmers to sell their goods was the unavailability of shipping. Although the advanced state of British navigation afforded some opportunities for export, the options for overland travel were quite poor. In 1816, it cost as much to ship a ton 30 miles overland as it did to ship it to England. In the early nineteenth century, there were no roads connecting many locations, and those that did exist were muddy, uneven, and filled with tree stumps and other obstacles. As a result, only the farmers who lived near the ocean or on navigable rivers found it worth their while to produce for the market.

But this situation changed markedly as a result of what George Rogers Taylor originally named the "transportation revolution."[22] The most significant development in this regard was the canal, of which the Erie, completed in 1825, was the first and most successful example. Connecting New York City with what is now the upper Midwest, the Erie Canal reaped a tremendous profit for its operator—the state of New York—and it proved an even greater boon for the larger society. According to Jeremy Atack and Peter Passell, "Pork that might have cost as much as $10 a barrel to wrestle over the Appalachians from Cincinnati to New York in 1820 could be transported by water for about $3.50 a barrel in the 1830s. . . . Over the same period, the differential in the price of flour was cut roughly in half."[23] Similar gains came from steam power, which allowed for goods to travel upriver. Antebellum railroads, though not yet occupying the dominant position they would achieve after the Civil War, provided cheap shipping to landlocked locations, and they could run in the winter and in bad weather. The nation's first railroad, the Baltimore and Ohio, was chartered in 1828, and by 1839, the United States could boast of 3,000 miles of operating track.

The cumulative effect of these developments was to bring greater integration of the country economically and to boost the significance of the market in the lives of more Americans. The more productive western farmers of the Ohio Valley now competed directly with easterners, accelerating the importance of commerce and industrialism in the latter area. With improved connectivity between regions and the possibility of wealth to be had in the newer areas, western emigration and land values both rose significantly. States became more involved in promoting local economies with the construction of transportation-related "internal improvements," while the more timid federal government generally restricted itself to projects that served some clearly defined and constitutionally sanctioned national interest, mostly those related to defense.

This period also saw the beginning of the trend toward industrialization in the American economy. New England was the first region of the United States to turn to manufacturing, as the relatively poor arability of its land made its citizens most susceptible to competition from western farmers. As early as 1790, the nation's first textile mill had opened in Pawtucket, Rhode Island, and the tremendously successful Lowell, Massachusetts, mills had begun operations (originally in nearby Waltham) in 1814. In 1820, an already low 58 percent of Massachusetts's labor force worked in agriculture; by 1850, that figure had decreased to 15 percent.[24] Though textiles were the most significant industrial product of the early nineteenth century, sectors such as iron, lumber, shoemaking, flour, and blacksmithing slowly but steadily grew until the Civil War. Often stimulated by high protective tariffs, industry became an increasingly prominent aspect of the American economy.

The net result of these developments was what Charles Sellers originally referred to as the "market revolution" in his 1991 book of the same name.[25] Despite the fact that historians have since taken issue with the sharp break in understanding signaled by the word *revolution,* most accept that the increase in commercial activity had a profound effect on American cultural and intellectual life in the Jacksonian era. John Lauritz Larson represented a more consensual view in his description of the changes wrought by the nation's economic growth. Though markets certainly existed in colonial and revolutionary America, in this period "greed was not normative, and an individual's behavior might as often contradict as conform to the dictates of economic interest." In earlier eras, Larson wrote, people "did not believe— or did not accept it as natural and inevitable—that the market should be the universal arbiter of interests." After the shift toward economic activity, many Americans, "whether happily or not, . . . came to believe that social and material life likely would not (could not?) be otherwise."[26] Rather than a definitive break in cultural understanding, the market revolution was "practically invisible to most individuals until, in hindsight, they recognized the difference between their future and a cherished past."[27]

During the antebellum years, the United States was buffeted by tremendous political and economic forces. Greater market participation brought opportunities for many while also creating social instability and economic inequality. At the same time, the rise of democracy introduced a parallel set of developments, introducing great uncertainty to American political institutions while newly empowering the so-called common man politically. These two developments would influence one another in the formation of the Jacksonian movement, whose primary function was to make the market revolution intelligible to legions of working-class voters.

What Was Jacksonianism?

Of the many points to emerge from Tocqueville's voluminous consideration of the antebellum United States, perhaps the most significant was that democracy, both as a form of government and as a guiding ideal, was a well-established feature of American life by the time of his writing. And in this period, one person served as both the potent symbol of this trend and the political vehicle for its implementation—Andrew Jackson. In *Democracy in America*, Tocqueville noted Jackson's tremendous popularity, going so far as to clarify the president's political views in order to counter the impression, evidently common in Europe, that he was a demagogue. Jackson, he said, "far from wishing to extend federal power, . . . wishes to limit that power to the clear and precise terms of the Constitution and never to allow it to be interpreted in a way favorable to the [u]nion's government." Though he was the leader of the national government, Tocqueville observed, Jackson did not favor centralization; rather, he served as "the spokesman of provincial jealousies." Most important, he did not retain power by consolidating it. Instead, Tocqueville stated, he "is the majority's slave; he yields to its intentions, desires, and half-revealed instincts, or rather he anticipates and forestalls them."[28]

Tocqueville did not present the president's views in the most flattering terms, but his characterization was largely accurate. Jackson believed in the people as much as they did in him, and consequently, he served as a significant bellwether of the change in American political ideals. Though Jackson's paeans to the ordinary American may sound empty and clichéd today, historian Harry Watson has pointed out that in nineteenth-century America, they represented a real ideological commitment. The many economic changes wrought by the market revolution "generated numerous demands by minority 'factions' for tariffs, subsidies and other special privileges from the government." Each party "promised public benefits in return for their private advantages," but Jackson viewed such arrangements as examples of "corruption, and he had them specifically in mind when he denounced the notion of special privilege." Additionally, argued Watson, Jackson viewed the slavery issue in similar terms: those with passionate views on either side of this increasingly divisive subject were not taking courageous moral stands as much as risking the survival of the very nation to impress their social vision upon others. "Majority rule was thus no platitude in Jackson's day; it was advocated as a controversial alternative to contemporary movements that seemed to threaten the [u]nion itself."[29]

Jackson was so popular that he spawned a movement that eventually transcended any particular person, one that became so influential that its name would signify the period itself. Jacksonianism and democracy arose concurrently in the United States. Though the second would eventually survive the passing of the first, becoming an essential feature of American self-identity, in the antebellum mind the two were intertwined and difficult to distinguish from one another. From the perspective of modern political understanding, then, the meaning of Jacksonianism is not as obvious as it might first appear. Jackson himself was the beneficiary of a subaltern turn in American politics, and the celebration of the lower classes was a central rhetorical aspect of the movement. When applied to political economy, though, this concern assumed a radically different form in the early nineteenth century than it would have today. Contemporary political categories tend to associate a concern for those at the bottom of the socioeconomic ladder with substantial government economic intervention: the construction of the "safety net" requires wages-and-hours laws, workplace protections, social insurance of various forms, and inevitably higher taxes. Jacksonians did make occasional moves in this direction—for example, Jackson's presidential successor and political heir Martin Van Buren issued an executive order limiting laborers on federal projects to a ten-hour day—but they generally embraced the market system and did not view as fundamentally unjust the fact that resources, talents, and opportunities were distributed inequitably by the accidents of birth. From their perspective, the major threat to democracy was not the free play of economic actors or the attendant disparities of wealth that followed in the wake of this activity but the perceived tendency of the wealthy and powerful to use their advantages to game the system. The major Jacksonian positions on political and economic issues—abolition of property requirements for the franchise, allowing business firms to incorporate without a specific act of the legislature, destruction of the Second Bank of the United States—reflected a core belief that government's role in uplifting the ordinary citizen centered on removing privileges that had accrued to elites, rather than providing comparable advantages to the masses.

Contemporary political categories, in particular those of "liberal" and "conservative," simply cannot be applied to the Jacksonian movement. The Jacksonians themselves certainly did not use these terms, seeing their movement instead as, in the words of Arthur Schlesinger, Jr., "a revival of Jeffersonianism."[30] Of course, the movement's political vehicle, the Democratic Party, was directly descended from the Republican Party of Jefferson and Madison. Yet the times had changed since the two founders originally formulated their political principles: the agricultural ideal had to give way in order to accommodate the nation's growing industry, Jeffersonian egalitarianism had never been meant to extend the franchise so far as to include those without property, and the (always somewhat hypocritical) concerns for republican virtue had been largely abandoned in the face of the increasingly characteristic American desire to better one's financial situation. It was not altogether obvious how Jeffersonian ideals might apply to the situation that characterized the 1820s and 1830s.

As a result, the fundamental commitments of Jacksonianism have often been difficult to explain to later generations. In 1945, Schlesinger's influential *Age of Jackson* challenged the previous historical consensus that positioned the movement as a sectional phenomenon influenced by the egalitarian conditions of the frontier. The book argued the primary concerns of the day did not pit regions against each other but classes. For Jackson, argued Schlesinger, "the economic problem, the balance of class power, overshadowed all the questions of the day."[31] According to this view, the Jacksonian outlook was premised on the belief "that there was a deep-rooted conflict in society between the 'producing' and 'non-producing' classes— the farmers and laborers, on the one hand, and the business community on the other." Taking the side of the producers, Jacksonians were committed to using the power of government on their behalf, as a counterweight to the influence of organized wealth, so that the United States could realize its promise of political and economic equality. The movement represented a "second American phase of that enduring struggle between the business community and the rest of society which is the guarantee of freedom in a liberal capitalist state."[32]

Schlesinger's extensive sourcing, sweeping scope, and compelling narrative established *The Age of Jackson* as the definitive work on the subject almost immediately, and the book won the Pulitzer Prize in 1946. Like many such ambitious works, however, no sooner was it showered with accolades than it began to attract heated criticism. The most common complaint was that Schlesinger himself, an FDR Democrat who would later serve in the Kennedy administration, was reading his present-day political commitments backward, imposing the ideology of the New Deal on the unwitting Jacksonians, most of whom would have recoiled in horror at the "big-government" tactics of the later Democratic administrations. A few years later, prominent historian Richard Hofstadter readily acknowledged that the movement owed its success to the increased participation of "the propertyless masses" and their "common feeling"—encouraged by political operatives—"that popular will should control the choice of public officers and the formation of public policy."[33] But he spoke for many historians in noting that the Jacksonians were not in any way opposed to business. On this view, Schlesinger had mistaken a movement that opposed privileges for the wealthy and well-connected for one that opposed capitalism itself. If an opposition between the lower and elite classes constitutes liberalism, then Jacksonianism was liberal. But a probusiness, laissez-faire "liberalism" so befuddles twenty-first-century political categories that the use of this term obscures far more than it clarifies. One year after Hofstadter, distinguished economic historian Joseph Dorfman issued a very similar criticism, arguing that Jacksonianism, being "antiaristocratic rather than anticapitalistic," could "combine both humanitarian and business elements." Though Dorfman proclaimed that "the movement [was] a liberal one," this was not by virtue of an opposition to capitalism but only because "it sought to eliminate or hedge law-created privileges."[34]

Historian Sean Wilentz later summarized many of these developments in the context of his magisterial history of democracy in the United States from the late eighteenth to the mid-nineteenth centuries. Though *The Rise of American Democracy: Jefferson to Lincoln* treated a broader period, at the book's heart was an appraisal of the Jacksonian era. Perhaps the book's most prominent contribution to the understanding of the period was its incorporation of previously neglected groups—African Americans both enslaved and free, women and suffragists, displaced Indians and their advocates, and working-class political activists—into the broad sweep of American democracy. In Wilentz's hands, a story that had, to that point, often been limited to the activities of larger-than-life founding heroes, philosophical theorists of government, and power-seeking politicians came to more accurately reflect the diversity of the population that had constructed the nation's democratic culture and government. Wilentz was fully aware of the many inadequacies of the Jacksonian project, in particular its indifference to slavery and its support for the forced removal of Indian tribes from the Southeast, but he nonetheless found much to admire in the movement and its leader. He dismissed the notion of Jacksonian anticapitalism, but in the end, he found that neither the addition to the narrative of previously neglected groups nor the significant historiographical revisions had "diminished the importance of the questions that *The Age of Jackson* asked about early American democracy."[35] Schlesinger's contribution, in Wilentz's view, had been modified but not overturned: "At bottom, the Jackson Democracy was chiefly what its proponents said it was—a political movement for, and largely supported by, those who considered themselves producers pitted against a nonproducer elite."[36] Wilentz seconded the emphasis on Jacksonianism as a "bottom-up," producerist movement rooted in class resentment, even while acknowledging that the Jacksonians enthusiastically supported the development of market-based institutions.

These political commitments led Jacksonians to a conception of political economy that does not assimilate well into contemporary analytical categories. The most succinct summary of this conception came from legal historian Herbert Hovenkamp. In his 1991 *Enterprise and American Law,* he followed in the footsteps of Hofstadter and Dorfman by arguing that the dominant nineteenth-century intellectual movement—which Hovenkamp called "classicism"—held as its "fundamental premise" the notion "that the government should not play favorites."[37] This idea had applications in economics, politics, and law and served as a unifying theory for much of the nineteenth century, but it was, in its essence, "a Jacksonian phenomenon."[38] Noting that "liberal critics today are inclined to view the classicists through the lens of the Progressives and the policy makers of the New Deal," Hovenkamp rejected as anachronistic the notion that the Jacksonians could not consistently serve as the champions of the working classes while opposing government market intervention. Though "Jacksonianism . . . was heavily supported by society's disfavored classes," he said, the causes they championed "were not welfare and subsidized education." Instead, they opposed "special corporate charters or licenses that gave unique privileges to engage in business to certain favored people while denying access to others." The Jacksonians remembered that Federalist market interventions had generally benefited the wealthy. "In such a regime," Hovenkamp observed, "arguments for a noninterventionist state leaned to the left, not to the right. To be a classicist in the 1830's was to be a liberal."[39]

This pivotal distinction summarizes both what was definitive about the wide-ranging intellectual commitments of Jacksonianism and why the movement confounds today's political categories. Jacksonianism retained the Jeffersonian hostility to elitism but did not share its distrust of markets more broadly; it favored the lower classes but did not oppose capitalism. At the core of this movement, which might be described as laissez-faire populism, was a simple principle: the federal government privileged the wealthy when it intervened in the market. Its mission, therefore, was to roll back Hamiltonian economic stewardship, and the word that best summarized this formulation was *divorce*. This idea, the animating principle of Jacksonian political economy, referred to the policy of keeping the workings of the federal government completely separate from those of the private market economy.

Hard Money

At the end of *The Age of Jackson* is a lonely, two-and-a-quarter-page appendix whose significance is so great that Schlesinger might have better aided his readers by placing it at the beginning of the book. With this appendix, the author intended to clear up a central ambiguity in the meaning of the term *bank*. For modern readers, a bank is an institution charged with the secure storage of the customers' money. Its incentive to provide this service comes less from the fees that those customers pay, which are relatively insignificant in quantity, than from the fact that the institution can pool the deposited funds and invest them, by making loans or purchasing financial instruments, in order to make money. But during the Jacksonian period, Schlesinger pointed out, "note issue was regarded as the characteristic function of banks, and an attack on the 'banking system' or on 'banks' meant generally an attack on the power of private note issue. It did not mean the elimination of the functions of discount[40] or deposit."[41]

But this explanation might only exchange one set of confusions for another, for "private notes" issued by banks are no longer in use, and they have no modern analogue. What may seem difficult for many contemporary audiences to understand is that during that period, the federal government was not circulating any currency: it did not print dollar bills or mint coins.[42] Thus, when individuals or businesses wished to conduct a financial transaction, the only obvious or standard medium of exchange available was precious metals. Gold and silver have a tendency to retain their value even during financial upheavals, and so, all other things being equal, most people preferred to transact in those media. But these materials are heavy, bulky, and cumbersome, and therefore, they were impractical for highly denominated exchanges or purchases made at a distance. Gold and silver presented another difficulty as well, for there was not enough of either to meet the many financial needs of the nation. To work around these problems, private banks issued notes that could be redeemed at that particular place of business for the amount of precious metals—referred to as "specie"—that corresponded to the value denominated in the note. Moreover, what made a note different from a "draft" (what we would today call a check) was that it was not addressed to any specific party. Anyone in possession of a note could, at any time, redeem it for specie at the issuing bank.

In the nineteenth century, these circulating notes came to perform the same function that government-issued currency does today.[43] But notes issued by private banks caused many problems. Since the various notes were, in fact, separate financial instruments, they were not interchangeable goods, and each bank's note generated a unique financial market. As a result, there was no guarantee—and actually little likelihood—that a note from one bank could buy the same value of goods as an equally denominated note from a different bank. This phenomenon also had a regional component: in the West, where there was little specie, the need for a medium of exchange prompted banks to issue too many notes, which caused inflation. As a result, notes from western banks were often simply worth less than similarly denominated ones issued in the East.

Additionally, the very nature of the banking business model was such that all banks—even those in very sound financial shape—circulated an amount of notes whose denominated value far exceeded that of the gold and silver the banks possessed. If, for whatever reason, a large number of a bank's customers appeared at once to exchange their notes for specie, the aggregate demand for precious metals could add up to a value greater than that of the specie held in the bank's vault. The least desirable scenario in this event would be what was called a *run* on the bank. This was a self-propelling catastrophe in which a bank's customers would panic when, for whatever reason, they came to believe that *other* customers wanted to redeem their notes. In such a situation, many who might otherwise have been perfectly content to hold the bank's paper would become convinced that they needed to get rid of it before it was too late, and everyone would attempt to exchange their notes for precious metals. More often than not, a run ended only with the failure of the bank; in such an event, nearly everyone involved lost everything.

To avoid such a fate, if the bank was owed money by other financial institutions it would begin calling for payment in order to meet the demands of its customers; this, in turn, would impair the ability of these other banks to provide specie to their own customers. The worst-case result would be a systemwide "panic," in which a problem at one institution would spread across the entire nation.

Jackson and his followers believed that this state of affairs was unacceptable, and a central tenet of their ideology was therefore a commitment to "hard money"—a deceptively simple phrase that referred most specifically to a policy preference for specie over banknotes. But this idea, requiring as it would a complete overhaul of the nation's banking system, stood at the center of a nexus of concerns. Wilentz described hard money as an "essentially political and democratic" doctrine that "insisted that no institutions independent of the sovereign people ought to be tolerated within the American government."[44] Under this view, notes were the provenance of banks, and banks worked to the advantage of the wealthy and well-connected at the expense of the laborers and farmers. Thus, Jacksonians believed that if the federal government did anything that encouraged the issuing of notes, it was violating the principle of divorce. As far as specific policy provisions, the "hard money men" supported a restriction on government acceptance of notes in payment of moneys it was owed and laws that would forbid banks from issuing notes in smaller denominations.

Jackson saw the hard-money position as little more than an extension of democracy into the economic realm. Yet the issue was far more complicated than he made it out to be. If it was the profit-seeking nature of banks that rendered them unreliable to carry out the quasi-public functions of circulating currency, then perhaps the most obvious solution to the problem would be to assign this function to an arm of the federal government. But Jackson deeply despised the government entity that had been given this responsibility, believing it to be inherently undemocratic. This institution was the Second Bank of the United States.

In 1811, many years before Jackson took office, a Republican Congress had narrowly voted against renewing the charter of the Bank of the United States, out of hostility to the remnant of Hamilton's financial system. Without the bank, the ensuing period was characterized by a weakening of the structure of the nation's commercial and financial systems. The number of state-chartered banks almost tripled, and the total quantity of banknotes doubled; at the same time, the amount of specie in the nation's vaults actually declined.[45] By 1814, the gross military and financial mismanagement of the War of 1812, combined with the omnipresent opportunities for wartime profiteering, created a climate of reckless financial speculation that culminated in a series of bank runs. Two years later, Congress and President James Madison set aside their opposition in order to start a new national bank. Only five years after Hamilton's bank had closed, the federal government chartered the Second Bank of the United States.

Despite its name, the Second Bank of the United States, like its predecessor, was not in any significant way a federal entity. Though the United States did own one-fifth of the bank's shares and the US president was empowered to appoint five of its twenty-five directors, what made the bank particularly "national" was only the fact that it was chartered by the federal government, rather than by one of the states. Nonetheless, its governmental affiliation and sheer size—it was capitalized at $35 million in order to serve a national economy that circulated around $70 million—gave the bank a disproportionate influence on the money supply. In the year before the bank was chartered, Treasury Secretary Andrew Dallas wrote to John C. Calhoun that "it is not an institution created for the purposes of commerce and profit alone, but more for the purposes of national policy, as an auxiliary in the exercise in some of the highest powers of government."[46] Many believed it would play a significant role in stabilizing the economy when necessary. By the time he became president, however, Jackson had come to hate the Second Bank of the United States, despite his clear-cut antagonism toward the system of private note circulation. Jackson believed, in the words of Sean Wilentz, "on strict Jeffersonian grounds . . . [that] the bank was constitutionally invalid, an entity that Congress had created by asserting powers not ceded to it by the framers"; additionally, he "perceived that the bank, by its very design, undermined popular sovereignty and majority rule."[47] The fight against what the Jacksonians called the "monster bank" would become the signature issue of the president's administration.

It is unclear just how much the view of Jackson and his followers regarding the Second Bank of the United States reflected a sober assessment of that institution's actual performance rather than a simmering emotional reaction: many, but not all, historians today agree with Bray Hammond's earlier assessment that the bank was a minor force for stability in an era of relatively primitive economic understanding.[48] But it is undeniably true that the Jacksonian attitude toward the bank was central to the movement's adherents' conception of the appropriate interaction between the federal government and the nation's economy. Jackson vetoed the congressional renewal

This 1835 note from the Second Bank of the United States "promises to pay . . . ten dollars on demand." (Courtesy Federal Reserve Bank of San Francisco)

of the charter of the Second Bank of the United States on July 10, 1832.[49] The message that accompanied the return of the bill to the Senate revealed a deep passion about the issue at hand. At 7,000 words, it was the longest veto message up to that time. And though historian Ralph C. H. Catterall's assessment that "its economic reasoning is in the main beneath contempt"[50] was a rather strong opinion, it is nonetheless safe to say that the message was not characterized by a thoughtful or nuanced approach to the issue.

One of the president's primary contentions was that a great number of the shares in the Second Bank of the United States were owned by foreigners. Should the United States find itself at war with the country from which these investors hailed, "all its operations within would be in aid of the hostile fleets and armies without. Controlling our currency, receiving our public moneys, and holding thousands of our citizens in dependence, it would be more formidable and dangerous than the naval and military power of the enemy."[51]

Jackson's concerns on this particular point approached the hysterical, but he offered other objections to the bank as well. One major reason for his veto was constitutional in nature. Jackson revisited the necessary and proper clause that had so occupied Hamilton, Jefferson, and Madison during the process of chartering the first bank. Claiming to concede that the federal government had the power to create a bank, Jackson instead quibbled with the particular powers granted to the bank according to the charter under review. His objections were so strenuous that any real-life institution guided by his restrictions would likely have had some difficulty in running a successful business. Practices that did not meet the high bar of Jackson's constitutional test included the charter's grant of monopoly, the ability of the bank to have branches throughout the country, the construction of buildings to house these branches, the amount at which the bank was capitalized, and (again) the selling of stock to foreigners.[52]

The bulk of the veto message seemed akin to political grandstanding, calculated to whip into a frenzy the president's supporters around the country. Nonetheless, a speech that was, in the main, little more than a long, polemical diatribe concluded with a broad exposition of the president's philosophical principles. This section of the speech, by far the most often quoted, was not terribly representative of the veto message, but it revealed much about the philosophy of Jacksonianism itself. The president noted that "it is to be regretted that the rich and powerful too often bend the acts of government to their selfish purposes." But Jackson was no leveler, observing that "distinctions in society will always exist" and that "equality of talents, of education, or of wealth can not be produced by human institutions." The fact that justice did not demand an equal distribution of goods, however, did not mean that all economic arrangements were acceptable. Injustice could ensue but only when "the laws . . . add to these natural and just advantages artificial distinctions" that "make the rich richer and the potent more powerful." At that point, "the humble members of society—the farmers, mechanics, and laborers . . . have a right to complain of the injustice of their [g]overnment." Were the state to "shower its favors alike on the high and the low, the rich and the poor," it would only be a force for good. Unfortunately, the bank charter presented "a wide and unnecessary departure from these just principles."[53]

Despite the fact that this influential passage was a poor representation of the overall address, it nonetheless illustrates two important points about Andrew Jackson and the movement that took his name. The first is that the president was no enemy of the nation's burgeoning capitalism: that the statements denying equality as a viable political goal came at such an arguably demagogic moment suggests that Jackson expected little disagreement with them. The president's objections to the Second Bank of the United States fit entirely within a framework that philosophically supported industry and even finance. Thus, the second point is, again, that the thread that ran through the various Jacksonian positions—the stance against hierarchy and aristocracy, the commitment to popular rule, the acceptance of the market, and of course the slew of hard-money positions—was the notion of divorce.

The economy was considered a purely private affair, and whatever accolades or wealth that people acquired there was their own business. What was illegitimate, however, were those policies in which government acted in a manner that was not neutral between parties, as distinctions acquired in this fashion were conferred rather than earned. And because there was no way for the state to pursue economic goals that were neutral between citizens, it had a positive duty to refuse to enter the economic arena at all.

To get a sense of how deeply Jackson opposed the Second Bank of the United States, one might consider that he brought up the subject again in his farewell address. Delivered four years after the veto was issued, the speech found Jackson still according to the bank a primary place among the threats to American democracy. Noting that the fifty-year anniversary of the Constitution was approaching, he remarked that nothing in that half-century period had "produced such deep-seated evil as the course of legislation in relation to the currency." Though the Constitution "unquestionably intended" that citizens utilize "a circulating medium of gold and silver," he said, Congress nonetheless established a national bank, "with the privilege of issuing paper money receivable in the payment of the public dues." This course of events unfortunately "drove from general circulation the constitutional currency and substituted one of paper in its place."[54]

The pernicious effects of paper money, Jackson continued, all stemmed from the tendency toward fluctuation in its value. In good times, when risks seem minimal, banks would succumb to the temptation "to extend their issues of paper beyond the bounds of discretion and the reasonable demands of business." Eventually, the public would learn that the notes were not well supported, and it would begin to redeem them. Next, the suddenly nervous banks would "immediately withdraw the credits they have given, suddenly curtail their issues, and produce an unexpected and ruinous contraction of the circulating medium, which is felt by the whole community."[55] This endless cycle was bad enough, but Jackson's most basic concerns echoed the Jeffersonian fear that the wild fluctuations in the value of various notes encouraged speculation in them. The culture that resulted from the prevalence of such pursuits would sap the moral strength of the nation itself, and in Jackson's view, "it is not by encouraging this spirit that we shall best preserve public virtue and promote the true interests of our country." The existence of paper currency would "foster this eager desire to amass wealth without labor," and the ensuing corruption, once penetrating the "public councils," would "destroy at no distant day the purity of your [g]overnment."[56]

Though private banks exerted far too much influence on the currency, Jackson continued, one brake on the system of concentrated power was the fact that no one bank was particularly large relative to the others. As such, their competition limited the amount of power that any particular bank could exert over the political system. Consequently, even if private banks did great injury to "the habits of business, the pecuniary concerns, and the moral tone of society," the inability of the banks to combine necessitated that "their power of mischief . . . be confined to a narrow space and felt only in their immediate neighborhoods."

The national bank, however, changed all that, and Jackson's description of its machinations can only be described as dystopian. The Second Bank of the United States had been able to "exercise despotic sway over the other banks," which became its "obedient instruments." At the same time, the "numerous class[es] of persons . . . who depend altogether on bank credits for their solvency" were necessarily bound "to propitiate the favor of the money power by distinguished zeal and devotion in its service." The untrammeled power of this colossus was such that it could "bring forward upon any occasion its entire and undivided strength to support or defeat any measure of the [g]overnment." Finally, its dominant position over the currency in circulation ultimately gave it "the power to regulate the value of property and the fruits of labor in every quarter of the Union, and to bestow prosperity or bring ruin upon any city or section of the country as might best comport with its own interest or policy."[57] The Second Bank of the United States had been killed not a moment too soon, as its very existence portended nothing less than the imminent demise of the republic.

Jackson remained popular as he clearly and unashamedly articulated his hard-money positions, but the doctrine of divorce was much easier to espouse than to practice. In the first place, if the situation ever came about that the people actually preferred the government to involve itself in economic affairs, then the democratic mandate could conflict with the powerful impulse toward hard money. Jacksonianism was ill equipped to deal with this contradiction. In the second place, it was not obvious that the best way to ensure fair and equal economic treatment of citizens was for the government to refuse to deal with the economy at all. Despite these tensions in the Jacksonian project of political economy, however, Old Hickory himself largely escaped any negative fallout from the bank veto. The repercussions would instead fall on the head of Jackson's protégé and successor, Vice President Martin Van Buren.

Pet Banks

Jackson's veto was upheld in Congress, but the "bank war" did not end with that action. The veto itself had been a result of an unwise gamble on the part of Nicholas Biddle, president of the Second Bank of the United States. Under the assumption that public opinion supported the bank, he asked his allies in Congress to introduce the bill renewing its charter nearly four years before the old charter was set to expire. Knowing that Jackson would soon be running for reelection and misjudging the popularity of his own institution, Biddle believed that the president would be unwilling to oppose the measure. But Jackson, who was much better at gauging the popular will, was delighted to run as the man who had defended the "humble members of society" against the "monster bank." As a result, with several years remaining on the bank's charter after the veto, the United States was left with a lame duck national bank.

During this period, Jackson had to figure out where to put the federal money, which at the moment was stored in Biddle's Philadelphia vaults. A little over a year after the veto, the president made his decision, ordering that the nation's specie be removed from the Second Bank of the United States and deposited in a series of designated state-chartered banks around the country. This move was not entirely popular. In the Senate, Jackson's political enemy Henry Clay proposed two motions, eventually successful, to censure the president for removing the deposits.[58] At the bank itself, Biddle called in loans and began redeeming more and more local banknotes at their home institutions. He hoped that these redemptions would prompt a greater need for specie among the banks, causing them in turn to circulate fewer notes. The currency contraction, Biddle believed, would prompt a greater popular understanding and appreciation of his bank's value.

As banks around the country began to fail, citizens pressured Congress and the administration for relief. The outcries only seemed to strengthen Jackson's resolve. "The bank, Mr. Van Buren, is trying to kill me," he told his vice president. "*But I will kill it!*"[59] Jackson did not waver, and the power of the bank was broken well before it ceased to exist legally. Yet the president's actions generated a political backlash. This reaction took shape in the founding of the opposition Whig Party, which competed with Jackson's Democrats during what political scientists call the second American party system.

The Whigs fare poorly according to contemporary popular memory.

The primary reason for this historical amnesia is that Americans generally think of politics in terms of the White House. The Whig Party elected only two presidents, and both of them died in office, serving for a total of only seventeen months. It is true that the party lacked executive influence, but this fact alone provided, in the words of Whig chronicler Daniel Walker Howe, "little sign of [the Whigs'] strength in congressional, state and local politics."[60] Two of antebellum America's most powerful congressmen— Henry Clay and Daniel Webster—were Whigs, and the country admitted of what Howe called a "fairly even distribution of partisan strength" between the two groups.[61] The ideas, values, and interests of the Whigs exerted a significant influence on the furious national debate, instigated by Jackson's bank veto, over the appropriate role of the federal government in the nation's financial affairs.

The central animating feature of the Whig Party was that its adherents feared Andrew Jackson, the principles that he represented, and the political network that his Democratic Party was building. Yet Howe argued in his study of the Whigs that these expressions of conspiracy and paranoia—a focus in no way foreign to the Jacksonians themselves—should not blind modern observers to the overall coherence of the Whigs' political philosophy. The Whigs held an optimistic belief in progress, technology, and entrepreneurialism that many Jacksonians, consumed with concerns over worker and farmer exploitation, could not share. Howe argued that the party did not crassly embrace the latter-day argument that "profitability itself is an indicator of social utility" but instead sincerely "justified not only the new technology but the system of industrial capitalism on the grounds of moral benefit to society." To the Whigs, the advantages of the modern system lay in "improving the quality of life and giving wider scope for the employment of talents and savings."[62]

The conception of industrial development as an unmitigated boon for all Americans led the Whigs to strongly reject Jacksonian class warfare. Moreover, since economic development was such an overwhelmingly positive force, they believed supporting it to be incumbent upon the federal government. At the center of this effort was Clay's "American system," which included high tariffs to stimulate domestic industry, a national bank that would support the nation's financial and credit systems, and federal funding for "internal improvements" in transportation infrastructure. All of these positions, of course, were in direct and fundamental opposition to those of the Jacksonians. Much like the Federalists and Republicans before them, both Democrats and Whigs tended to view the other side less as misguided or mistaken than as corrupt, conspiratorially using the political system to reward its friends and punish its enemies.

Sean Wilentz generally positioned the Democrats in a more favorable light than the Whigs, whom he presented as comprising a fundamentally conservative party devoted to the protection of property from the Jacksonian mob. His analysis, however, squared with Howe's on the points most relevant to political economy. The Whigs, in Wilentz's view, reacted to the increasing prevalence of democratic presumptions in American politics by developing a new philosophy in which "all freemen shared a basic harmony of interests that had effectively banished the existence of classes." The abundant land and tremendous economic opportunity that characterized the United States meant that "the idea of the few and the many had been banished, and, contrary to the Democrats, rendered permanently antithetical to the genius of American politics." For the Whigs, then, the "true oppressors of the people" were not the wealthy but those politicians whose economic programs served only to enrich themselves and to harm entrepreneurial and business-minded citizens. These policies, in turn, limited the possibility of economic expansion and hurt the workers and farmers who depend on a growing economy. No offender fared worse in this schema than "King Andrew," and no particular policy was more indicative of his corruption than the system of local banks that he installed after killing the Second Bank of the United States.[63]

These institutions were referred to disparagingly by the Whigs as "pet banks," and they did not work out for Jackson exactly the way he had hoped. In contrast to the Whig characterization, these banks were profit-seeking institutions and not political organs. As such, they were happy to get specie from the government without the requirements that had formerly accompanied the deposits of the Second Bank of the United States. Unfettered by such stipulations, they issued more and more notes, flouting the hard-money orthodoxy in the process. Jackson, now beginning to look at the end of his presidency, enacted a series of smaller reforms in an attempt to impose this philosophy on the deposit banks.

During this period, two government initiatives were of particular importance in moving the country toward a hard-money policy, but the first was not Jacksonian in origin. It was the deposit bill, a measure sponsored by the Whigs that required each state to have at least one deposit bank and that designated a greater number of such institutions overall. After the bill became law, the number of deposit banks nearly tripled, literally overnight. Furthermore, the bill set the mandated ratio of required specie on hand to issued notes lower than that which had been in effect in many states, which would allow the banks to circulate more notes without having to obtain more precious metals. Additionally, the bill sought to combat the pet bank phenomenon by forbidding banks from holding more·than three-fourths of their reserves in the form of government deposits. In effect, this bill required that the government remove specie from a smaller number of banks that tended to have conservative note-issuing policies (because they were friendly to the Democrats) and disburse the precious metals among a larger group of banks with expansionist tendencies. Finally, the recent retirement of the federal debt—an achievement of which Jackson was very proud—had combined with other economic developments to leave a bit of "extra" money in the federal accounts. The deposit bill mandated that this money be distributed to the states in four payments of approximately $9 million each. Its purpose was frankly and obviously to expand currency circulation.

Once Congress passed and submitted the deposit bill, Jackson's first impulse was to veto it. But he believed the action would be unpopular with voters, who might see him as favoring the pet banks as a form of patronage. Moreover, Jackson feared for the political future of Van Buren, who would be heading the Democratic ticket in 1836 and would not want to be saddled with such unpopular legislation. With the president's signature, the bill passed into law. The Deposit Act, however, backfired for its Whig supporters. In compliance with the law's provisions, millions of dollars left New York banks, which were already reeling from an unrelated tightening of credit from England. While in transit, this money was not available to its destination banks, which might have used it to ease the strains of contraction. The unintended effects reduced the money supply overall for a period of time and moved much of the nation's specie to places where it could do little good.

The other significant contractionary policy was initiated with Jackson's issue of the so-called Specie Circular. In an effort to combat both the speculation in federal land and the consequent accumulation of nearly worthless paper in government accounts, Jackson directed his secretary of the Treasury, Levi Woodbury, to accept only specie for the sale of government real property. This policy was intended to contract the money supply, and it did just that. Jackson had thought that it might combat the presumed expansionary effects of the Deposit Act, but the unforeseen and unintended contraction put into place by that law meant that the government, in effect, was putting its weight behind a second set of contractionary policies at a time when the national economy desperately needed the amount of circulating currency to expand. When this was combined with the English credit squeeze, many financial actors found the cumulative effect unbearable. On May 10, 1837, several New York banks ran out of specie and stopped redeeming their notes; within a few days, only 6 of the nation's 800 banks would still be making payments.[64] The ensuing national economic collapse, the worst the nation had ever seen, became known as the Panic of 1837. It would define the presidency of Martin Van Buren.

"Evils of Great Magnitude"

Martin Van Buren is usually cited as the first professional politician in the history of the United States. Born in Kinderhook, New York, in 1782, he began to practice law as a young man, shortly thereafter becoming involved in state politics. Van Buren quickly demonstrated an affinity for the backroom deals and patronage arrangements that served as the coin of the realm in the rough-and-tumble world of New York politics; given his small stature, at 5'6", and his political wizardry, Van Buren was soon nicknamed "the Little Magician." By 1820, he was the leader of the dominant faction in that state, a machinelike organization called the Albany Regency, which secured his election to the Senate in 1821.

Once on the national stage, Van Buren hitched his star to Andrew Jackson, eventually emerging as the future president's political point man in the North. Upon his election, President Jackson rewarded Van Buren's loyalty by appointing him secretary of state. As the next election approached and Vice President John C. Calhoun emerged as a political rival for Jackson and ultimately resigned, Jackson named Van Buren to the ticket. Van Buren became vice president in 1832, and upon the end of Jackson's second term, he emerged as the popular president's handpicked successor.

After defeating three Whig candidates in the 1836 presidential election, Van Buren had been in office only about two months when the Panic of 1837 began. Within five days of the initial bank failures, public pressure forced him to call for a special session of Congress to meet in September, some four months hence. In the meantime, Van Buren ordered Treasury Secretary Woodbury to remove government deposits from any private banks that had discontinued specie payments. That fall, Van Buren opened the congressional "panic session," as it became known, with an address. The president assessed the various options for dealing with the crisis and declared, in true Jacksonian faction, that the solution lay in separating completely the functions of government from those of private banks. The practical manifestation of this claim, in terms of policy, was that the government would remove all its money from any such institution. Federal specie would, from that point forward, be stored in an institution newly proposed by the president—an "independent treasury" made up of several smaller depositories around the country.

Van Buren's address began by delineating the particular nature of the crisis at hand and the tasks with which Congress was now charged. He proffered an exhaustive list: the regulation of "the safe-keeping, transfer, and disbursement of the public moneys"; the designation of "funds to be received and paid by the government"; the enabling of "the Treasury to meet promptly every demand upon it"; the collection of revenue; and any "further measures . . . as will be best calculated to revive the enterprise and to promote the prosperity of the country."[65] Thus, the president implied none too subtly, if someone saw any greater responsibility for the government of the United States, that individual not only was mistaken but also was essentially violating the ideals of the Constitution. Many of the more ambitious tasks that some would have liked to see the government undertake were outside its purview and consequently a threat to liberty. What was needed in this crisis, argued Van Buren, was not more federal intervention in the economy but less. The exigencies of the day, he contended, presented three options: keeping federal money in the state-chartered banks, bringing back the national bank, or eliminating the governmental need for private banks entirely. He admitted that each of the first two options had their supporters, but he noted that "it is apparent that the events of the last few months have greatly augmented the desire, long existing among the people of the United States, to separate the fiscal operations of the [g]overnment from those of individuals or corporations."[66]

Taking the options in turn, the president began by presenting his arguments against a national bank. Judging by the failure of the two previous national banks, he confidently claimed that the people simply did not want such an institution: "Again to create a national bank as a fiscal agent would be to disregard the popular will, twice solemnly and unequivocally expressed."[67] Van Buren would return to this point several times throughout the speech, and his case for divorce was not merely political in the narrower partisan sense of the term but also ideological. The president argued that a national bank would have failed to prevent the Panic of 1837, but his larger point was that whatever benefits such an institution *could* provide were illegitimate ones, gained by using governmental power to enrich some specific group of citizens.

Van Buren, in short, denied that the federal government and in particular its chief executive had any responsibility for the performance of the nation's economy. To him, even the "derangement alleged at present to exist in the domestic exchanges of the county"—that is, the Panic of 1837—did not present to the government a situation that demanded its action or attention. He noted many complaints regarding "an omission to aid and regulate commercial exchange," but these objections, he said, "only serve to exemplify the constant desire among some of our citizens to enlarge the powers of the [g]overnment and extend its control to subjects with which it should not interfere."[68] Arguing that the federal government "was not designed by the Constitution" to "assume the management of domestic or foreign exchange," the president took a position that today would be simply unimaginable. He argued on constitutional grounds that the nation's economic misery was not a concern of the federal government. He based his argument on what he saw as a moral truth deeper than the need to alleviate suffering: that commercial enterprise had no claim on the attention of the government. The government's "province" was not "to aid individuals in the transfer of their funds otherwise than through the facilities afforded by the Post Office Department." Business and commerce "ought to be conducted by those who are interested in them in the same manner that the incidental difficulties of other pursuits are encountered by other classes of citizens."[69] On this view, the economy was of no more particular concern to the government than was any other purely private pursuit.

Van Buren expressed his hostility to a national bank much as Jackson did in his veto message: by asserting a much broader principle in order to justify that opposition. The Jacksonian premise contained two interrelated assertions—that the government was unauthorized to assume the kind of power that a national bank represented and that, whether justified or not, taking on such a responsibility would be a mistake of gigantic proportions. Such discrimination would nearly always work to the advantage of the well-off against the "humble members of society."

Experience had shown, Van Buren continued, that state banks had also failed to meet the nation's purposes, and their mismanagement was a substantial cause of the panic. Such banks had performed quite well in good times, but "when it became necessary, under the act of June, 1836, [the Deposit Act] to withdraw from them the public money . . . they found it in many cases inconvenient to comply with the demands of the Treasury." The maintenance of these government requirements "increased the general distress and contributed, with other causes, to hasten the revulsion in which at length they, in common with the other banks, were fatally involved."[70] The president thus concluded that the state banking system was inadequate to the financial needs of the federal government.

Having therefore considered and rejected the only two available options, Van Buren appeared to be without a solution. But he did not accept such a conclusion, arguing instead that the apparent choice between the use of a nationally chartered bank and several state-chartered institutions was a false one. Both options, he declared, operated under a premise that he would reject—that it was necessary or advisable for the federal government to involve itself with banks at all. The mere act of acknowledging this presumption, in Van Buren's rhetorical pronouncement, was tantamount to rejecting it: "Under these circumstances it becomes our solemn duty to inquire whether there are not in any connection between the [g]overnment and banks of issue evils of great magnitude, inherent in its very nature and against which no precautions can effectually guard."[71]

Of course, Van Buren meant to suggest that such an inquiry would yield the conclusion that the federal government had no business involving itself with private financial enterprises. The reasons for this rejection of standard practice, which he claimed to have evolved more as "a measure of emergency than of sound policy,"[72] were twofold. In one direction, the vagaries of financial markets could impede the government's ability to perform its core functions, and in the other, the opportunities for gain presented by banks could compromise the motivations and actions of federal officials.

The Panic of 1837 had clearly demonstrated that a dependence upon private financial institutions could render impotent a government suddenly deprived of its funds. As Van Buren put it, "a sudden act of the banks intrusted [sic] with the funds of the people deprives the Treasury, without fault or agency of the [g]overnment, of the ability to pay its creditors in the currency they have by law a right to demand." Yet the potential consequences of such upheavals could inflict even greater damage. To prove this point, Van Buren, as Jackson had done in his bank veto message, asked the members of Congress to imagine the harm such a crisis could have inflicted had the nation been involved in a war. In invoking such a scenario, he argued that governmental functions, including even seemingly mundane ones such as those involving finance, were far too important to allow any entity not beholden to the people to perform them. In converting "the money raised for and necessary to the public service . . . into a mere right of action against corporations intrusted [*sic*] with the possession of them,"[73] the federal government would give away the means to perform its public duties.

Van Buren's first set of objections concerned banks hampering the government's ability to perform its functions, but he noted that risks also ran in the other direction as well: government officials could interfere with financial markets. Though the purpose of keeping federal money in these banks was to enable the government to better serve the people, "its effect may be to introduce into the operations of the [g]overnment influences the most subtle, founded on interests the most selfish." In such a scenario, the people's money, rather than being used for the projects that the citizens had prioritized through their elected representatives, instead would serve as "a fund on which discounts are made for the profit of those who happen to be owners of stock in the banks selected as depositories."[74]

Van Buren summed up his commitment to bank divorce with another rhetorical question. "Experience has shown," he stated, that lending "public money to the local banks is hazardous to the operations of the [g]overnment," "[offers] doubtful benefit to the institutions themselves," and "[produces] disastrous derangement in the business and currency of the country." Under such conditions, he asked, "is it the part of wisdom again to renew the connection?"[75]

The fear that the power of government could be used to benefit some specific group was a strong concern of Jacksonianism. Though other American ideologies have certainly shared this particular anxiety, what was uniquely constitutive of the Jacksonian worldview was the belief that the only way to prevent this from happening was to completely separate the public sector from the private sector. The conclusion to Van Buren's speech made clear that this premise underwrote his request for bank divorce. After declaring that he did not expect Congress to resume deposits to banks that were not making specie payments and that the state banks would not receive the final payment due them, he summarized his program with a philosophical flourish. "Those who look to the action of this [g]overnment for specific aid . . . to relieve embarrassments arising from losses by revulsions in commerce and credit lose sight of the ends for which it was created and the powers with which it is clothed," he stated. The government was not "intended to confer special favors on individuals or on any classes of them, or to create systems of agriculture, manufacturers, or trade." Echoing Jacksonian principles, Van Buren declared that if "its operations were to be directed for the benefit of any one class, equivalent favors must in justice be extended to the rest." This system would impose logistical difficulties that would render it impossible.[76]

The president's reading of US history offered similar lessons. The "framers of our excellent Constitution," he observed "wisely judged that the less government interferes with private pursuits the better for the general prosperity." Divorce represents the fullest articulation of this principle, one from which the nation had obviously strayed. "It is not [government's] legitimate object to make men rich or to repair by direct grants of money or legislation in favor of particular pursuits losses not incurred in the public service. This would be substantially to use the property of some for the benefit of others."[77]

Van Buren's articulation of the reasons for bank divorce clearly demonstrated an application of Jacksonian principles. Yet the appeal of Jacksonianism was waning. A little over a week after Van Buren's speech, the independent treasury bill was introduced in the Senate. The next month, the bill narrowly passed that body before being tabled in the House as the special session ended. The next year, the House would debate its own version of a divorce bill before defeating it on June 25 by a margin of 125 to 111. In each of his next three annual messages to Congress, Van Buren restated the need for such a bill. (Since the proposal also called for the establishment of a network of federal depositories around the country, run by the Treasury Department, it was often referred to as the "sub-treasury bill.") The arguments that he gave for these policies never varied significantly from the one he presented in the panic session. Congress had given Van Buren's bill a chance, and it had failed. In spending so much political capital on his idea, the president unwittingly showcased the limits beyond which the American people were not willing to accept the Jacksonian philosophy.

The bill would eventually become law—but not because of Van Buren's steadfastness. Instead, the political and economic situation of the country altered significantly around the independent treasury issue, affording the president another chance to press for his proposal. Few banks had resumed paying specie, and under those conditions, the federal government refused to deposit its funds. Thus, the country was gaining some experience with a de facto divorce of government and private finance, even if not the de jure one desired by Van Buren. Then, on October 9, 1839, under the strain of the economic conditions, Biddle's Bank of the United States—now a Pennsylvania-chartered institution—ceased redeeming notes for specie. The bank had been declining in influence and revenue since Jackson's veto, but it was still an important player, and its default prompted that of many other banks in

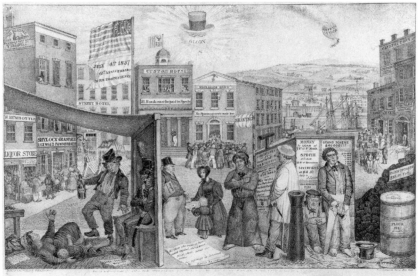

This 1837 lithograph blamed Jacksonian favoritism for the difficult economic times. In the cartoon, a mother and her child are reduced to begging and the mason and carpenter are unable to work, while the banker and attorney prosper. The hard-money customhouse provides no help in the crisis, and panicked customers make a run on the Mechanics Bank, which does not back its notes with specie. (Courtesy Library of Congress)

succession. The resulting economic catastrophe was unlike any the nation had seen to that point. Commodity prices plummeted, and they would continue to do so for the next several years. In one example, cotton fell from an 1839 price at New Orleans of 12.4 cents per pound to 5.7 cents by 1843. In the same period, US imports dropped from $159 million to $43 million annually; by 1842, nine states had defaulted on interest payments on loans they had taken out for internal improvements.[78] The collapse of these banks revived interest in, and political possibilities for, Van Buren's original divorce idea.

On January 23, 1840, the independent treasury bill was passed in the Senate by a 24-to-18 vote. Two months later, it was reintroduced in the House, and the controversial proposal was debated there at length. One congressman, Charles G. Atherton (D-NH), motioned that the measure come up on the floor, arguing that the bill was not new "either to members of the House or to the country." The president, Atherton reminded his colleagues, had several times recommended the bill in his annual messages. It had been amply studied by both houses of Congress, and "every member of the House was sent here by his constituents, either for or against this bill."[79]

The arguments offered by the bill's supporters reiterated that the central premise of Jacksonianism was a fervent desire to keep government out of the nation's economic affairs. Isaac Leet (D-PA) echoed a familiar Jacksonian refrain on the floor of the House. If left to their own devices, he contended, banks would consistently overextend themselves, issuing notes that they could not support. Though this might have been a necessary part of the commercial and economic system, there was every reason to keep the government far from such doings. If banks already had a tendency "without the aid of the public treasure" to "excite speculation and overtrading," leading them to "expand their issues and afterward be under the necessity of contracting them, thereby affecting the value of produce and of all articles of trade," then, he asked, "how much less will it be the case if you . . . refuse to loan the public treasure at all? It is this very principle of refusing to loan the public treasure which is to save you and the country from all this feverish excitement and speculation for money's sake which we see resulting from these institutions."[80]

Another Democrat, John Smith of Vermont, articulated the concern that opponents of divorce had designs on reinstituting a national bank. Billing the issue as a clear-cut contest between the forces of the people and those of naked privilege, Smith addressed his concerns to the Speaker of the House. "If, sir, the people are worsted in this contest, the second war of revolution, another national bank will be chartered and made the 'high tower' of the aristocracy, from which mandates to control the vast associated and individual wealth of the nation are to emanate."[81]

On June 30, 1840, the House passed the bill by a vote of 124 to 107. Believing the new law to be a significant advance for American democracy, Van Buren waited until July 4 to sign it. Yet the law did not have the effect the president had hoped because the people had moved away from his policies. Running to reclaim his office in the presidential election that same year, Van Buren was proud to present himself as the champion of the Independent Treasury Act. But he faced an opposing candidate, William Henry Harrison, who ran on a campaign of paper money and a (somewhat inconsistent) support for the reinstatement of a national bank.

During the election, the Whigs highlighted their opposition to hard-money Jacksonianism, arguing that their desire to have government support the economy made *them* the party of entrepreneurialism. On this view, the

Democrats were little more than scolding schoolmarms, telling the voters that they simply should not want what an expansive currency policy could bring. And the Democrats occasionally seemed willing to play this role. One telling example appeared in the Democratic *Richmond Enquirer*: "What!" the paper exclaimed. "Surrender all your principles, because you cannot command the highest prices for your corn and flour[?]!"[82] By 1840, many Americans realized they no longer wanted to champion principles that kept them from participating successfully in the market economy. Perhaps of equal importance to the campaign was that the Whig candidate was a western military hero who appropriated a popular "man of the people" persona, associating himself with the symbols of hard cider and log cabins. Evidently, popular acclaim was no longer the sole province of the Democrats. William Henry Harrison defeated Martin Van Buren to become the ninth president of the United States. His victory signaled that the Jacksonian theoretical framework had become outmoded. Harrison and a Whig Congress eliminated the independent treasury in 1841.[83]

At its core, Jacksonianism still reflected the world of Thomas Jefferson and the ideal of a party of the people doing battle with the representatives of aristocratic privilege. This conception simply could not adapt to the democratic reality of two competing popular parties, each with a distinct yet equally broad base of support. Even more damaging to the Jacksonian project of separating federal functions from those of the private economy, however, was that a growing number of Americans did, in fact, want the government to help them sell their corn and flour, and they saw no philosophical contradiction in asking it to do so. As the nineteenth century progressed, the people of the United States became increasingly certain that government should be a major player in supporting the nation's economic health. What role it should play was not entirely clear, for when Jacksonianism faded as a tenable theory of democratic capitalism, nothing emerged to take its place for a long while. More important, in the middle part of the century, the nation's intellectual and political attention focused on the issues and events generated by the controversy over slavery: nullification, secession, the Civil War, and Reconstruction. These developments also served as the impetus for the creation of the modern-day Republican Party, which was founded in 1854 to oppose the spread of slavery. As philosophical concerns turned away from economic matters, the postbellum political culture would find itself unprepared for the rise of the large and wealthy corporation. The most pivotal question of the succeeding era, therefore, would have to be settled in the courts.

Chapter Three

Property

As the leader of all the Allied forces in Europe, Dwight David Eisenhower had little trouble translating his status as a World War II hero into political success. Running for president as a Republican in 1952, the man known to millions of Americans by his childhood nickname, "Ike," won a landslide victory over Democrat Adlai Stevenson. But the new president quickly learned that his popularity, as great as it was, did not protect everyone with whom he was associated. His nominee for secretary of defense, Charles E. Wilson, had been the president of General Motors (GM); upon his nomination for the cabinet post, Wilson resigned his GM job but was reluctant to sell his many shares in that company. This refusal proved to be a major sticking point at his confirmation hearings. Some senators, noting that General Motors was one of the Defense Department's major contractors, saw a potential conflict of interest in the fact that Wilson would be in a position to influence his former company's prospects and would also benefit personally from an increase in the company's share price. During the hearings, Senator Robert C. Hendrickson (R-NJ) asked the nominee to address this issue specifically. Acknowledging that Wilson had repeatedly told the committee he saw no conflict in his roles as a stockholder at GM and a potential defense secretary, the senator asked him to consider the possibility anyway: "If a situation did arise where you had to make a decision which was extremely adverse to the interests of your stock and General Motors Corporation . . . in the interests of the United States government, could you make that decision?"

Wilson's immediate reply was in the affirmative. Certainly, he said, he would take into consideration only the needs of his country and not those of his former employer. But he also continued to emphasize that he could not imagine a scenario pitting the two entities against each other. Wilson's additional response was no doubt intended to be reassuring, but for many observers, it had exactly the opposite effect. Wilson claimed that he could not conceive of a situation that would position the United States against the automaker "because for years I thought what was good for our country was good for General Motors, and vice versa. The difference did not exist. Our company is too big. It goes with the welfare of the country."[1]

To some, Wilson's "vice versa" implied that it was in the interests of the United States to ensure the continued welfare of General Motors, prompting the troubling conclusion that the future secretary of defense believed the federal government bore a responsibility to enact specific policies to that end. Thus, the frequent and popular misquotation of Wilson's statement as "what is good for General Motors is good for America" has come to symbolize larger fears regarding the possibility of an inappropriate relationship between the nation's government and its largest businesses.[2]

Wilson's statement, independent of the fact that he did not truly utter it in its most controversial form, does raise an essential question. Large corporations have come to play a significant and arguably irreplaceable role in the United States, and their influence is widely felt not only with regard to necessities such as food, clothing, and housing but also in such central aspects of life as telecommunications, finance, defense, and employment. Might it not, then, actually be true, metaphorically speaking, that what is good for General Motors *is* good for America? And if this situation does not hold, then should large corporations be allowed to command the wealth, power, and authority that they do? "Clearly democratic theory needs to be extended," observed political scientist Charles Lindblom, "to take account of what we will call the privileged position of business."[3]

The question is largely shunted aside today. But the issue of the appropriate privileges that should be accorded to the corporation, as well as the obligations to be expected from it, was among the most significant of the late nineteenth century. The defeat of Martin Van Buren in the 1840 presidential election effectively ended Jacksonianism as a dynamic domestic political philosophy. It also marked the conclusion of the debate regarding federal involvement in the nation's economy, which had essentially been settled in favor of the positions of Hamilton and the Whigs. From that point forward, various sectors of the American electorate would not hesitate to use the political system to exert influence on the shape of the economy, elected officials would feel responsible for providing a successful economic climate, and the political and intellectual class would offer a plethora of opinions on how best to execute this charge. Yet the emerging consensus on the necessity of fed-

eral economic stewardship did not end the debate over appropriate government policy, for different groups of Americans had sharply divergent opinions about just what purpose the economy was to serve.

The words that usually command nearly universal support when applied
to a national economy—words such as *strong* and *robust*—can actually mask
a great deal of disagreement. These terms leave unstated the fundamental
question of what the most basic purpose of the economy itself actually is.
Should the nation's economy be oriented toward growth, fairness, stability,
or liberty? Who should be its primary beneficiaries? What, if any, obligations accrue *from* the winners or *to* the losers? What behaviors should be
encouraged and discouraged? After settling the question of *whether* the government should intervene in the economy, Americans have never stopped
debating the end to which it should do so.

As Jacksonianism declined in the 1840s and disappeared by the 1850s,
the nation's attention slowly turned away from questions of political economy and toward the myriad issues raised by the enslavement of black Americans. During the Civil War, there was little debate as to the function of the
Northern economy. Its purpose was to win the war, and the achievement of
that goal relied heavily on federal economic intervention. For example, it
was during the Civil War that the United States, for the first time, levied an
income tax and printed paper money. The subsequent Reconstruction era
continued to see the nation's attention captivated by the issues that had been
raised by the war and the end of slavery, including the contested status of
African Americans, the viability of states' rights, and the limits of federal
jurisdiction.

It was not until the Gilded Age that Americans' attention returned to
political economy, and then, the emphasis was decidedly on the *economy* side
of the term. The new industrial technologies—advances in railroads, steel
production, manufacturing processes, and the like—captured the imagination of a new cohort of businesspeople, who became the first generation of
American millionaires. Individuals such as Andrew Carnegie, John D.
Rockefeller, and J. P. Morgan, though often derided as "robber barons" for
their frequently unsavory business practices, aroused in millions of Americans both admiration and resentment. The nation was preoccupied with
business, and many Gilded Age commentators, as well as later historians,
found this had a negative influence on the practice of American politics.
Richard Hofstadter represented this view in 1948 when he wrote of the
Gilded Age: "There is no other period in the nation's history when politics
seems so completely dwarfed by economic changes."[4] On this view, politics

was not where the action was during the period, and enterprising young individuals on the make were less likely to enter the political field. As a result, those who did serve in government often lacked talent and, frequently, integrity. Meanwhile, corruption was rampant, both businesspeople and politicians viewed government as the handmaiden of commerce, and Congress did little to address the most pressing issues of the day.

More recently, however, historians have modified this view somewhat, arguing that the corruption of the Gilded Age has been overblown and misrepresented. Historian Charles W. Calhoun, for instance, acknowledged that "the roster of politicians in the late nineteenth century did include some brazen spoilsmen who seemed to crave office for its own sake or for the money it might bring," but he rejected the notion that this characterization was typical of the Gilded Age officeholder. Instead, he argued that "in large measure, the attractiveness of political life, especially for leaders at the national level, lay in the sense of accomplishment public service offered them"; further, he observed that most of these politicos "remained convinced that their labors sustained and promoted firmly held principles."[5] From that perspective, the lack of legislative productivity from the federal government during the Gilded Age had much more to do with the fact that the electorate—and, consequently, the Congress—was evenly divided between Democrats and Republicans.

Whatever the reason, the fact remains that the political branches of the US government did not effectively serve as the venue for the debate over the most significant concern of the day: the increasing power of corporations. Instead, those who argued for the expansion or limitation of the power of business turned to the legal system. The Supreme Court, in particular, played a very powerful role in adjudicating the competing visions of the function and powers of the corporation during the Gilded Age. "Since the gravest problem facing America [after the Civil War] was government regulation of business," wrote Supreme Court historian Robert McCloskey, "that problem gradually became the major interest of America's constitutional court."[6]

One of the more significant decisions to address this issue was handed down in the 1886 case of *Santa Clara County v. Southern Pacific Railroad*, in which the court found the American corporation to have the legal rights of a "person" as delineated by the US Constitution. In this decision, the court considered the issue of whether the protections of the Fourteenth Amendment should extend to "artificial persons," that is, to corporations. Though the amendment had been written and ratified to guarantee the equal treat-

ment of recently freed slaves, the justices declared that its protections should
be extended to corporations as well. In other words, for the purposes of the
Fourteenth Amendment, a corporation possessed the same rights and privileges as a flesh-and-blood human being. The decision itself was quite brief
and, upon reading, seemingly rather insignificant. Yet it has acquired great
import over time. Indeed, the major finding of *Santa Clara* has repeatedly
been affirmed by the Supreme Court, and corporate litigants have continually cited this decision to gain access to constitutional protections.[7]

Santa Clara consequently provides an excellent window into the reasoning that supported (and still supports) the grant of political and economic
privileges to the corporation in the American system of democratic capitalism. That position held, first, that private property is sacred and inviolable,
immune to adjustment by the democratic process, and, second, that a corporation, as a form of property, is entitled to the protection of the courts
against the incursions of those who might threaten it. This conception of the
corporation, however, was greatly at odds with the prevailing understanding
of the subject. As a result, the attribution of personhood to the corporation
represented less a legitimate application of widely held Liberal principles
than a massive government intervention in the economy on behalf of
wealthy individuals and companies.

What Is a Corporation?

Its name derived from the Latin word for "body," a corporation binds
individuals into a business entity that assumes a separate legal identity from
any of its owners. The individuals are not *part of* the corporation, but
instead—as owners—they occupy a separate legal status from it. Definitive
of the corporate identity is the selling of shares in the business, in the form
of stock certificates. Possession of these shares conveys to their bearer the
ownership of a small fraction of the company; since the corporation maintains a legal existence distinct from that of its owners and managers, its stock
is a portable form of property that can be traded on a market without the
need to constantly renegotiate the responsibilities assumed by each new
owner. Another characteristic of the corporate form is that the business itself
assumes perpetual life: a corporation, unlike a partnership, survives the death
of any of its owners. Firms limited in their temporal existence to the life span
of their oldest owner would find it impossible to enter into businesses that
required long-term commitments, either by their very nature (for example,

life insurance) or because of the great length of time required to recoup the initial investment (such as railroads). Beyond the relative fluidity of ownership symbolized by the stock market and the immortality of the corporation, however, the single most significant advantage to incorporation stems from the doctrine known as *limited liability*. According to this understanding, a corporation's owners cannot lose any more money than what they have already invested in the business.

Imagine the legal status of a small business that a woman starts, say, in her garage. She would own it outright, in the same way that she might own a house or a car. But unlike those items, a business can run up debts. It can borrow money that it cannot repay, manufacture an unpopular product that generates more costs than revenue, produce environmentally hazardous products that create legal liability, and so on. Regardless of the reason, it is not impossible or even unlikely for the business to come to owe more than it is worth. The fact that the business is the possession and therefore the responsibility of one particular person means that the owner's obligations to her creditors are not discharged in the event the firm exhausts its funds. Creditors who are still owed money will have every right to seize and liquidate the personal assets of the owner in order to claim the funds that are owed them. This dynamic is known as *unlimited liability*: the owner is responsible for any and all obligations incurred by her property (the company), just as she would be if her dog had bitten someone or her house had caught fire and damaged another person's home.

A partnership complicates this arrangement, but the basic point remains the same. If two persons each own half of a business, then, generally speaking, each of them is liable for all of the debts that it incurs, not merely half of them. A third party who is owed a sum of money is not, and should not be, responsible for sorting out the partners' finances: if, to cite one scenario, the business and one of the partners have gone bankrupt, this creditor is entitled to hit up the remaining partner for any moneys owed. Complicating matters further, nothing alters the situation if the partners are not equal owners or if there are twenty partners instead of two. In other words, once the firm's finances are exhausted, each of the partners is obligated to make good on any liabilities that it has incurred. Under this system, it is quite likely that the partner with the deepest pockets, not necessarily the one with the most responsibility or the biggest share in the company, will foot the most substantial part of the bill. That is what it means to *own* something: one not only reaps the benefits that the object brings but also suffers the consequences of unfortunate developments. As an owner of a business firm, a person is liable for its actions; the size of a person's stake does not matter at all. Taking this principle to its logical, if extreme, conclusion, then the man who invests, as a partner, $100 in a million-dollar firm could conceivably find himself in a situation where he is liable for far more money than he possesses. This $100 investment could, at least theoretically, lose the person his life savings, his house, and so on.

Moreover, in earlier times the consequences for bankruptcy could include drastic punishments such as imprisonment or slavery. Under those circumstances, few wanted to make a small investment in an expensive enterprise or, indeed, in any business over which they could not exert control. Even one who believed in the prospect of a given project's success enough to risk losing the initial investment would not have been terribly willing to take on the responsibility of paying all the firm's creditors should the business fail. But an entrepreneur needing to raise, say, $100,000 for a new venture would presumably have found it far easier to find 1,000 people willing to risk $100 than to convince 2 donors to contribute $50,000 apiece. Thus, the traditional legal doctrine of unlimited liability was a major impediment to businesses that required large amounts of start-up capital.

The doctrine of limited liability— and the consequent invention of the joint-stock company and later the corporation—was an attempt by imperial European governments to address this problem. The extended sea voyages by which nations amassed their colonial empires were extremely expensive and carried great financial risk. Thus, rather than bankrolling these voyages themselves, governments generally preferred to operate their empires by allowing independent or at best semiprivate companies to undertake the voyages on behalf of the state.[8] But why would an investor wish to put his or her own money into such a risky venture? Considering the possibility of being liable for all the expenses incurred if a ship did not return, potential investors were not terribly sanguine about investing in such an enterprise.

In order to induce investment in the voyages that they wanted to see continue but no longer wished to fund, European governments in the age of exploration introduced limited liability into their concept of the corporation. Individuals who considered putting money into a risky mission of colonization and exploration would have been far more likely to capitalize a voyage if they knew that, in the best case, profits could potentially grow as much as the venture would allow but, in the worst case, losses would not exceed the amount of their initial investment. Of course, this governmental grant did not come without a cost: in limiting the risk of the investor, it increased the risk of the creditor (including, potentially, the company's workers), who would, in the event of the debtor company's bankruptcy, simply be out of luck. In other words, limited liability reduced the uncertainty in investing in a company but also increased the risk in providing supplies or labor to, or contracting for a product with, such an organization. It was, in short, a state-sponsored legal construct that privileged the difficulty in raising capital over other commercial concerns.

Another key benefit that often accompanied corporate status was a state grant of monopoly privilege. Monopoly grants were fairly common in the corporation's early days, and they played a significant role in the development of the institution in the United States. During the age of exploration, companies undertaking expeditionary voyages received a charter from the crown that granted them the sole right to sail to a specific part of the world; the lack of competition obviously increased the likelihood that any given trip would bring back riches. Under this arrangement, one corporation in particular acquired tremendous power and wealth. In the seventeenth and eighteenth centuries, the British East India Company had its own army and navy, and it literally governed India. The company lasted for some 274 years and is perhaps best known to Americans as the firm that was granted a monopoly on the sale of tea in North America, prompting as a protest the Boston Tea Party of 1773.

Later, most grants of incorporation in the United States were based on the widely held premise of the "natural monopoly." According to this idea, competition did *not* lead to a more efficient allocation of goods in industries of a specific nature—that is, industries that required a disproportionate outlay of capital to get the business up and running. Under those circumstances, after making this initial investment the company only recouped its money slowly during the course of ordinary business. Thus, any price competition that would ensue from another business entering the market would fail to provide lower-cost goods for the customer, as it would instead ensure that both companies would eventually go out of business. In those circumstances, so the theory went, the government could grant monopoly status to a business not because that business should not have to compete fairly but because fair competition was essentially impossible. Only with such a government-granted privilege would citizens be provided with a service that could not be otherwise supplied by a free market. The paradigmatic example of a natural monopoly in the nineteenth-century United States was, of course, the railroad, but public works such as bridges and toll roads, gaslight companies, and eventually electric utilities and the telephone industry all frequently received protections under this doctrine.

By allowing incorporation under such terms, the state provided a bene-fit to entrepreneurs doing business as corporations that it did not grant to other types of businesspeople. Thus, the shifting history of the various jus-tifications for the existence of the corporation in the United States and of the particular privileges and responsibilities that have characterized it is a history of government economic intervention.

Antebellum Understandings of the Corporation

The earliest understanding of the corporation in the United States was perhaps the most straightforward. According to this conception, called the *grant* or *concession* theory, corporate status was a privilege that the state bestowed upon a number of people who petitioned it for the right to be treated as a group rather than as a collection of individuals. The state gen-erally did not see fit to grant the privileges that flowed from incorporation unless it viewed the project that those individuals wished to undertake as one that would advance a public interest. Under this interpretation, the state created a new, "artificial" being—so called because it came into existence not by normal social interaction but by legal fiat—and the charter of incor-poration was essentially a contract between two parties: the state and that entity. Should the corporation have broken the contract—by ceasing to operate, for example, or by overcharging its customers—it could have been dissolved. In the early national period, two corollaries flowed naturally from this understanding: first, that a given corporation would be allowed to exist only as long as it provided some service to the citizenry and, second, that corporations, more so than other business forms, would reasonably be sub-ject to heavy regulation by the state.

As a result, the vast majority of corporations in the early United States fulfilled some obviously public need; examples included toll bridges, gaslight companies, and eventually railroads. Additionally, state governments kept close tabs on their interests. Therefore, each application for a corporate charter was required to be individually approved by a state legislature, and these contracts usually expired after a finite period of time (typically twenty or twenty-five years), at which point the state might or might not see fit to renew them. Because of the strict governmental supervision, most busi-nesspersons preferred not to avail themselves of the corporate form unless circumstances absolutely necessitated doing so: in 1789, for instance, the United States could boast of only six nonbank corporations.[9]

From a legal perspective, the most influential and representative decision in this tradition was issued in the 1819 case *Trustees of Dartmouth College v. Woodward,* an opinion delivered by Chief Justice John Marshall.
Dartmouth had received an English royal charter in 1769; the act granted
the school corporate status in perpetuity and provided for the trustees themselves to select the members to replace those who had died or resigned.
Thus, the college operated independently of state supervision, and so its
charter had never been granted or renewed by its home state of New Hampshire. Some fifty years after Dartmouth's founding, the state sought to establish greater control over the college by passing a law that would establish a
board of overseers to govern the trustees, increase the membership of the
board, and allow the governor to fill future vacancies.[10] The original trustees
took the state to federal court on the grounds that these laws violated Dartmouth's initial charter.

The court ruled in favor of the plaintiffs. Chief Justice Marshall, in writing for the majority, invoked the grant theory by establishing that he viewed
Dartmouth's charter as nothing more or less than a contract between the
corporation and the state. "The American people," he noted, "have said in
the Constitution of the United States that 'no State shall pass any bill of
attainder, *ex post facto* law, or law impairing the obligation of contracts.'"
Since "it can require no argument to prove that the circumstances of this
case constitute a contract,"[11] the decision was deemed to be a straightforward one.

Despite his claim as to the open-and-shut nature of the case, Marshall
provided substantial argument to support his conclusion. He directed his
energies against an idea advanced by the defendants: that the specific nature
of corporate charters burdened their holders with uniquely public responsibilities. Under this interpretation, even if a charter was a contract, it was
of a fundamentally different sort than, say, one between a buyer and a seller.
Because the corporation's founders received special benefits from the state
and because the state only granted those privileges to those who were providing a service to the people, all corporations were, in some sense, public
entities. The force of the *Dartmouth College* decision was oriented toward
the rejection of this view.

"A corporation," Marshall argued, "[is] the mere creature of law," and
as such, "it possesses only those properties which the charter of its creation
confers upon it." Such an entity "does not share in the civil government of
the country, unless that be the purpose for which it was created." The fact
that the state granted a corporation "the power to take and to hold property,

in a particular form," did not give it "a consequent right . . . to change that form, or to vary the purposes to which the property is to be applied."[12] Marshall did not contest the notion that states had the right to expect or even demand a civic orientation from incorporated firms. Corporations unquestionably were granted special privileges, he argued, and the state had to ensure that the people would receive adequate compensation for granting them. But the only legal place to do that was in the initial charter, and states could not pass subsequent legislation to make up for unwise contracts that they might have consummated in the past. Marshall did not argue that the state was obligated to or restricted from any particular terms in its corporate charters. But once those terms were offered and accepted by the incorporators, the state was bound by its own word. As he put it, "From the fact . . . that a charter of incorporation has been granted, nothing can be inferred which changes the character of the institution, or transfers to the government any new power over it."[13]

Today, *Dartmouth College* is often viewed as a "procorporate" decision that limited the power of the state over incorporated businesses. But neither its reasoning nor its import should be read so narrowly. The state was not prevented from imposing restrictions on the corporation, as long as it did so through the vehicle of the charter. Indeed, in the years after *Dartmouth College*, that was just what most states did, issuing increasingly restrictive charters that served as the de facto corporate code.[14]

The understanding of the corporation as an artificial entity, however, would not stand. "From the Civil War until the end of the century," wrote historian Herbert Hovenkamp, "the notion that the corporate charter was a contract according vested privileges to the corporation substantially fell apart. Business corporations lost contract clause arguments in the great majority of cases, usually on rationales that were flatly inconsistent with Marshall era interpretations."[15] This change in understanding was motivated primarily by a change in political conditions, for the ascendant Jacksonianism assailed grants of corporate charters as evidence of widespread corruption in the state legislatures. Jackson himself decried "the multitudes of corporations with exclusive privileges which they have succeeded in obtaining in different [s]tates," and often enough, such charges were well founded. "Lobbying expenses, delay and bribery," testified economic historian Stuart Bruchey, "often attended appeals to state legislatures for acts of incorporation."[16] Viewing the charter as a vehicle by which well-connected individuals obtained unfair privileges, the Jacksonians' most prevalent demand was to eliminate the opportunity for corruption and unfair competition by streamlining and formalizing the incorporation process, effectively allowing anyone to incorporate. New York adopted a so-called general incorporation law as early as 1811, and several states had done the same by the time of the Civil War. Though many states that adopted these laws also continued to charter corporations through legislative acts, Louisiana amended its constitution in 1845 to forbid this practice, and many other states soon followed suit.

The streamlining of the incorporation process led to a rapid increase in the number of corporations. In New England, for instance, 27.8 percent of charters during the nineteen-year period from 1844 to 1862 were established through general acts; the shorter subsequent period of 1863 to 1875 witnessed not only a significant increase in the number of incorporations (4,575, up from 3,533) but also a rise in general incorporations to nearly half the total number of charters.[17] "Incorporation by the 1870s," wrote Alan Trach - tenberg, "had become more of a right than a privilege," and this trend fueled the growth of the corporation in the late nineteenth century. "Freed from encumbrances often attached to special charters and from the pre- sumption of public service," he continued, "the corporation swiftly dis- placed unincorporated forms . . . as the most significant organization of business."[18]

Against this new reality, the legal and philosophical understanding of the corporation embodied in the *Dartmouth College* decision—that it was a state- created entity granted special powers because its goals were deemed to be in the public interest—became more and more difficult to defend. Since gen- eral incorporation laws made the corporate form available to many differ- ent kinds of businesses, one could no longer assume that such firms were generally, or even usually, oriented toward civic purposes. Additionally, as a grant of incorporation became little more than perfunctory, the notion that corporations owed their very existence to state largesse ran counter to expe- rience. "Incorporation," stated legal historian Morton J. Horwitz, "eventu- ally came to be regarded not as a special state-conferred privilege but as a normal and regular mode of doing business."[19]

But if corporations operated outside of normal market practices and if the state did not specifically create them, then how and why did they exist? And why were they allowed special privileges if they were not doing the people's business? The answer that probusiness jurists developed over the latter half of the nineteenth century was that the benefits of incorporation were not grants from the state at all. Rather than justifying corporate ben- efits, they denied their existence. Instead, they claimed that these alleged privileges were merely examples of individual rights long enshrined in the Liberal tradition. Often, these rights were derived from a dubious philosophical lineage that incorporated the Fourteenth Amendment to the Constitution in the United States. This systematic justification of corporate privileges on the grounds of individual rights was most clearly shown in the 1886 *Santa Clara* decision, and it served as a primary example of federal (in this case, judicial) economic intervention during the Gilded Age.

"Privileges or Immunities"

The famous proclamation in the Declaration of Independence that "life, liberty and the pursuit of happiness" are "unalienable rights" was, in fact, a gloss on a refrain from John Locke's *Second Treatise*. There, Locke invoked an innate "title to perfect freedom" that granted an individual a "power" to "preserve his property, that is, his life, liberty and estate, against the injuries and attempts of other men."[20] Locke saw property as an overarching moral concept, under whose umbrella even freedom was included. Despite this distinguished pedigree, however, the right to own property has had an ambiguous history in American constitutional law.

Central to this history was the legal and intellectual reception accorded the Fourteenth Amendment. As one of the three "Reconstruction amendments," its immediate purpose was to address the fallout of the Civil War. Slavery was officially banned upon the ratification of the Thirteenth Amendment in 1865, but many former Confederate states responded to this development by passing what were known as *black codes*. Such laws restricted the civil rights of African Americans and functioned as the reinstitution of antebellum racial stratification without the legal device of slavery. The Fourteenth Amendment was a response to these developments, and its 1868 ratification eliminated the states' legal prerogative to impose such inequities. The first provision of the Fourteenth Amendment repudiated the notorious holding of the *Dred Scott* decision—that African Americans had "no rights which the white man was bound to respect"[21]—by specifically declaring "all persons born or naturalized in the United States" to be "citizens of the United States and of the State wherein they reside." Finally establishing, once and for all, that former slaves and, indeed, all persons of color would be citizens, the amendment denied to the states the ability to "abridge the privileges or immunities of citizens of the United States." Its two other major injunctions forbade a state from "depriv[ing] any person of life, liberty, or property, without due process of law" and "deny[ing] to any person within its jurisdiction the equal protection of the laws."

This amendment first came before the Supreme Court in the 1873 *Slaughter-House Cases*. Significantly, the issues brought to trial had little to do with racial discrimination but instead concerned possible limitations on the ability of the states to charter corporations. Consolidating three separate suits involving any number of parties, the *Slaughter-House Cases* involved a Louisiana statute passed in response to a public health crisis in New Orleans. During the Reconstruction era, New Orleans was among the most prominent centers of meat production in the nation, and the relatively low financial barriers to entry in that business attracted many former slaves and other entrepreneurs of limited means. The need for moving water to keep one's operation clean placed nearly all of these butchers on the banks of the Mississippi. Thus, wrote Hovenkamp, "New Orleans became overrun with small, economically marginal, grossly unsanitary slaughterhouses,"[22] whose waste created a polluted and unsafe river.

Additionally, New Orleans's prospects for remaining an important center for beef production hinged upon the city's ability to incorporate a new refrigeration process that would allow it to ship meat year-round. But this infrastructure had such high start-up costs that any firm wishing to use it would have to operate at a much larger scale than that of the typical New Orleans slaughterhouse. Taking all of these issues into consideration, the state passed a law, at the city's request, to charter a new corporation. This new entity, the Crescent City Live-Stock Landing and Slaughter-House Company, was to receive a monopoly on all of the "landing, slaughtering or keeping of any animals."[23] The law also required the new corporation to build a slaughterhouse large enough to accommodate all of the area's butchers, mandated that the corporation make these facilities available to anyone at a price set by the statute, and provided for salaried inspectors to ensure the quality of the outgoing meat. The monopolistic charter of this corporation, in other words, was designed both to alleviate a growing public health crisis and to aid the area's economic development by giving butchers the means to take advantage of economies of scale that they could not otherwise enjoy.

Not all of those affected by the law, however, saw it as such judicious legislation. Several butchers got together and sued on the grounds that "the act of the legislature had made a monopoly and was thus in violation of the most important provisions of the thirteenth and fourteenth amendments to the Constitution of the United States."[24] Their counsel was John A. Campbell, a former Supreme Court justice who had resigned his position prior to the Civil War in order to join the Confederacy. The plaintiff's attorney presented a powerful argument that positioned the new Fourteenth Amendment as a protection of economic rights against federal restrictions.[25] Though Campbell's presentation did not ultimately carry the day, Robert McCloskey characterized the court as "visibly shaken" by it.[26]

Campbell's argument picked up on a slight ambiguity in the amendment's language and exploited it on behalf of his clients. Since the Fourteenth Amendment declared that all people born on US soil were citizens of both the country and "the [s]tate wherein they reside," any American citizen living in a particular state would automatically have two concurrent sets of rights—those of a US citizen and those of a citizen of a particular state. So when the amendment went on to forbid states to pass laws that "abridge the privileges or immunities of citizens of the United States," it arguably did not articulate clearly which set of rights was being guaranteed. Though this distinction might appear to be of truly Scholastic moment, its consequences were of the utmost importance. If the Fourteenth Amendment forbade states from limiting the privileges or immunities of *state* citizenship, then it required only that states apply their own laws in a fair manner, in such a way that each person under their jurisdiction received similar treatment.[27] But if the purpose of the amendment was to secure those rights held by virtue of *national* citizenship, then it was imposing a much greater burden on the states—that of not trampling on the rights that the federal government had determined the state's citizens to have. Such an interpretation would have shifted the balance of American federalism clearly and obviously away from the states and toward the federal government.

Campbell argued that the rights guaranteed by the privileges and immunities clause were, in fact, those of national, as opposed to state, citizenship: the "privileges and immunities . . . are undoubtedly the personal and civil rights" that formed "the basis of the institutions of the country."[28] Though he correctly noted that the clause did not specifically mention the states, he never specifically indicated which of the butchers' federal rights had been violated by Louisiana's issue of a corporate charter.[29] Moreover, his reference to extraconstitutional precedents such as "tradition" and "the common sentiments of people" suggested that he was aware of no specifically enumerated federal right that could support his claims.

Campbell's implication seemed to be that the right being compromised related to the ability to pursue a livelihood: "By an act of legislative partiality [the Louisiana charter] enriches seventeen persons and deprives nearly a thousand others [the number of butchers in the New Orleans area, according to Campbell] of the same class, and as upright and competent as the seventeen, of the means by which they earn their daily bread."[30] Even when characterized this way, however, the state's action did not appear to represent a denial of the butcher's federal rights. The power to charter corporations had traditionally been a state prerogative, and Louisiana believed the existence of such a corporation was in the best interests of its citizens. Thus, the burden was on Campbell to show that the particular charter issued to the Crescent City Live-Stock Landing and Slaughter-House Company violated a specific federal right. This he failed to do.

Campbell's inability to articulate a compelling federal right that was compromised by the state charter of the slaughterhouse left the justices in a state of disarray. Although they all rejected the notion that the privileges or immunities clause guaranteed state rights rather than national ones, they substantially disagreed about what specific rights it protected. Justice Samuel F. Miller, writing for the majority, found very few specific rights articulated in the Constitution and offered no relief for the butchers. Miller's majority decision buttressed the grant theory of the corporation by noting that the state ability to endow individuals with corporate status was a long-accepted and uncontroversial feature of the common law. Responding to Campbell's claim that the legislature had overstepped its authority, Miller pointed out that little controversy would have ensued had Louisiana given to the city of New Orleans the same rights that it granted to the Crescent City Live-Stock Landing and Slaughter-House Company, even though the butchers would have been placed in the same disadvantageous position. "Why," he asked, "cannot the legislature confer the same powers on another corporation, created for a lawful and useful public object, that it can on the municipal corporation already existing?" This rhetorical question led the justice to his most general conclusion, the overarching principle that "wherever a legislature has the right to accomplish a certain result and that result is best [obtained] by means of a corporation, it has the right to create such a corporation, and to endow it with the powers necessary to effect [*sic*] the desired and lawful purpose."[31]

Without the recent ratification of the Fourteenth Amendment, the *Slaughter-House Cases* would have been a rather straightforward matter, unlikely to be taken up by the Supreme Court. But the new amendment had altered the legal terrain; Campbell's argument relied heavily upon it, and the court had split on its import. On Justice Miller's restrictive reading of the meaning of the privileges and immunities clause, the Fourteenth Amendment issued no threat to the state prerogative of incorporation. Since he wrote for the majority, the grant rationale for the corporation was left significantly intact. This doctrine, however, was on its last legs, for in the same case, Justice Stephen F. Field issued one of the most significant and influential dissents in the court's history. His decision announced that the Constitution contained a host of previously unacknowledged economic and property rights, powers that were now guaranteed by the Fourteenth Amendment. Field's decision did not carry the day in the *Slaughter-House Cases*. But within a decade, his position would become the norm, eventually receiving, in the *Santa Clara* decision, the imprimatur of the Supreme Court of the United States.

"The Liberty of Citizens to Acquire Property and Pursue Happiness"

Justice Miller wrote the decision on the *Slaughter-House Cases* for a narrow, five-to-four majority that included Chief Justice Salmon P. Chase. Campbell had claimed to be discussing federal rights in the trial, but Miller found that the attorney was invoking rights relevant to the states. Consequently, he believed the plaintiffs were attempting to apply the Fourteenth Amendment inappropriately.

This argument left Miller with the burden of explaining and justifying his own interpretation of the amendment. He began with an obvious but important point: even though the circumstances of the Civil War and Reconstruction provided the immediate background of the Fourteenth Amendment, the measure had to apply to all cases that were covered by its wording. In particular, this meant that people who were not black were still covered under its provisions. Obviously aware that the "pervading purpose" of all of the Reconstruction amendments was "the freedom of the slave race," Miller nonetheless pointed out that one could not therefore conclude that "no one else but the [N]egro can share in this protection."[32] Though some might take offense at the fact that a right conceived in order to protect society's most vulnerable members could be extended to some of its most powerful, the restriction of the Fourteenth Amendment to African Americans would have been logically incoherent and legally undesirable. The amendment as written left no other interpretation realistically possible.

Miller thus established that the mere fact that not all of the butchers were black did not invalidate their claim to Fourteenth Amendment protections.

He then turned to the central issue of what specific rights the amendment did and did not protect. Here, he accused Campbell of confusing the rights that inhered by virtue of federal citizenship with those that came with state citizenship. The plaintiffs' argument, wrote Miller, "rests wholly on the assumption that the citizenship is the same, and the privileges and immunities guaranteed by the clause are the same."[33] He was accusing Campbell, therefore, of claiming that the Fourteenth Amendment established federal oversight of state laws only to smuggle in specific rights that were not derived from the US Constitution. He stated, "If, then, there is a difference between the privileges and immunities belonging to a citizen of the United States as such, and those belonging to the citizen of the [s]tate as such[,] the latter must rest for their security and protection where they have heretofore rested [that is, with the states themselves]; for they are not embraced by this paragraph of the amendment."[34]

Since the privileges or immunities clause forbade the abridgement of federal, rather than state, rights, it could not legitimately be used to compel a state to respect its own laws in dealing with any given citizen. To understand the clause otherwise, argued Miller, would be to grant the federal government an effective veto over many state actions, and the sweeping consequences of that interpretation were so odious that they simply could not have been what the writers of the amendment intended. "Was it the purpose of the [F]ourteenth [A]mendment," he asked rhetorically, "to transfer the security and protection of all the civil rights which we have mentioned, from the [s]tates to the [f]ederal government?" Such an interpretation would have given Congress the power to forbid states from enacting certain laws, making the US Supreme Court "a perpetual censor upon all legislation of the [s]tates, [and] on the civil rights of their own citizens." The court, he wrote, is "convinced that no such results were intended by the Congress which proposed these amendments, nor by the legislatures of the states which ratified them."[35]

In dissent, Justice Field would take issue with Miller's interpretation in the strongest possible terms. If the majority was correct, he wrote, and the language of the Fourteenth Amendment only applied to those rights "specially designated in the Constitution or necessarily implied as belonging to citizens of the United States," then it was "a vain and idle enactment, which accomplished nothing, and most unnecessarily excited Congress and the people on its passage."[36] Evidently anticipating such an objection, Miller had articulated several federal rights in order to show that his interpretation actually did give the Fourteenth Amendment something to do. His rather anemic list of such privileges and immunities, however, might have made his opponents' case rather than his own: it included, among a few others, the rights to travel to the seat of government and transact business there, to access federal seaports, and to demand federal protection when traveling abroad. Though Miller was technically correct in maintaining that his interpretation did not render the clause in question completely without content, the rights that he cited did not seem robust or controversial enough to have motivated a constitutional amendment.

Field's minority opinion exerted a much greater influence on subsequent legal thought than Miller's actual decision. A proponent of the laissez-faire theory that was becoming more and more popular throughout the late nineteenth century, Associate Justice Stephen J. Field had been raised in Connecticut as the son of a minister in the waning Puritan tradition. His later success in gold rush—era California would support his convictions—shared by many in the era of social Darwinism—that commerce was the arena in which the cream could rise to the top. Protection of private property, he concluded, was among the most significant of governmental responsibilities. As he began a career in California politics and law, Field was consistently distressed at the scant protections that these liberties received, not only from the Constitution itself but also from American legal precedent. Though a Democrat, Field had opposed Southern secession, and Abraham Lincoln rewarded his loyalty with a nomination to the Supreme Court. Once there, Field aggressively began to write opinions echoing his laissez-faire convictions—at first in the minority but later, as the court became more protective of property rights, increasingly speaking for the majority.

Early in his *Slaughter-House* dissent, Field expounded, with great confidence, his belief that morality was on the side of the butchers. "No one will deny the abstract justice which lies in the position of the plaintiffs in error," he claimed, seemingly oblivious to the fact that a majority of his brethren on the court expressed little sympathy for them. He continued by pointing out, however, that his task in writing the dissent was legal and not moral; it was to "show that the position has some support in the fundamental law of the country."[37] Field acknowledged that the state of Louisiana had the right to exercise what jurists refer to as the "police power"—to pass and enforce legislation in the interest of public health and safety. But he denied that the terms under which the state chartered the Crescent City Live-Stock Landing and Slaughter-House Company qualified as an expression of that power. In Field's view, only two of the legislation's regulations—a provision fixing appropriate locations for slaughtering and another requiring that the animals be inspected—fell within that category. But, he added, "in all other particulars the act is a mere grant to a corporation created by it of special and exclusive privileges by which the health of the city is in no way promoted. . . . The pretence [*sic*] of sanitary regulations for the grant of the exclusive privileges is a shallow one, which merits only this passing notice."[38]

Field's real concern closely tracked the one Campbell voiced in his arguments before the court: that in establishing a corporation with special privileges, Louisiana had disallowed other would-be butchers from practicing their trade. "The act of Louisiana," he wrote, "presents the naked case, unaccompanied by any public considerations, where a right to pursue a lawful and necessary calling, previously enjoyed by every citizen . . . is taken away and vested exclusively . . . in a single corporation."[39] As a result, Field saw this case as being about much more than slaughtering animals in Louisiana. On the reasoning of the majority, he argued, there would be no check on arbitrary state power in the economic realm. If the Louisiana law granted a corporation a monopoly right to slaughter animals for twenty-five years, he argued, then there was no reason that another law could not give such rights to one person rather than several; in any industry whatsoever; or, at the logical extreme, in perpetuity. Field therefore found Miller's position to be of dangerous import. "Upon the theory on which the exclusive privileges granted by the act in question are sustained," he declared, "there is no monopoly, in the most odious form, which may not be upheld."[40]

Field's *Slaughter-House* dissent, then, was nothing less than an attack on the grant theory itself. Though he clearly found the monopoly provision to be the most unjust, his argument would have applied to any privilege granted to a corporation. But incorporation was an economic benefit bestowed by the state, so one might have expected Field to come out against incorporation itself. Whether because of his probusiness inclinations or because the state ability to charter corporations had long been established, Field did not move in this radical direction. To build a compelling case against state economic intervention without challenging matters of settled law, his objection to the Louisiana charter would have had to have been based upon a new development, one that altered the legal calculus regarding corporations. This he found in the federal rights guaranteed by the recently ratified Fourteenth Amendment.

Field's dissent agreed with the majority opinion on one major point, for both posited that the purpose of the privileges or immunities clause was to guarantee federal, not state, rights. Miller had not denied that the Fourteenth Amendment was intended to aid in the individual expression of federal rights, but he had narrowed the scope of those rights to the point that no plausible scenario would ever find a state violating the terms of the amendment. Field, by contrast, found a much greater number of relevant rights at issue. His rather expansive conception of federal privileges and immunities encompassed "those which of right belong to the citizens of all free governments." Field had borrowed that phrase from Justice Bushrod Washington's circuit court decision in the 1823 case *Corfield v. Coryell*. This characterization had become influential among jurists, but it was not binding on the Supreme Court because it had been decided in a lower venue. (Miller had cited it in his decision but rejected its authority, claiming that Washington's description was a delineation of state, rather than federal, rights.) Washington, a nephew of the first president, had been appointed to the Supreme Court by John Adams. He had described the extension of the term *privileges and immunities* (which also appears in Article IV of the Constitution) as "more tedious than difficult to enumerate," before giving an expansive list of such privileges, which included "the right to acquire and possess property of every kind."[41]

Arguing that Washington's broad understanding of privileges and immunities "appears to me to be a sound construction of the clause in question," Field applied this definition to the *Slaughter-House Cases*. Among the rights at issue, he asserted, "must be placed the right to pursue a lawful employment in a lawful manner, without other restraint than such as equally affects all persons."[42] On this reasoning, the Louisiana statute was obviously unconstitutional. "The privileges and immunities of citizens of the United States," he wrote, "[are] secured against abridgment in any form by any [s]tate. . . . All monopolies in any known trade or manufacture are an invasion of these privileges, for they encroach upon the liberty of citizens to acquire property and pursue happiness."[43]

Field was not terribly rigorous in delineating the legal grounding for these economic rights. Though he did argue that monopolies ran afoul of the common law, he offered no rebuttal to Miller's claim that state-chartered corporations were firmly rooted in that tradition. Field appeared to prefer grounding these economic rights in another legal tradition—natural law. Under this conception, human beings possessed specific rights by their very nature, and these rights took priority over any lesser claims, including those of other human beings or of social and political organizations. In contrast to Miller's limited view of the scope of the Fourteenth Amendment, Field saw it as expansively guaranteeing all natural rights: "[It] was intended to give practical effect to the declaration of 1776 of inalienable rights, rights which are the gift of the Creator, which the law does not confer, but only recognizes."[44] Such an interpretation of the Fourteenth Amendment would have given it sweeping powers indeed and would have essentially ended the American experiment in federalism. Moreover, even if the purpose of the Fourteenth Amendment had been to enact such a revolution, the rights mentioned in the Declaration of Independence—which pointedly supplanted the Lockean "life, liberty and estates" with the more humanistic "life, liberty and the pursuit of happiness"—did not include these economic rights of which Field wrote.

Rather than a reflection of serious legal scrutiny, then, Field's assertions about the existence of economic rights pointed to a trait of character. Robert McCloskey wrote of Field that his "belief that there *were* eternal verities, that they were absolute and unshaded, and that he was endowed with special insight into their nature—this belief never wavered."[45] Indeed, his belief in such truths, such as the unalienable right to pursue a profession, seemingly trumped even his political convictions. As a states' rights Democrat, Field might have been expected to oppose the expansion of the federal mandate to invade the prerogatives of the states. Yet, as McCloskey pointed out, "evidently, the desirability of protecting economic rights outweighed in his mind the disadvantage of detracting from state autonomy. It is also important to observe that he was attempting to bring a substantive protection of economic liberty into the Constitution by way of the privileges or immunities clause."[46]

The majority decision in *Slaughter-House Cases* was unpopular from nearly the moment it was issued. Miller's biographer appropriately summarized the literature in claiming that "other than *Dred Scott v. Sandford, Plessy v. Ferguson*, and *Roe v. Wade*, few opinions have received more withering attacks from historians and legal scholars."[47] Though some have more recently begun to reevaluate the decision in light of the terrible public health conditions in New Orleans and the precarious position of African Americans in Louisiana,[48] the overall take on the opinion remains that the court stepped in to stem the tide of Reconstruction by limiting the role of the federal government in demanding respect for civil rights from the states. The immediate effect of the decision entailed, in the graphic words of legal scholar Akhil Amar Reed, "strangling the privileges-or-immunities clause in its crib."[49] Its medium-term legal significance, however, was that those seeking to establish federal protections for civil or property rights began to turn to the due process clause in order to achieve those ends.

In this context, Field's *Slaughter-House* minority opinion appears to have been a vital step in the development of the American corporation. Though Miller's decision affirmed the grant theory, Field's dissent, had it been successful, would have scuttled this approach in its entirely. But as an advocate of laissez-faire seeking to expand the reach of business, the justice would have had to figure out how to square his conviction that the federal government should protect innate human economic rights with the obvious fact that the very existence of corporations depended upon unequal privileges bestowed by state governments. By the time of *Santa Clara*, he had done so.

"We Are All of the Opinion That It Does"

Santa Clara County v. Southern Pacific Railroad was fundamentally a tax case. California law stipulated that one who took out a mortgage in order to purchase a piece of property was liable only for the taxes on the portion of that property that he or she actually owned. For example, the day that an individual purchased a home using a mortgage, that person would owe only the fraction of the taxes that corresponded to the value of the initial down payment; the rest of the taxes would be due from the bank that had provided the loan. As the purchaser made more payments, his or her share of the taxes due for that property would increase and the lender's share would decrease. To complicate matters, however, the California constitution specifically singled out "railroad and other *quasi* public corporations"[50] as an exception to this policy. Thus, if the land in question was the property of a corporation, then that company would be liable for the tax on the entire value of that piece of real estate, whether mortgaged or not. So if a railroad and an individual found themselves in exactly the same situation with regard to an identically valued piece of land mortgaged at the same time under the same terms from the same bank, the railroad would owe more taxes on the land than the individual would. The railroads unsurprisingly believed this state of affairs to be unjust, and one of them, the Southern Pacific, brought to trial several arguments to that effect. Many of these alleged that the state of California had denied them the equal protection of the laws, in violation of the Fourteenth Amendment.

Though the Supreme Court did rule in favor of Southern Pacific in the *Santa Clara* case, it did not reach this conclusion by finding that the company had been discriminated against by virtue of being a corporation rather than an individual. Instead, it decided the case on narrow, technical grounds: that California's initial assessment of the railroad's property had been inflated because it included the value of fences that were actually part of the neighboring parcels. Writing for the court, Justice John Marshall Harlan directly stated that the decision carried no greater weight for other cases. "As the judgment can be sustained upon this ground," he wrote, "it is not necessary to consider any other questions raised by the pleadings and the facts found by the court."[51]

Another reason that *Santa Clara* might have seemed an unlikely candidate for the basis of a new tradition of constitutional interpretation is that the most far-reaching aspect of the court's finding appeared not in the actual decision but in the case's headnotes. Typically, this is a place that includes summaries of the facts relating to a case rather than the findings of the justices. The headnotes of the *Santa Clara* decision, however, contained an unusual declaration. Under the heading "prior history," the clerk wrote that the defendant's brief had "discussed at length" the proposition that "corporations are persons within the meaning of the Fourteenth Amendment to the Constitution of the United States." In response, Chief Justice Morrison Waite had declared that "the court does not wish to hear argument on the question" of whether the Fourteenth Amendment's equal protection clause applied to corporations. "We are all of the opinion," he added, "that it does."[52] In American jurisprudence, the source of the idea that corporations are entitled to the same rights as persons was this unremarkable declaration.

Since the court never ruled on this interpretation as part of its decision, it should not have set a precedent. But, in fact, it did. After *Santa Clara*, corporations were entitled to Fourteenth Amendment protections under US law, and the Supreme Court has consistently reaffirmed this finding until the present day.[53] Four years after the decision, the Sherman Antitrust Act included language stating "that the word 'person,' or 'persons,' wherever used in this act[,] shall be deemed to include corporations and associations."[54] Nearly a half century after the decision, Supreme Court Justice Hugo Black unhappily acknowledged this new reality in an important dissenting opinion. "Of the cases in this court in which the Fourteenth Amendment was applied during the first fifty years after its adoption," Black wrote, "less than one-half of one percent invoked it in protection of the Negro race, and more than fifty percent asked that its benefits be extended to corporations."[55]

This development was significant because considering corporations as persons for Fourteenth Amendment purposes required a major rethinking of the very nature of these associations. The grant theory had been based on the assumption that the state could bestow upon an association of individuals a collective identity and specific powers in exchange for some benefit to the people. But the criterion of public purpose—and the attendant expectation of greater regulation—could not be applied to a corporation with Fourteenth Amendment guarantees of equal protection and due process. The trend toward general incorporation laws had meant that the vast majority of corporations were no longer held to such high standards. With these understandings in place, the corporation had become "nothing more," in the words of Herbert Hovenkamp, "than a device for assembling large amounts of capital so it could be controlled efficiently by a few active managers."[56] Had the court refused to extend Fourteenth Amendment protections to corporations, another business form without the historical or theoretical baggage of the corporation, such as the limited partnership, might have arisen to solve the problems of capital formation more effectively. But in providing these rights to corporations, the court intervened in the economy in order to privilege the needs of some—those desiring to raise large amounts of capital with minimal risk—over the needs of others, such as debtors, competitors, and those without access to a large pool of investors.

Because the justices heard no argument on this point, their reasons for adopting what turned out to be a critical precedent are largely unknown. Additionally, the few mentions of this issue in the *Santa Clara* decision actually confused, rather than clarified, it. Referring to Southern Pacific's argument that the value of the fences was improperly included in the value of the railway, Justice Harlan wrote, "If these positions are tenable, there will be no occasion to consider the grave questions of constitutional law" regarding Fourteenth Amendment protections for corporations. If the case were decided on that basis, then "the judgment can be affirmed upon the ground that the assessment cannot properly be the basis of a judgment against the defendant."[57] Yet the court *did* decide the case based on the argument about the fences, and it *also* affirmed the idea that the Fourteenth Amendment applied to corporations.

The clearest indication of the justices' possible thinking might have come from the court of appeals that had earlier ruled on the *Santa Clara* case. In a strange twist of nineteenth-century legal custom, Supreme Court justices also rode circuit as chief judges of the various appellate courts. Presiding over the jurisdiction in which *Santa Clara* had originally been heard was none other than Stephen J. Field, the justice who had previously dissented so strongly in the *Slaughter-House Cases*. In his capacity as *Santa Clara* appellate judge, Field had written a lengthy and detailed decision in which he strongly argued that the Fourteenth Amendment should apply to corporations as well as persons. Indeed, his finding in favor of the railroad was based largely on that conviction. The decision was an impassioned, thirty-page diatribe whose main purpose was to warn against the dangers of governmental oppression that would result from failing to treat corporations equally under the law. The first part of the decision emphatically made the point that the California tax law *did*, in fact, impose an unequal burden upon railroad corporations. Field wrote, "In fixing . . . the liabilities of parties to pay the tax assessed and levied upon properties subject to a mortgage . . . a discrimination is made between the property held by railroad and *quasi* public corporations, and that held by natural persons and other corporations."[58] To make the point perfectly clear, Field drew several hypothetical scenarios, all making the claim that identically situated property owners would face different tax liabilities depending on the legal structures that characterized their ownership.[59]

Field's claim reflected a significant break that had taken place in the prevailing theory of the corporation. When he pointed out that California law treated the natural person differently than the corporation, he was of course correct. But such a distinction could only fairly be called discrimination if there was some reason to assume that the state should be disposed in identical ways toward corporations and individuals. In suggesting that the state had an obligation to treat these businesses exactly as it treated particular people, Field directly, if implicitly, attacked the logic of Marshall's *Dartmouth College* decision. If incorporation was a contract between the state and the individuals who formed the corporation, as that decision articulated, then any terms that the state imposed were appropriate, since no one was forced to incorporate. Under that scenario, the concept of equal protection could not be meaningfully applied.

But Field applied it nonetheless, simply ignoring the prevailing grant theory. In perhaps the decision's most rhetorically passionate section, he indulged in the same slippery-slope argument he had used in the *Slaughter-House* dissent. Today, he argued, it was railroads that suffered from the "discrimination . . . against their property." But if the Fourteenth Amendment allowed states to play favorites in this fashion, then this unequal treatment would soon apply to "the property of churches, of universities, of asylums, of savings banks, of insurance companies, of rolling and flouring mill companies, of mining companies, indeed, of any corporate companies existing in the state." Moreover, once it was decided that the amendment sanctioned disparate treatment of natural and artificial persons, it would not remain limited to those particular categories: "Any difference between the owners, whether of age, color, race, or sex, which the state might designate, would

be a sufficient reason for the discrimination. . . . To levy taxes upon a valu-
ation of property thus made is of the very essence of tyranny."[60]

Field was aware, however, that such a diagnosis, no matter how pas-
sionately argued, depended for its legitimacy upon the premise that the
Fourteenth Amendment was appropriately applied to the *Santa Clara* case.
On this point, many modern-day commentators—most of them on the
left—have mercilessly criticized the *Santa Clara* decision, claiming that its
application of the Fourteenth Amendment declared corporations to be persons. Yet Field did not hold this view. Such a position was both offensive to
the human self-image and obviously untrue, yet neither the appellate finding
nor the Supreme Court decision made this claim. Both ruled that corporations were entitled to Fourteenth Amendment protections, rather than that
they were persons. Such a finding was less offensive and more reasonable
than is often assumed. Though corporations are obviously not people and
just as obviously do not possess all the rights of human beings, it was not
outrageous to consider the question of whether they possessed the specific
right to equal protection of the laws.

Another salient point regarding Field's use of the Fourteenth Amendment in the *Santa Clara* decision is that Field, like Miller in the *Slaughter-
House Cases,* was very much aware that the amendment's purpose was to
protect former slaves. He did not crassly ignore that fact but instead followed the logic of the amendment itself: though African Americans were
most in need of a guarantee of fairness at that particular point in history, that
did not mean that they were the only ones who should ever receive such
assurances. Despite the fact that the amendment "undoubtedly had its origin in a purpose to secure the newly-made citizens in the full enjoyment of
their freedom[,]" he wrote " . . . it is in no respect limited in its operation to
them." Further, he asserted, the Fourteenth Amendment "is universal in its
application, extending its protective force over all men, of every race and
color, within the jurisdiction of the states throughout the broad domain of
the republic."[61]

Given that laws had to be applicable to all relevant parties or be inherently unjust, the question still remained as to who should receive the benefits of this guarantee. Certainly, not all American entities received this
assurance. It did not apply, for instance, to children, animals, works of art,
or natural resources. But none of these exceptions implied that the amendment was ineffectual or that it had been violated. Thus, the significant question with regard to the legal status of the corporation vis-à-vis the
Fourteenth Amendment was whether a specific type of existing entity was

more similar, for the purposes of determining whether it was entitled to equal protection and due process, to an adult human being in full command of all of his or her faculties or to something like the Grand Canyon or the Golden Gate Bridge.

Justice Field's answer was, in short, that a corporation was not only *like* a natural person but was *in fact* such an entity. Yet he made this leap not by endowing a corporation with personhood but by refusing to see the corporation at all. As a shorthand device for treating the interests of the partners, or shareholders, he argued, the concept of incorporation had some uses. But this convenient legal fiction, in Field's view, should not obscure the fact that what was at stake when considering corporate property was really the property of the individual owners of that corporation. "Whatever affects the property of the corporation—that is, of all the members united by the common name—necessarily affects their interests." Thus, "whenever a provision of the [C]onstitution or of a law guaranties [*sic*] to persons protection in their property . . . the benefits of the provision or law are extended to corporations." Such legal privileges applied, he wrote, "not to the name under which different persons are united, but to the individuals composing the union. The courts will always look through the name to see and protect those whom the name represents."[62]

To understand Field's view of the corporation is to see how he could imagine that the Fourteenth Amendment might appropriately apply to it. Field correctly pointed out that no matter what the historical origins of the amendment, for it to be meaningful it had to serve as a vehicle to combat discrimination in general, rather than as a narrow boost for black Americans. And if corporations were merely collections of individuals, then treating them differently than natural persons was, in fact, denying those individuals the equal protection of the laws. "Surely," wrote Field, "these great constitutional provisions . . . cannot be made to read as counsel contend, 'nor shall any state deprive any person of life, liberty, or property without due process of law, *unless he be associated with others in a corporation*, nor deny to any person within its jurisdiction the equal protection of the laws, *unless he be a member of a corporation*.'"[63]

What was at stake in this issue, as Field saw it, was not merely the status of the corporation but that of property itself. Under this view, the corporation was just a placeholder for one of the most basic human rights. If property could be "subject to unequal and arbitrary impositions," then "it follows that corporations hold all their property . . . at the will of the state; that it may be invaded, seized, and the companies despoiled at the state's pleasure." To Field, such a conclusion was as undesirable as it was preposterous: "Whatever power the state may possess in granting or in amending their charters, it cannot withdraw their property from the guaranties [*sic*] of the federal [C]onstitution."[64]

In articulating this conception of the corporation, one which clearly influenced the Supreme Court in its *Santa Clara* decision, Field supplanted the grant theory of the corporation with an entirely new understanding. He did not see the corporation as an artificial entity created by the state but only as a sort of placeholder for individual interests. He argued that the special privileges accorded to a group of people doing business together were justified by the rights that the individuals had possessed before they joined the group. Field successfully provided a Liberal, individualist justification for what was effectively an illiberal, collectivist enterprise.

This line of reasoning, however, was contradictory to its core. If, as Justice Field argued, the court saw only individual rights when it looked at a corporation, then it would be impossible to explain why individuals working together as a corporation enjoyed more rights, such as limited liability, than did singular citizens on their own. The answer to this seeming conundrum appeared to be that Field was prepared to retain those aspects of the grant theory that worked to the advantage of the corporation. Thus, when the Supreme Court in 1886 ratified the idea that incorporation was a right guaranteed by the US Constitution, rather than a privilege bestowed by the state in exchange for some public gain, it intervened in the economy in a specifically procorporate direction. As the size, wealth, and power of corporations in the United States increased throughout the twentieth century, these institutions became a simple fact of American life. Those concerned about this development could propose various regulations and reforms, but precious little intellectual space was to be found from which to mount a meaningful theoretical, political, or legal challenge to the existence, purpose, or justification of the corporation itself.

Santa Clara in the Gilded Age

Though the logic that underwrote the *Santa Clara* decision was arguably eccentric, it is important to note that the ruling represented more than the idiosyncratic view of Justice Field. The court's finding was unanimous, and it has not been overturned to this day. Moreover, many Gilded Age thinkers viewed the corporation as a major force for social progress; consequently, in battling against potential restrictions to the corporation's sphere of activity, *Santa Clara* was very much in step with its time. Legal scholar Jeffrey Rosen has argued that "when the courts act unilaterally, their efforts are likely to be ineffective, to provoke backlashes, and ultimately to threaten the legitimacy of the courts."[65] The lack of any of these reactions suggests that a decision that might today seem radical actually provided an excellent encapsulation of Gilded Age thought.

The first point to consider in this regard is that the decision itself provoked no denunciation or controversy. In fact, it was accorded very little reception at all. Reporting the news one day after the decision was announced, for example, the *New York Times* printed a six-paragraph summary of all the Supreme Court decisions rendered the previous day under the headline NO JURISDICTION IN POLYGAMY CASES/CALIFORNIA RAILWAY TAXES. *Santa Clara* was mentioned in the final paragraph.[66] Field's earlier— and much more explicit—appellate decision on the case received a bit more attention from the *San Francisco Daily Examiner,* but that paper's headline stated VALUE OF THE MORTGAGES MUST BE ASSESSED TO THE HOLDERS rather than anything about the application of the Fourteenth Amendment to corporations.[67] The paper editorialized against the decision, but it expressed little consternation about the personhood of corporations. Its concerns, instead, were with the state's overburdened treasury; the editors hoped that the state would "collect, finally, every dollar that these rapacious corporations owe us."[68]

More broadly, the pursuit of wealth was predominant in the minds of many Americans during the Gilded Age, and the corporation was widely understood as a legitimate and even necessary means to that end. Though it would be inaccurate to say that all segments of American society welcomed the rise of these businesses, one must note that corporate industrialism, in the words of business historian Martin Sklar, "was not only something Americans responded to; since at least the early nineteenth century, it was also something they were doing."[69]

Certainly, many influential Gilded Age thinkers had concerns over the growing power of corporations. Walt Whitman wrote in the 1870s that "exceptional wealth . . . countless manufactures, . . . [and] capital and capitalists . . . form, more or less, a sort of anti-democratic disease and monstrosity."[70] Nor was such anticorporate sentiment restricted to the romantic criticisms represented by the poet. The year after the court decided *Santa Clara,* economist Henry Carter Adams would mock the sort of reasoning that supported the decision, observing that "the tyranny of corporations,

THE CURSE OF CALIFORNIA.

In 1882, cartoonist G. Frederick Keller's "The Curse of California" took aim at the Southern Pacific Railroad, which was soon to be the defendant in the *Santa Clara* case. Comparing the company to an octopus, Keller depicted its many tentacles exerting control over government, finance, farming, and mining. (Courtesy Bancroft Library, University of California–Berkeley) which grew naturally from conditions of 'industrial freedom,' was as griev-ous as any tyranny ever established by government agency."[71]

But overall, such complaints were in the minority. Many Americans rev-eled in the power of these new corporations to promote economic and tech-nological change. Quite common was the view of the corporation as a progressive development in economic life, one to which, in Sklar's words, "society in its sociopolitical, intellectual, and cultural dimensions must adjust . . . in an appropriate way or suffer regression."[72] Many agreed with the somewhat later claim of the Republican vice presidential candidate, Colum-bia University president and Nobel Peace Prize recipient Nicholas Murray Butler, that "the limited liability corporation is the greatest single discovery of modern times."[73]

Richard T. Ely was an economist who, along with Adams, founded the American Economic Association in 1885. Two years later, he wrote for *Harper's* magazine a series of articles that focused on the corporation. Though Ely was sympathetic to the labor movement and had flirted with socialism, these pieces were noteworthy for their contention that "corpora-tions are a good thing and ought to be encouraged."[74] Rather than viewing the corporation as a tool of plutocracy, Ely saw it as a great leveler that would allow those of limited means to participate in industrial and financial life, gradually bringing about "the progress of democracy in industry."[75]

Though Ely might have shared with Justice Field a reverence for the corporate form, their reasons for this admiration could not have been more in opposition. First, the economist's understanding of the corporation was entirely rooted in the grant theory. Seemingly unaware of the Supreme Court's holding from the prior year, Ely noted that corporations were "crea-tures of the state" that were "endowed by sovereign power" with unique abilities, and he stressed that a governmental body was justified in creating such entities "only to promote the welfare of the people; otherwise its action would be inexcusable." Since the state did not "dare . . . create an artificial person which may injure the people . . . [t]here is no limitation whatever to the right of the state to determine the character of corporations."[76] Second, where Field saw the corporation as an institutional instantiation of individ-ual rights, Ely thought that "the evolution of the race has reached that point where the supremacy of the individual is neither needed nor desired," and he viewed the corporate entity as the embodiment of a new communalism. Rejecting the notion that "co-operation either through some public body or through some voluntary agency involves curtailment of individual rights," Ely argued that corporations represented the culmination of the spirit of

"fraternalism" over that of "paternalism" and that they embodied economically the democratic political principle of which Americans were justly
proud.[77]

Ely did not claim that corporations were free from problems. He noted
the frequent antagonism between capital and labor, as well as the many
unfair competitive benefits that might accrue to large corporations. But he
specifically argued in favor of "these useful industrial forms" and against
the notion that "there are evils inseparably connected with corporations as
they exist today in the United States."[78] Though there were certainly cases
of the abuse of the corporate structure, they could all be traced, in Ely's
view, to the exploitation of natural monopolies. Thus, the problem was not
with corporations per se but with the "application of the principles of private business concerns to what are in their nature essentially public under-
takings."[79] Corporations, argued Ely, could greatly aid in the hoped-for
extension of industrial democracy as long as their principles were restricted
to their proper sphere, which was to say, outside the realm of unlimited natural monopoly.

Therefore, even one whose reasoning, positions, and values were significantly out of step with those of the *Santa Clara* court resisted an attack
on corporations themselves. By and large, the mainstream of political and
intellectual classes in US society during the Gilded Age rejected any program that would significantly restrict the growth and influence of these
firms. Corporations had already become an essential part of American economic life: Ely estimated in the *Harper's* series that one-quarter of the
nation's wealth was held by corporations, and in his *Santa Clara* appellate
decision, Field claimed, perhaps less plausibly, that corporate property
"embraces the greater part of the wealth of the country."[80] Regardless of the
correct figure, the point is that corporations had become a fixture of the economic and political landscape and that the task for the American political
system was to construct a justification of them. The significance of *Santa
Clara* lies less in Justice Field's somewhat tortured logic than in the fact that
the decision intellectually and legally cemented the place of the corporation
in American political economy.

Consequences of the Property Conception

Santa Clara ushered in a new age of jurisprudential permissiveness with
regard to corporations. About a decade after the decision, the court invali-

dated a state law on the basis of "liberty of contract." Robert McCloskey characterized this decision as the culmination of a "process of constitution-making" that traced its origin to the *Slaughter-House* defenses. After the "Court had conceded, rather offhandedly, that corporations were 'persons' within the meaning of the Amendment," he observed, businesses realized that this "concession" was of "epic importance and of incalculable value." From 1886 onward, McCloskey argued, "business, whether incorporated or not, was no longer wholly at the mercy of the popular will."[81] *Santa Clara* helped to enable businesses to supersede the democratic process itself.

In addition to permanently fixing the primacy of the corporation, *Santa Clara* brought about other consequences. As Herbert Hovenkamp has pointed out, "Corporate personhood" was more than merely the articulation of laissez-faire values. More important, it was a response to a problem or, more accurately, two interrelated problems. The first was how to determine that property held in the name of the corporation would receive the same constitutional protections as that held in other arrangements; in other words, incorporation should not actually *weaken* such protections for those who held property in this form. By characterizing the corporation as itself a person, the court effectively solved this problem by allowing the corporation to hold the property itself. The second issue was both more complicated and potentially more troublesome. Despite its newly awarded personhood, "the corporation" was a mere abstraction. Once it had been determined that corporate property was also subject to constitutional protections, it was no more clear than before who was, specifically, able to claim or utilize these rights on behalf of the firm. If the shareholders owned the corporation but the corporation was a legal entity that was entitled to own property itself, then it did not seem that the stockholders could claim the actual corporate property. The managers of the firm directly controlled the corporation's resources, but they did not own either the resources or the company. The doctrine of corporate personhood potentially created new problems once it solved the old ones.

In securing property rights to the corporation by declaring it a person, rather than through some other legal mechanism, the court resolved this conundrum by effectively prioritizing the company's managers over its shareholders. As Hovenkamp pointed out, the grant of legal personhood gave corporate managers "the power to assert the corporation's constitutional claims," but it also implied conversely "that the shareholders *lacked* standing to assert these rights." As a result, "an important effect of the *Santa Clara* decision . . . was to enlarge the gap between ownership and control that characterized the development of the classical corporation."[82] Shareholders would own the corporation, but managers would actually control it. Commonsensical notions of ownership simply did not apply, and the resulting relationships appeared beyond the power of ordinary citizens to understand, much less limit or regulate.

Santa Clara demonstrates the extent to which corporations themselves, today the building blocks of the market economy, represent not the absence of government regulation but one of the more intense forms of government economic intervention. They are state-created entities that privilege some economic interests over those of others. Originally, US states bestowed these benefits in exchange for services of some value to the citizenry. But by the time of *Santa Clara County v. Southern Pacific Railroad,* mainstream opinion among jurists and intellectuals had changed. The ability to incorporate was no longer viewed as a privilege; it was now seen as a right. As such, the notion that corporations were required to justify their existence by providing a public service, rather than merely seeking the highest returns for their shareholders, became a quaint relic of a bygone age. That this shift in understanding was marked by court decisions rather than popular or electoral politics suggests that during the Gilded Age, the always difficult balance between democracy and capitalism in the United States weighed a bit more heavily on the side of business. This situation would change, however, with the advent of the Great Depression.

Chapter Four

Employment

Hubert Humphrey died in 1978, at the age of sixty-six. The Minnesota Democrat had spent much of his adult life—twenty-one years—in the US Senate. A longtime liberal, Humphrey had been an early supporter of civil rights; it was his proposal that prompted the Dixiecrats to walk out of the 1948 Democratic National Convention. He ran for his party's presidential nomination in 1960, served as vice president of the United States under Lyndon Johnson, and secured the Democratic nomination for president in 1968. Though unable to win the nation's highest office, Humphrey was held in high esteem by senators of both parties. When he succumbed to pancreatic cancer, many in Washington hoped to honor him by passing the last piece of legislation that he had championed.

That bill, however, was a controversial one. Designed to bring about full employment, it had originally been proposed in the House in 1974 by Augustus Hawkins (along with Wisconsin Democrat Henry Reuss), an African American Democrat from Los Angeles. Though Hawkins was particularly concerned about the effect of joblessness on the black community, his proposal was designed to address a broader dynamic: the number of jobs created by the American economy was simply not as large as the number of people seeking employment. Hawkins rejected the typical government approach to unemployment, which was to address the problem indirectly by stimulating economic demand through tax cuts and public spending in the hope that private industries would produce more and hire more workers. He sought to replace it with the more direct policy of a straightforward guarantee of a job for every working citizen. For Hawkins, "an authentic full employment policy" would not be based on broad stimulation of the overall economy but on "the more human and socially meaningful concept of personal rights to an opportunity for useful employment at fair rates of compensation." At the bill's core, therefore, were two unprecedented innovations: the requirement that the federal government itself provide a job to any individual who was unable to find one and the establishment of a legal right to work, enforced by granting individual citizens the right to sue the government for a job.[1]

To many, the notion of eliminating unemployment seemed utopian and Hawkins's quest a quixotic one. The bill appeared to be going nowhere until Humphrey introduced a version of it in the Senate, immediately giving it the imprimatur of a well-known, "establishment" liberal. Many Democratic constituencies were nonetheless uncomfortable with the bill, which addressed what some felt was a "black" issue. Of those groups that hesitated to support what was now called Humphrey-Hawkins, the most significant was the American Federation of Labor and Congress of Industrial Organizations (AFL-CIO). The organization opposed the provision guaranteeing the right to sue for a job, believing it was impractical, cumbersome, and expensive. Without the support of organized labor, the most important Democratic interest group, the bill simply would not pass.[2]

In response to these concerns, Hawkins and Humphrey negotiated with representatives of the AFL-CIO and introduced a revised version of the bill. The new bill eliminated many of the most innovative aspects of the older legislation, including the individual right to gainful employment. In the 1976 Democratic presidential primaries, Jimmy Carter, the party's eventual nominee, distanced himself from Humphrey-Hawkins. After Carter won the presidency, then, the bill's sponsors had to rework it again in order to gain executive support. The final version, reintroduced in November 1977, relaxed the time limit within which unemployment had to be reduced; gave the president the ability to request that Congress alter the employment goals; and required that the "last resort" government jobs agenda be authorized again, separately from the rest of the bill.[3]

Enthusiasm for the bill was waning when the Ninety-Fourth United States Congress session ended. Early in the next session, however, Humphrey died, and the outpouring of grief and appreciation was expressed in a wave of support for the senator's final bill. Minnesota's governor appointed Humphrey's widow, Muriel, to finish his term, and she soon submitted Humphrey-Hawkins in the Senate. The *New York Times* noted that the bill had "wide appeal" after "several false starts" in Congress and referred to it as "unassailable."

Yet the editors of the *Times* did not endorse Humphrey-Hawkins. Having opposed earlier versions of the bill because they "promised too much," the paper declared in an editorial that the current iteration "promises too little." The "vague" bill, it continued, "ducks" the jobs issue "by making a promise that no one knows how to keep," perpetuating a "cruel hoax on the unemployed."[4] The editors' concerns, however, did little to derail the bill, and President Carter signed Humphrey-Hawkins into law on October 27, 1978. The new law mandated that the unemployment rate would not be higher than 4 percent and "translat[ed] into practical reality the right of all Americans . . . to full opportunity for useful paid employment." But its final text also committed the country to other economic goals, some of which appeared to complicate the task of job creation: "full . . . production and real income, balanced growth, adequate productivity growth, proper attention to national priorities, and reasonable price stability."[5] With such a wide range of objectives, the bill was exactly what the *Times* had said it was— little more than an economic wish list.

The Humphrey-Hawkins Act is still on the books today, but it has had a minimal effect on federal employment policy. In that regard, the watered-down bill perfectly exemplifies the US approach to unemployment. Elected officials rhetorically commit to addressing the issue, but they shy away from comprehensive solutions to the problem. Though the reticence and confusion generated by this issue can be frustrating, it is nonetheless understandable. Unemployment carries tremendous human costs, and many would like to see the government help the jobless to bear those burdens. But the idea that the government should be responsible for finding or creating jobs does not fit comfortably in the tradition of political or economic thought in the United States. The labor market, like the rest of the economy, is ostensibly a private affair, with buyers, sellers, employers, and workers all self-interestedly interacting for their own individual benefit. On that interpretation, there is no particular distribution of jobs that would transform a private concern into a social problem that requires government attention.

For much of the nation's history, few would have seen it any other way. Jobs did not become a necessary part of life for most Americans until the early twentieth century. Soon thereafter, the Great Depression legitimized the idea that minimizing unemployment was an appropriate goal of government economic intervention. President Franklin Delano Roosevelt, embodying the brand-new political orientation known as liberalism, responded to that economic crisis with a set of ambitious policies and programs known as the New Deal. Yet the ambivalence that liberals would manifest decades later in their hesitant embrace of Humphrey-Hawkins was apparent from the days of the New Deal itself. Perhaps the best example of this confusion can be found in the writings of Henry Wallace, onetime Roosevelt vice president. FDR had said that every American had a right to a job, and Wallace's 1945 book, *Sixty Million Jobs,* advocated specific policies to make the recently deceased president's claim into a reality. But the law that resulted from these considerations failed to incorporate the most central prescriptions from the book. Ever since, the American political consensus has held politicians accountable for high unemployment while forbidding to them the tools that would directly address the problem.

The Progressive Era

From the nineteenth century to the twentieth, the predominantly agricultural economy of the United States transformed into something far more urban, industrial, and corporate. In 1880, the vast majority of Americans—73 percent of the nation's population—lived in rural areas. Fifty years later, only 43 percent did so.[6] The typical American of the twentieth century was far more likely to be a factory worker, utterly dependent on wages for his or her subsistence, than the self-sufficient farmer imagined by Thomas Jefferson.

This shift caused tremendous changes in American political thinking. The integrity of the independent yeoman image had always been undermined by the dependence of actual agriculturalists upon urban and foreign markets, government land grants, and slave labor. Nonetheless, that ideal occupied an important place in American cultural, intellectual, and political life. Perhaps its most significant role in setting economic policy was providing a yardstick against which the economically unsuccessful could be found wanting. If abundant land and hard work could always provide a person with a satisfactory living, then the hardships of the less fortunate were no one's fault—and no one's problem—but their own. In the latter decades of the nineteenth century, followers of Herbert Spencer reapplied this logic to their own time. The figure of their veneration, however, was not the farmer but the businessperson. Appropriating the insights of evolutionary biology to explain political and economic phenomena, the social Darwinists concluded that government aid to the less fortunate would only allow the unsuccessful to reproduce when they might otherwise have died off. Such outcomes would harm the human race itself, diluting the qualities that had allowed the successful to thrive. Russell Conwell, the minister who later founded Temple University, was among the most influential voices of the period. Beginning in 1890 and continuing for two decades, he presented to thousands of audiences his popular address "Acres of Diamonds," which featured as its central point the notion that "the opportunity to get rich . . . is here . . . now . . . within the reach of almost every man and woman."[7] The corollary of the claim that wealth was available to everyone was, of course, that idea that those without wealth were lacking in some critical personal quality. Though the rich, Cromwell continued, were virtuous in character, among the "most honest men you find in the community," the poor were those "whom God has punished for [their] sins." Since "there is not a poor person in the United States who was not made poor by his own shortcomings," to "sympathize" with the less well off, he concluded, was actually "to do wrong."[8]

Social Darwinism turned on the premise that a person's economic station was primarily a function of that individual's level of talent, initiative, and work ethic. Yet the changing patterns of American life posed problems for this understanding. The typical American increasingly worked for someone else; lived in property built and owned by someone else; and purchased food, clothing, and other necessities from someone else. In such an environment, the notion that economic self-sufficiency was entirely a function of individual drive was difficult to maintain.

As the new reality took hold, wrote historian Richard Hofstadter, "the need for political and economic reform was now felt more widely in the country at large."[9] The power of social Darwinism began to wane, giving way to a new political orientation known as Progressivism. This movement flourished in the first two decades of the twentieth century, the period known today as the Progressive Era. *Progressivism* was an umbrella term that denoted no formal group membership, and the movement claimed members from both the Democratic and Republican Parties. As a result, identifying its central meaning can be difficult, and historians today still argue about the definitive Progressive attribute. What is unquestionably true, however, is that Progressivism was a response to the changes that industrialization had wrought upon American life. Richard Ely, the economist whose 1887 series of articles had lauded the corporation, wrote in 1903 that "the momentous changes resulting from the industrial revolution" had created a need to "control and take advantage of these new forces." Since industrialism was widely considered inseparable from progress, the issue was not one of undoing these changes. Instead, Ely saw the "industrial prob-

lem" as determining how to "retain the advantages of associated effort"—
that is to say, incorporation—while continuing to provide the "freedom of
movement and a socially desirable distribution of products."[10]

Progressivism articulated a new political understanding necessitated by
the economic conditions of modernity. The movement's adherents believed
that modern institutions, foremost among them the urban political machine
and the monopolistic corporation, had already compromised the freedom of
the American citizen. Liberty, in their view, was not well served by the laissez-faire that had characterized Gilded Age attitudes. Nor were Progressives taken with the calls for revolution issuing from socialist and anarchist
quarters. Neither radicals nor conservatives, Progressives adopted as their
watchword the decidedly moderate term *reform*.

Though their reforms were aimed in many different directions, one
theme that united a great deal of Progressive activism was the integrity of
government. Reacting against the corruption and graft that characterized
the "smoke-filled rooms" of the political parties and the big-city machines
of many major urban centers, Progressives believed that the best way to
ensure the honesty of government officials was to make them more directly
accountable to the citizens. "Sunlight," wrote jurist Louis Brandeis in 1913,
"is said to be the best of disinfectants."[11] In a two-decade period, twenty-
two states adopted some aspect of the "Oregon System," named after the
state that had adopted the initiative, referendum, party primary, and direct
election of senators by the voters (rather than, as was common up to that
time, the state legislatures). In 1913, the US Constitution was amended to
require that senators be elected in this fashion. That same year, Congress
established the Federal Reserve, whose intended function was to remove
politics from the management of the nation's money supply. Perhaps the
ultimate realization of the Progressive impulse was achieved with the ratification of the Nineteenth Amendment in 1920, when *feminists*—a word
coined during this period—finally secured for women the right to vote.

Another major concern of Progressives was reining in the power of the
corporation and the wealthy more broadly. In 1877, Congress established
the Interstate Commerce Commission, the first federal agency charged with
regulating big business. Three years later, it passed the Sherman Antitrust
Act, which "declared to be illegal" every "contract, combination . . . or conspiracy, in restraint of trade or commerce."[12] This law has served as the basis
of federal monopoly regulation ever since. Progressives believed that local
utilities—companies delivering gas, water, electricity, and other necessi-

ties—were particularly exploitative: between 1887 and 1921, for instance, thirty-seven states established electric regulatory commissions.[13] Public health was another area in which Progressives sought to limit the power of corporations. In 1906, Upton Sinclair's novel *The Jungle* caused a national sensation by raising awareness of the dangers that the meat-packing industry posed to both its employees, through its working conditions, and its customers, via the rotten and disingenuously labeled food that it sold. Under public pressure, Congress passed the Meat Inspection Act and the Pure Food and Drug Act that same year.

President Theodore "Teddy" Roosevelt (TR), a Republican Progressive who first took office in 1901, sued the Northern Securities Company for antitrust violations under the Sherman Act. In 1904, the Supreme Court ordered that the trust be dissolved, and Roosevelt earned a reputation as a "trustbuster" by bringing suit against a total of forty-four companies during his presidency. In the most significant of these, the court ordered the Standard Oil Trust to be broken up into dozens of separate companies. Two years later, in 1913, the Sixteenth Amendment to the Constitution established the first peacetime federal income tax, in order to ensure that the wealthy contributed some of their earnings to the national Treasury. The Clayton Antitrust Act, which followed one year later, exempted labor unions from the antitrust provisions of the Sherman Act and outlawed specific business practices that the earlier law had left in place. In the same year, Congress established the Federal Trade Commission, the first national agency charged with regulating interstate commerce from the perspective of consumers rather than competing businesses.

In 1917, the United States entered World War I and in so doing effectively ended the Progressive Era. Progressives themselves were divided on the merits of the Great War, but the militarism, jingoism, and xenophobia that characterized public discourse during that period left little room for consideration of the domestic matters that served as the movement's primary concern. Additionally, during the Red Scare of 1917–1918, many Americans became suspicious of these activists. "Businessmen and conservatives," wrote historian Michael McGerr, "quickly learned to denounce [P]rogressive academics, churchmen and journalists as 'parlor Bolsheviks.'"[14] The factor that contributed most strongly to the demise of Progressivism, though, was the same one that ultimately finished similar programs through American history—success. Having achieved many of the goals that they set out to accomplish, Progressives lost much of their energy and direction. After lying dormant for a decade, spurred on by the Great Depression, Progressivism would again animate American political life. But it would do so under a new name.

From Progressivism to Liberalism

As much as the Progressives altered the country's policies and practices, their influence on the tradition of political thinking in the United States had an even greater significance. The intellectual framework that they introduced came to form one of the dominant patterns of political thinking in twentieth-century America. By the time this influence had arrived, however, Progressivism had acquired a new name: liberalism.

In early nineteenth-century England, the Liberals were a radical wing of the Whig Party. The smaller faction grew to the point that it overshadowed the larger organization, and the resulting Liberal Party was soon one of the two major political parties in the United Kingdom. By midcentury, Liberalism generally stood for three things: a radical individualism best represented in the utilitarian philosophy of Jeremy Bentham, an economic wing that was influenced by Adam Smith, and a strong commitment to religious liberty. This philosophy, today often called classical Liberalism, was oriented toward battling limitations to individual freedom such as slavery, religious establishment, and colonialism. Yet it was not liberal in the modern sense of the term. Classical Liberalism did not favor, for example, restricting child labor or other government economic interventions, seeing the contract as an example of individual liberty.[15]

By the early twentieth century, however, Progressives in the United States had developed a way of thinking that took the commitments, if not the name, of classical Liberalism as a starting point. But Progressives also believed that Liberalism was inadequate to the new wage-oriented, industrial, urban economy. Whereas the earlier English Liberals had concerned themselves primarily with the claim that more people *should* be free, their twentieth-century American counterparts found that the new environment made it necessary to reimagine the meaning of freedom itself. In the modern polity, they argued, the mere absence of coercion did not render the typical American urban worker "free." With few options other than working sweatshop labor, living in tenement slums, voting for ward bosses, and ingesting unsafe food and medicine, the urban worker found that his or her voluntary choices did not feel like a genuine expression of liberty.

One who influentially expressed the new Progressive philosophy was Herbert Croly. Born to two successful journalists in 1869, Croly attended Harvard University three separate times but never took a degree. He worked on and off as an editor before writing *The Promise of American Life*, which was published in 1909. The book soon "catapulted" Croly, in the words of historian David W. Noble, "from obscurity into the forefront of [P]rogressive thinkers."[16] But *The Promise of American Life* was not a Progressive platform or a wish list of policy positions. Croly, as characterized by political scientist David K. Nichols, owed his significance and lasting influence to the fact that he "was less concerned with specific reforms than he was with the establishment of an intellectual context for reform." In order to "change the system," Nichols wrote of Croly, "it was first necessary to change the ideas that animated it."[17]

Those ideas, Croly argued, had been profitable ones for much of the nation's history. They had animated the arrangement that had delivered, until recently, on the promise of American life that gave his book its title. The widespread economic opportunities of the eighteenth and nineteenth centuries, Croly asserted, allowed Americans to believe that those whose efforts had not met with success lacked some native virtue or talent. More recently, however, the changes wrought by industrialism had made such an outlook more difficult to sustain. "The discontented poor," wrote Croly, "are beginning to charge their poverty to an unjust political and economic organization," and he thought they were correct to do so. "The traditional American confidence in individual freedom," he argued, had come to underwrite a series of institutions and practices that produced "a morally and socially undesirable distribution of wealth."[18]

In Croly's view, the same values that had once made the United States a land of opportunity now supported a brutal plutocracy. At the center of this intellectual system were the ideas of nationalism and democracy. By the first, which he associated with the ideas and influence of Alexander Hamilton, Croly meant a communitarian sense of common purpose, one that might necessitate individual sacrifice for the country's greater good. With the second, he referred to the dignity of the individual, a position for which he invoked the patronage of Thomas Jefferson. Both schemas, he argued, had been central to the greatness of the American experience, but each of them had a negative aspect as well. In the Hamiltonian ideal, "the central government is to be used . . . to promote the national interest and to consolidate the national organization." Yet Hamilton "did not seek a sufficiently broad, popular basis for the realization of those ideas."[19] Jefferson, by contrast, "was filled with a sincere, indiscriminate, and unlimited faith in the American people,"[20] which led to a "conception of democracy [that] was meager, narrow, and self-contradictory," in which "persistent governmental interference implied distrust in popular efficiency and good-will." Still, because Jefferson's political success was longer lasting than Hamilton's, "the consequences of Jefferson's imperfect conception of democracy have been much more serious than the consequences of Hamilton's inadequate conception of American nationality."[21]

Croly explained that these two ideas had created tensions throughout American history. In the middle part of the nineteenth century, slavery exposed the contradictions in the two approaches, as the nationalist principle supported the western expansion of slavery and the democratic impulse opposed it. Abraham Lincoln, who was Croly's great hero, resolved this tension by showing that the "legal Union was being threatened precisely because American national integrity was being gutted by an undemocratic institution."[22] For Croly, the later "pioneer period" was a Jeffersonian idyll in which "millions of Americans of much the same pattern were rewarded for their democratic virtue in an approximately similar manner." This democratic condition led to an unforced communal bond among Americans, one that was soon threatened by the industrialism of the late nineteenth century. The "economic forces making for specialization . . . , for social classification, and . . . for greater individual distinction" destroyed this "early national consistency."[23] Thus, the American emphasis on Jeffersonian individualism first fostered and then destroyed Hamiltonian nationalism. By the time in which Croly was writing, it had become apparent that the disintegration of nationalism had brought about "the establishment in the heart of the American economic and social system of certain glaring inequalities of condition and power."[24]

Croly's criticisms of contemporary life focused on two related issues: the limited opportunities available to the poor to actualize their own potential and the power of the corporation. In his view, however, these specific problems were merely manifestations of more fundamental misunderstandings of the American promise. Under conditions that fostered "the perpetuation of unearned economic distortions" and legitimized "extreme poverty, whether deserved or not," the very "integrity of a democracy is injured."[25] Nonetheless, Croly was not a romantic looking back toward a "restoration of American democracy to its former condition of purity and excellence."[26] Such a project was naive and impossible, in his view, because the economic distortions were a manifestation of Jeffersonian individualism, rather than an aberration from it. Since "the automatic harmony of the individual and the public interest, which is the essence of the Jeffersonian democratic creed, has proved to be an illusion," he stated, both individualism and nationalism required activist government in order to maintain their integrity.[27]

The core of *The Promise of American Life* was Croly's belief that the nation's democratic potential was best realized in the capacity for self-improvement. To this extent, an economic system that animated the "industrial leader" by providing only "the motive of amassing more millions than can be of any possible use to himself or his children" was a failed one. "If an economic democracy can purchase efficient industrial organization on a huge scale only at the price of this class of fortunes, then it must be content with a lower order of efficiency."[28] What the state should be doing, Croly argued, was setting the conditions by which those persons "of exceptional ability" would have "an exceptional opportunity of exercising it."[29] The emphasis on Jeffersonian individualism over Hamiltonian nationalism had allowed for the creation of monstrous distortions of wealth, which had paradoxically destroyed the democratic character of economic life in the United States. He believed that a centralized, Hamiltonian federal government was necessary to foster and preserve the individualized, democratic Jeffersonian character of the American people themselves. "In the complete democracy a man must in some way be made to serve the nation in the very act of contributing to his own individual fulfillment."[30]

Like many Progressives, Croly was enamored of Teddy Roosevelt, whose presidency he interpreted as an ideal fusion of the Hamiltonian and Jeffersonian traditions. Roosevelt's "nationalism," he wrote, "really implies a democracy of individual and social improvement," which was, of course, exactly Croly's recipe for maximizing American potential.[31] Roosevelt declined to run for office in 1908, entrusting his Progressive legacy to his friend, fellow Republican, and handpicked successor William Howard Taft. Over the next four years, TR became increasingly disillusioned with Taft, and in 1912, he decided to run for president again. Roosevelt performed far better than Taft in the Republican state primaries, but in those days, party bosses at the convention, rather than the voters in the state contests, chose a party's nominee. Taft controlled the party machinery and so was able to secure the nomination. Incensed at this turn of events, Roosevelt and others founded a new political organization—the Progressive Party—and mounted a third-party run. Many of his supporters came from Republican ranks, so his candidacy split the Grand Old Party (GOP) vote. In the end, Roosevelt got more votes than Taft—but the winner was Democrat Woodrow Wilson.

Roosevelt considered the third-party attempt a failure. He returned to the Republican fold and urged his supporters to do likewise. But the Progressive Party's very existence was based on dissatisfaction with the Republican Party; its members were not likely to rejoin that organization. The Progressive Party itself limped along in an uninspiring fashion, electing the occasional congressperson or state official before officially disbanding in 1916. Meanwhile, the Democratic president, Woodrow Wilson, came to believe that Progressives were a Republican constituency that he might be able to capture. He began to adopt much of Roosevelt's old program and to bring some Progressives over to the Democratic Party.

As a result of this sequence of events, Progressive values lacked a political vehicle after 1912, even as they energized a significant section of the electorate. In 1914, three prominent Progressive journalists—Croly, Walter Lippmann, and Walter Weyl—founded a magazine to carry the movement's banner. Called the *New Republic*, the weekly magazine quickly became an important journal of political opinion, publishing many influential political writers, thinkers, and activists. But to describe the philosophy to which they were committed, the journal's editors needed a new term. At this point, Progressives were not particularly committed to any party, so they did not identify as either Democratic or Republican. Moreover, the word *Progressive* itself was tarnished by its association with political defeat. In 1916, the magazine issued a typically unsigned editorial regarding Woodrow Wilson.[32] Sounding a tentative, guarded note, it mixed praise for Wilson's adoption of the magazine's favored positions with concerns that these shifts represented no more than politically expedient partisanship. The president's move to the left had confused political categories, the editors noted, and consequently "deprived the liberal of any alternative to Democracy except Republicanism or Socialism." Before committing to Wilson, however, "liberals need to obtain" from Wilson "some assurance that during a second term he will not think and act too much as a Democrat."[33] In this article, the editors of the *New Republic* apparently used the word *liberal* in its modern sense for the first time.[34] The influence of the magazine was significant enough that liberals soon began to describe themselves as such, and eventually, the term entered the general lexicon.

The word *liberalism* came to describe the belief that an activist government was charged with the responsibility of addressing the nation's economic problems. Liberals tended to favor labor unions, support federal regulation of business, and assign responsibility to the government for the plight of society's less fortunate. Though the relationship between the new usage of the word and its original meaning, as a defense of freedom, might be difficult to trace, such a connection does exist. It was perhaps explained most effectively by philosopher John Dewey in a series of lectures he gave that were published under the title *Liberalism and Social Action*. Dewey, a frequent contributor to the *New Republic*, was a prominent and influential public intellectual: the most well-known philosopher in the country during a period that actually included well-known philosophers. Political theorist Alan Ryan referred to Dewey as "*the* philosopher of American liberalism in the first half of [the twentieth] century."[35] In his lectures, Dewey expressed a clear awareness that, as late as 1935 (the year in which the book was published), some who called themselves Liberals still subscribed to the older sense of the word. Such people thought "in terms of the old opposition between the province of organized social action and the province of purely individual initiative and effort." This form of thinking, Dewey said, "still provide[d] the intellectual system of apologetics for the existing economic régime," which its adherents "strangely, it would seem ironically, uphold as a régime of individual liberty for all."[36]

By contrast, he observed, the "new" liberals "are committed to the principle that organized society must use its powers to establish the conditions under which the mass of individuals can possess actual as opposed to merely legal liberty."[37] The choices and actions available to the typical modern citizen were structured so that merely being allowed to choose between them did not render a person free. As Dewey explained it, the new liberalism operated in the tradition of Progressivism by noting that, in the modern era, liberty was no longer a condition that was satisfied merely by removing impediments to individual choices and actions. The "new" liberals, he argued, recognized that specific times and places would generate their own unique threats to freedom and that "liberty is always relative to forces that at a given time and place are increasingly felt to be oppressive." Throughout history, people had identified liberty with emancipation from many different factors: serfdom, slavery, clericalism, and monarchy are but some of them. Dewey believed, however, that in his own day, freedom connoted "liberation from material insecurity and from the coercions and repressions that prevent multitudes from participation in the vast cultural resources that are at hand."[38] As such, liberalism was defined by the position that a strong central government was a condition of freedom rather than an obstacle to it.

Throughout the early twentieth century, Progressivism and then liberalism slowly took hold as one of the two major political orientations in the United States. With regard to government intervention in the economy, the battle lines became rather easy to draw after that point. Liberals were, generally speaking, frankly and unabashedly for it. They believed in using government to impose competition on firms through antitrust actions, to keep prices affordable for consumers, to ensure the safety of workplaces, to provide for the health and viability of labor unions, and to mitigate the effects of economic inequality. These things were all necessary for the full flowering of individual freedom as liberals understood it, but it was impossible to deny that they also required a great deal of economic intervention. The dominant economic note sounded by the century's *other* major political system, movement conservatism, was that the costs of liberal interventionism were far too high. The liberal notion of freedom, argued conservatives, could come about only with the imposition of a good deal of regulation, taxation, and restriction. These government activities would significantly limit freedom of action, which constituted the understanding of liberty that tended to matter most to conservatives.

Despite their willingness to embrace government economic intervention, early twentieth-century liberals thought little about unemployment. The working conditions of the time were so poor and exploitative and the urban political patronage so corrupt that reformers were far more concerned about the perils of having a job than with those associated with lacking one. Nonetheless, concern for individuals without employment eventually became a prominent characteristic of twentieth-century liberalism. The cause of this shift was a tragedy that threatened the viability of the capitalist system itself.

The Great Depression and the New Deal

In the time before industrialization, everyday people made many of their own goods, and they purchased few items. Thus, the nineteenth-century economy necessarily catered primarily to the needs of industrial producers and the very wealthy. In the early twentieth century, technological changes in manufacturing allowed for a much greater emphasis on the mass production of goods. The ability of firms to sell a large number of comparatively inexpensive items, as opposed to the small number of expensive products that characterized an industrial economy, prompted tremendous economic growth in the United States. By the 1920s, a decade in which the gross national product (GNP) increased by 43.4 percent, this process had reached its mature stage.[39]

The booming economy transformed ideas about the commercial enterprise itself. In the words of historian Maury Klein, "Business itself was fast becoming the new religion." Led by a trio of probusiness Republican presidents—William H. Taft, Calvin Coolidge, and Herbert Hoover—many Americans came to believe that they were living in a "new era" that spelled the end of the boom-and-bust rhythm of the business cycle. Nothing signified this attitude more clearly than the national obsession with the stock market. Though Klein declared it impossible to know the number of Americans who invested in the market, "even in small towns," he wrote, "people put money into it or heard stories of it or knew someone who knew someone who had made a killing in it. . . . There was something almost mystical in popular attitudes toward the bull market."[40] This confidence kept the whole scheme afloat for most of the decade: people who believed the market would continue to rise bought more stocks, stoking the engine by which the market would, indeed, continue to climb. "To the speculating public," reported the *New York Times* in 1929, "the picture has apparently come to be that of a continuous rise in prices which nothing can interrupt more than momentarily."[41]

Two months after the *Times* described the ebullience of the financial investor, the stock market crashed. Though popular memory imagines the crash of October 1929 as the cause of the long-term economic catastrophe that followed, historian David M. Kennedy, author of a magisterial history of the Depression and war years, referred to that impression as a "misconception." Summarizing the scholarship on the issue, he concluded that "the most responsible students" of the market collapse "have been unable to demonstrate an appreciable cause-and-effect" between it and the Great Depression.[42]

The truth is that small pockets of the economy had seen problems even in the prosperous twenties. Agriculture had been underperforming, automobile production and construction both began to slow in the middle part of the decade, and the Florida real estate boom crashed in 1926. Consumption dropped slowly but steadily, and by the end of the decade, business inventories had increased significantly.[43] These unsold goods would eventually become a major problem: firms with stock on hand had no need to produce more, and hence, their demand for workers was diminished. But during most of the 1920s, other sectors of the economy continued to perform well. Unemployment was particularly low in the latter half of the decade, and the stock market continued to rise. Facing good times overall, few Americans expressed concerns about these seemingly minor issues.

The stock market crash, regardless of its actual economic impact, marked a major cultural shift. It demarcated the border between a period in which most Americans were generally confident about their economic futures and one defined by tragedy and anxiety. After October 1929, problems seemed to swell in size and number, whereas bright spots receded. President Hoover struggled to contain the damage from the stock market crash, attempting to keep it away from the broader economy. But Hoover's plans failed, and his popularity sagged. In 1930, the gross domestic product (GDP) shrank by 8.6 percent, and the Republicans lost their majorities in both houses of Congress.[44] At the end of that year, a series of bank runs and failures began in Kentucky, and they quickly spread across the Midwest. Customers demanded the return of their deposits, and banks sought to stay afloat by calling in moneys owed them by other financial institutions. The cascade of bank failures exposed the weakness of the nation's financial system, and soon, the crisis had spread to well-known institutions. The failure of New York City's Bank of the United States, which had held $286 million in deposits, was the largest in history.[45]

"From the spring of 1931 onward," wrote Kennedy, "it began to be clear that this depression was not just another cyclic valley, but a historic watershed, something vastly greater in scale and more portentous in its implications than anything that had gone before."[46] With Adolf Hitler on the rise in Germany, tensions in Europe exacerbated the economic problems of the United States. In the fall of 1931, the British government defaulted on its gold payments to foreigners. The world's economies were tied together by the gold standard, and foreign investors in need of precious metals began withdrawing their assets from the United States. Production continued to decline, and unemployment climbed to 15.7 percent. By the end of 1931, nearly 3,000 banks had failed.[47]

The crisis, by now truly a great depression, worsened, and Hoover responded as best he could. Believing that the problem was primarily a liquidity crisis that could be addressed by greater access to credit, the president started the Reconstruction Finance Corporation (RFC), an organization that would make federal loans available to financial institutions. He supported legislation to loosen the restrictions on the generally unresponsive Federal Reserve and began programs to provide credit for construction firms and mortgages for new home buyers. But he contradicted the expansionary effects of these policies by cutting government spending and raising taxes, out of concern for the growing federal deficit.

Succeeding generations have widely derided Hoover as a man whose ideological intransigence blinded him to human suffering. Nearly a century later, the historical verdict is less damning, if still somewhat mixed. Today, his policies appear generally well intentioned and occasionally prescient, if also somewhat unimaginative. At the same time, President Hoover was limited by his personal style, which was neither sufficiently flexible to embrace new approaches nor warm enough to calm an anxious nation in need of leadership. "No [p]resident ever worked harder in the White House than Herbert Hoover," wrote historian William E. Leuchtenberg, "but he was never able to convince the nation that he cared deeply how people were suffering."[48] Whatever the merits of his overall strategy, his actions failed to mitigate the crisis or endear him to the public. "By early 1932," assessed historian Martin L. Fausold, "the president seemed to have lost all but his most devoted followers."[49] In July of that year, thousands of impoverished World War I veterans marched on Washington to demand payment of bonuses that were not due to be paid to them until 1945. The president's order to have them dispersed resulted in soldiers mounting a military-style attack on the unarmed protesters, to the great dismay of the voting public. Hoover campaigned for the presidency in the 1932 election as a deeply unpopular incumbent.

His defeat was a foregone conclusion. The Democrat who reaped the political benefit of the president's unpopularity was Franklin Delano Roosevelt, a fifth cousin of President Theodore Roosevelt. A former assistant secretary of the navy and the 1920 Democratic candidate for vice president, he had contracted polio as a young man and lost the use of his legs. Despite this setback, Roosevelt resumed his political career and was elected governor of New York. Like his famous cousin, FDR was descended from a Dutchman who emigrated in 1664 to what is now New York. "Insofar as there is an American aristocracy," noted biographer Roy Jenkins, "both Roosevelts clearly belonged to it."[50] Despite this privileged background, Franklin had a gift for connecting with the everyday citizen. Significantly, the language he employed in doing so was that of the new liberalism.

His campaign against Hoover was generally a cautious one, described by the *New Republic* as being "without much flavor," in the service of a "program" the magazine labeled as "vague."[51] But when Roosevelt did give voice to political principles, they were recognizably Progressive ones. The clearest example of this tendency was a speech delivered at the Commonwealth Club in San Francisco, which the *New Republic* labeled as "the high point . . . of his campaign."[52] It stands as one of the most important philosophical expressions of a president who generally disdained theorizing. Roosevelt began this address by reviewing American history. Like Croly, he positioned Hamilton and Jefferson as the key figures at the nation's founding. The election of the latter to the presidency in 1800, Roosevelt continued, inaugurated the period in which "individualism was made the great watchword in American life." The abundance of land and economic opportunity made this era a "long and splendid" one, and the United States was seen as a vehicle of advancement, even for those who had been born in other lands. The middle part of the nineteenth century, however, brought the new technologies associated with the Industrial Revolution. Roosevelt noted that the generation of businesspeople usually associated with the Gilded Age could be "ruthless," "wasteful," and "corrupt," but he believed that the "advantages of the machine age" were so great that the country was wise when it "accepted the bitter with the sweet." Under conditions of rapid economic growth, in which "our industrial plants were insufficient to supply our own needs," the nation, Roosevelt said, "chose to give the ambitious man free play and unlimited reward" in exchange for producing the goods that the growing country needed.[53]

Times changed with the advent of the new century. With the closing of the frontier came the end of free land, and large corporations "had become great uncontrolled and irresponsible units of power." Teddy Roosevelt fought to limit the size of trusts, and Woodrow Wilson opposed the "centralized economic system" that he saw as "the despot of the twentieth century . . . whose irresponsibility and greed" could impose "starvation and penury" on "great masses of individuals." World War I limited Wilson's ability to combat this emerging power; as a result, by Roosevelt's time, "equality of opportunity as we have known it no longer exists."[54]

"Clearly," Roosevelt concluded, "all of this calls for a re-appraisal of values." Like the Progressives before him, he urged new ways of thinking rather than a radical redesign of society. By way of analogy, he noted that when many in the nineteenth century believed that government threatened their liberties, they did not seek to abolish it in favor of anarchy. Instead, monarchies were "modif[ied] gradually into a constitutional democratic government." Similarly, Roosevelt's new values did not underwrite the abolition of the corporation or, by extension, the end of capitalism. What they did require, he argued, was a new understanding of the relationship between the state and private enterprise: "As I see it, the task of government in its relation to business is to assist the development of an economic declaration of rights" that would constitute a "minimum requirement of a more permanently safe order of things." Listed among these would be "the right to make a comfortable living." This formulation reflected both the necessity of gainful employment in a modern society and the realization, imposed by the Depression, that the private economy could not always provide for the needs of the American citizenry.[55]

Not quite six months later, as he addressed the nation for the first time as its president, Roosevelt sounded many of the same themes. In his 1933 inaugural address, the new chief executive set the task for the country: to "restore . . . the ancient truths" to the "temple" from which "the money changers have fled." He argued that success in this endeavor would be judged by the extent to which "we apply social values more noble than mere monetary profit." But he also claimed that shifts in thinking and attitudes were not going to be enough. "Our greatest primary task," he proclaimed, "is to put people to work."[56] This statement charged the government with the responsibility for finding or creating jobs for millions of unemployed Americans.

He did not make this commitment idly. In the speech he gave to the Democratic faithful in 1932 when accepting that party's presidential nomination for the first time, candidate Roosevelt had "pledged [him]self to a new deal for the American people."[57] The phrase soon came to describe his campaign and presidential administration. Roosevelt himself was elected to the presidency four times, and he led the nation through the Depression and, later, World War II. He became the dominant political figure of the United States in the twentieth century. As a result of his tremendous influence, the period covering the Depression and war years is known today as the New Deal era.

The New Deal encompassed so much that it came to refer to a variety of loosely related concepts: a massive expansion of government; an explosion of previously unimagined federal responsibility; the new liberal philosophy; and a Democratic political strategy that united African Americans, southern segregationists, the labor movement, and urban political machines. But it also put into place a significant new understanding of the role of government in the economy. Beginning as a response to a specific economic crisis, the New Deal grew to the point that it defined a new set of baseline assumptions regarding government economic intervention in the United States.

The Philosophies of New Deal Liberalism

Upon taking office in 1933, Roosevelt immediately began putting into place a series of policies and projects that were unprecedented in their scope and volume. His first priority was to work with Congress to reform the financial industry, and he began by declaring a "bank holiday." This was a polite name for an order, almost certainly unconstitutional, for banks to close while the government frantically revamped the financial system. The resulting legislation was the Emergency Banking Act, a law that, in addition to many other provisions, subjected banks to government scrutiny before allowing them to reopen. The measure was so desperately needed that the House approved it even before copies were available to read; without such an action, the crisis might have continued indefinitely. In the words of Roosevelt adviser Raymond Moley, "Capitalism was saved in eight days."[58] Later that year, the Glass-Steagall Act required the separation of commercial banks, which take deposits from customers who generally do not anticipate the possibility of their money being lost, from investment banks, institutions that specifically put individuals' money into stocks and other risky assets. The law also established the Federal Deposit Insurance Corporation to safeguard the accounts of the nation's savers. The Securities Exchange Act of 1934 required publicly traded corporations to make public certain financial information, and it set up the Securities Exchange Commission to police Wall Street. Roosevelt also continued and greatly expanded Hoover's RFC. The reforms of the banking and financial industries are among the great successes of the New Deal.

Americans who lived in rural areas had been hit especially hard by the Depression, and they were a particular focus of the New Deal. The Agricultural Adjustment Administration (AAA) sought to boost the prices of agricultural products by paying farmers not to grow crops and raise livestock. Electricity, which by the 1930s had been firmly established in urban centers, lagged behind in rural areas. Private utilities had not found it profitable to extend power to such places, and their unwillingness to serve those who lived on farms and in small towns effectively condemned such people to living in the nineteenth century. In 1935, Congress passed the Rural Electrification Act, which allotted federal money to provide electric power to farms and small towns. One of the New Deal's most ambitious programs, the Tennessee Valley Authority (TVA), put the government directly into the business of providing electricity. The area around Muscle Shoals, Alabama, was among the poorest in the nation and subject to constant flooding.

Instrumental to Franklin Roosevelt's ability to fashion a rapport with the American people were his "fireside chats." In the very first of these casual presentations, pictured here, the president explained the causes of the banking crisis and outlined the actions that his new administration had taken to address it. (Courtesy Franklin D. Roosevelt Library, Hyde Park, NY)

The TVA addressed several problems at once with what the president called "one great, comprehensive plan."[59] It built a network of hydroelectric dams along the Tennessee River, which not only helped the flooding problem but also generated electric power that the government sold inexpensively to the area's residents. Additionally, the construction itself provided a good number of much-needed jobs. The TVA, along with the other programs aimed at helping rural citizens, showcased the direct government intervention into the market that often characterized the New Deal.

The New Deal also mitigated the unemployment crisis by providing jobs directly. Among the most popular of Roosevelt's programs, the Civilian

Conservation Corps (CCC) took young men from the cities and boarded them in camps in the countryside. The employees worked outside in forests and national parks, building such things as campgrounds, bridges, and museums. In just under a decade of its existence, the CCC employed 3 million people who built 125,000 miles of road, constructed 300,000 dams, and planted 3 billion trees.[60] Public works constituted what historian Jason Scott Smith called "the central enterprise of the New Deal," representing not only a strategy for providing employment but also "a strikingly effective method of state-sponsored economic development." The central agencies in this agenda were the Public Works Administration (PWA) and its successor organization, the Works Progress Administration (WPA). The amount of the initial appropriation for the first (in 1933) equaled 5.9 percent of the gross domestic product that year; the second (in 1935), 6.7 percent. Their payrolls in those years, wrote Smith, "easily dwarf[ed]" those of the largest private employers.[61] The PWA built, among many other installations, the Lincoln Tunnel, La Guardia Airport, and the San Francisco–Oakland Bay Bridge. The WPA, which took on smaller-scale projects, employed 8.5 million people in its lifetime, building, among other projects, 500,000 miles of highways, 100,000 public buildings, and 8,000 parks.[62]

Finally, the New Deal was instrumental in giving labor a legal standing and in creating an American social safety net. The Wagner Act (1935) established union recognition as a right, banned employer interference in union organizing, and required firms to bargain collectively with the workers' chosen representatives. In 1938, Congress passed the first federal minimum-wage law. Perhaps the most far-reaching program of the New Deal, however, was introduced via the Social Security Act of 1935. This law put in place a series of programs designed to mitigate the loss of wages that might come from unemployment, disability, old age, or (in the case of children and, given gender norms in 1935, widows) death. Most of its programs were based on the ideal of "social insurance." Insurance of all types is essentially a perverse sort of lottery: everyone buys a ticket by paying a premium to the insurance company, but only those who "win"—by getting in a car accident, suffering an injury, losing their house to a fire, and so on—receive payment. Everyone else loses the money they spent on the premium, just like someone who bought a losing lottery ticket. Social Security was set up on the same principle: all workers (and employers) were required to pay a tax on their earnings, but only those who became unable to work would be paid through the program. (Of course, in the case of old age, that included everyone who lived long enough.) On signing the bill, Roosevelt echoed the Progressive theme that liberty in the modern era required government economic intervention: the act would provide "at least some protection," he asserted, against the "startling industrial changes" that had taken place in the "last hundred years."[63] Far too many of life's necessities were now tied to employment, and the Depression had proven that the ability to find gainful employment was not correlated with a person's level of industry or talent. In such an environment, the Social Security Act served as a statement that the federal government, which had only recently taken on the responsibility of helping people work, also owed something to those who were unable to do so.

The first few years of the New Deal were characterized by a barrage of disjointed impulses moving in many directions at once, searching in vain for a broad, coherent program, to say nothing of a new articulation of the proper role of government in the economy. Indeed, many have found that no such principles existed. Richard Hofstadter wrote in 1955 that "nothing revolutionary was intended" in the New Deal, as it was "simply a matter of politics" for "the federal government to assume primary responsibility for the relief of the unemployed."[64] On this interpretation, the New Dealers were simply overtaken by events. The programs and policies instituted by Roosevelt and his administration had such an incredible impact on the economy that the broader ideas and expectations regarding government intervention could not help but have changed; those changes, however, were not intended and perhaps were not even welcome. More recently, historian Alan Brinkley tempered this analysis somewhat. Though not going so far as to say that the New Deal represented no principles at all, Brinkley did point out that the ideas that are today associated with "New Deal liberalism" are "related to, yet substantially different from, the cluster of ideas that had shaped the earlier stages of the Roosevelt administration."[65] The contemporary meaning and significance of the New Deal, for both its liberal supporters and its conservative detractors, should not be confused with the intentions of the men and women who put Roosevelt's programs into place. The Roosevelt administration, Brinkley argued, served as a contested battleground for several different philosophies. Each of these had its moment in the sun, and so the historical New Deal, as opposed to the one of popular political memory, stood for different approaches at different times.

In characterizing the New Deal this way, Brinkley followed the earlier insights of economic historian Ellis Hawley, whose 1966 book, *The New Deal and the Problem of Monopoly*, detailed the complex history of the conflicting economic attitudes that characterized the Roosevelt administration. For Hawley (and, later, Brinkley), three major schools of thought were contained within the New Deal. Two of them competed for primacy during the period until approximately 1937, and then the third effectively took over. The first of these was historically rooted in Progressive antitrust thinking. Hawley described "antitrusters" as those who believed that the Depression had been caused by the "market power" of monopolistic firms, which allowed large corporations "to maintain prices even though their costs of production were falling." Their solution was to restore economic competition through "rigorous antitrust prosecution, . . . limits on size, . . . a tax on bigness," and "controls over business financing and competitive practices." Characterizing the people in the other camp, Hawley said they began from the opposite premise: they believed that competition was the problem. In an age of large-scale efficiency, companies that cut costs by lowering wages and undercut their competitors by dropping prices were "chiselers" who were doing long-term damage to the economy. Since "concentrations of economic power were inevitable," the problem could only be addressed through "systematic organization and planning, in conscious and rational administrative control of economic processes."[66] Rather than position the federal government adversarially against large companies, these "planners" believed that the government and the economy should work together to keep wages high, profits sustainable, and resources and goods efficiently distributed.

The latter approach enjoyed an early peak in influence and was embodied most conspicuously in the National Recovery Administration (NRA). Established in 1933 by one part of the National Industrial Recovery Act, the NRA developed "codes" that would apply to all firms working in a specific industry. Government and industry wrote these codes together, reaching agreements that would determine wages, resource allocation, production levels, and sale prices. Those firms that declined to participate not only faced public disapprobation but also the possibility that the government would write their industry's codes with their competitors or without any business input at all. Crucially, the antitrust laws were for the most part suspended in industries that worked with the NRA. Participating firms were allowed to post the NRA logo, the "Blue Eagle," on their premises and products. This display would symbolize to customers that these businesses were doing their part to bring about economic recovery.

From the modern vantage point, the NRA's emphasis on reducing competition and partnering business with government in the establishment of cartels looks less like saving capitalism than abandoning it. But such a perspective, as political scientist Ira Katznelson has pointed out, fails to capture the options as they appeared in the early 1930s. The Great Depression had cast serious doubt on the viability of capitalism, and the rise of communism in the Soviet Union and fascism in Germany suggested that Liberal democracy was not the only available path. Sincerely believing that their choices could determine whether the American form of democratic capitalism would survive, the New Dealers were willing to consider alternatives that might today seem unimaginable. In this environment, Katznelson wrote, they "never thought the USSR or Nazi Germany could provide workable models. But they were drawn to Mussolini's Italy, which self-identified as a country that had saved capitalism." In the years before World War II, Americans did not automatically associate fascism with the racist elements and territorial ambitions that characterized Nazism, and many viewed it with curiosity and even approval. In this context, the NRA exemplified the alliance between government and private firms that the Italians called "corporatism." The New Dealers hoped to institute a domestic version of this approach but, as Katznelson pointed out, "on American terms for American purposes." [67]

Yet the New Deal did not come to stand for the imposition of corporatism on the American economy, and it is today remembered as a liberal movement rather than a fascist one. The corporatist approach did not carry the day because the NRA was a colossal failure from almost the very moment of its inception. Its director, Hugh Johnson, was a bombastic hothead with a serious drinking problem and a tremendous hostility toward organized labor. Critics charged that the codes that emerged from the negotiations between the NRA and the various industries consistently favored larger firms over their smaller competitors and labor unions. In response to these charges, Roosevelt appointed an investigative commission chaired by aging attorney Clarence Darrow, of the Scopes "monkey trial" fame. Though the final report of Darrow's committee was, in David Kennedy's opinion, "slapdash" and inconsistent, it concluded that there could be "no hope for the small business man [sic] or for complete recovery in America in enforced restriction upon production for the purpose of maintaining higher prices"—and that hurt the NRA. Amid the widespread perception that the agency was merely a tool of management, Johnson's increasingly erratic personal behavior led to his forced resignation fifteen months after assuming office. A new director could not, however, erase the stigma that had attached to the NRA. The agency tottered along for nine more months until the Supreme Court unanimously declared, in the case of *Schecter Poultry Corporation v. United States*, the entire National Industrial Recovery Act was in violation of the Constitution. In the time it took Chief Justice Charles

Evans Hughes to read the decision, which he did "vehemently" according to Arthur Krock of the *New York Times,* the 750 codes that characterized the NRA were invalidated.[68] Roosevelt had no choice but to comply with the decision. Over the coming weeks, he had some parts of the law redesigned to meet the objections of the court. But the beleaguered and unpopular NRA enjoyed no such fate.[69]

The Supreme Court had previously struck down smaller parts of New Deal legislation, but *Schecter* was significant for what journalist Michael Hiltzik described as its "complete and uncompromising" destruction of an agency that was central to the president's agenda.[70] Moreover, *Schecter* marked the beginning of a trend. In the next two years, the Supreme Court would declare unconstitutional the Agricultural Adjustment Act (which was later recast in a form more acceptable to the court) and issue a large number of less momentous yet equally decisive rulings against the president's programs. New Dealers feared that all their achievements were in danger.[71] More and more frustrated, Roosevelt proposed a new law that would increase the total number of Supreme Court justices. Of course, the president would be appointing the new members, so the plan was a transparent effort to tilt the court in a direction more friendly to the New Deal. Many Americans viewed this proposal as a violation of the principle of separation of powers: the plan went nowhere in Congress, and the president's personal popularity suffered. Other events also threatened the long-term viability of the New Deal. As the economy had recently picked up a bit, Roosevelt had raised taxes and cut spending in an attempt to balance the budget. The stock market crashed soon thereafter, the fragile economic recovery stalled, and the country entered what became known as the Roosevelt recession. Finally, the events in Europe and Asia that would lead to World War II increasingly turned the attention of the nation's political and economic decision makers away from issues regarding the domestic economy.

Thus, the year 1937 was a true turning point for the economic philosophy of the New Deal. Roosevelt's personal popularity was at a low ebb, and the country's attention was shifting from economic matters toward military ones. For this reason, many historians agree with David Kennedy's observation that "the New Deal petered out in 1938," when defense-oriented "preparedness" production began to put people back to work.[72] But the New Deal's lasting influence did not turn on the achievements of the programs, important as they were, that passed when the economy was in its worst shape in history and Roosevelt was incredibly popular. Its long-term influence on the expectations of government economic intervention in the United States would not have been possible had its policies and principles not endured until later times. "If the New Deal developed only modestly as a program after 1937," argued Brinkley, "it continued to develop as an idea."[73]

This shift in the political fortunes of the Roosevelt administration inevitably affected the economic philosophy that animated the New Deal. "As a matter of practical politics," wrote Hawley, "the death of the NRA marked the end of serious attempts to repeal the antitrust laws and establish a general program of publicly supported cartelization."[74] From that point forward, the power of the planners waned, and the antitrust approach enjoyed greater influence within the administration.

The peak of the antitrust influence was marked by the appointment of Thurman Arnold as the assistant attorney general in charge of the Department of Justice's Antitrust Division. Arnold had once been the mayor of Laramie, Wyoming, and was, at the time of his appointment, a Yale Law School professor. He had captured the attention of liberals with the publication of two important books, *Symbols of Government* (1935) and *The Folklore of Capitalism* (1937), and many administration liberals were eager to find a place for him. From 1938 until 1943, Arnold brought a vigor to the Antitrust Division that had not been present since the days of the Progressive presidents. With an eye toward using antitrust as a statement and application of policy, Arnold aimed to change, rather than punish, corporate behavior. He employed innovative methods to reach that end. Believing that the goal of creating a stable and predictable body of antitrust law through litigation was best served by investigating and bringing suit against all the major players in a business sector at once, he frequently targeted entire industries for prosecution, rather than aiming at the specific anticompetitive practices of a particular firm. Another important tool that Arnold used was the consent decree. After bringing a case, he would present the firm being targeted with an offer to drop the litigation in exchange for the company agreeing to cease its monopolistic practices, generally on terms that were very favorable to the public.[75] These tactics, among others, helped Arnold raise the profile of antitrust, making it a central part of the New Deal approach. At the end of his five-year tenure, the Sherman Act was fifty-three years old. Of the total number of prosecutions under that law, 44 percent had been brought during Arnold's time as director.[76] He achieved high-profile victories over the automobile, medical, and motion-picture industries. During his tenure, the budget of the antitrust division increased by a factor of five, and it came to employ 300 attorneys, up from the original 58. This bureaucratic success no doubt owed something to the fact that the division generated in settlements three times as much money as it spent.[77] Arnold's record was, in short, spectacularly impressive.

As a philosophy of government economic intervention, however, the antitrust approach suffered the same fate as had planning before it. The president had always been ambivalent about antitrust and, more broadly, about the relationship between his administration and the business community. In the late 1930s, however, Roosevelt increasingly needed to cultivate his ties with industry in order to boost the nation's level of military preparedness in anticipation of possible hostilities in Europe and Asia. After the Japanese attack on Pearl Harbor and the US entry into World War II in 1941, any ambivalence was gone. Arnold faced pressure to go easy on those firms that were doing business with the United States. The centers of power in Washington were moving from the New Deal agencies to those dealing with preparedness, many of which were headed by corporate executives. As a result, wrote Brinkley, Arnold was "forced to give the military and the war agencies the right to veto antitrust initiatives that they believed would interfere with the war effort."[78] He was ordered to give up several high-profile prosecutions, some of which he had been developing for years. In 1943, the president kicked Arnold upstairs by appointing him to the First Circuit Court of Appeals. Arnold saw the writing on the wall and resigned from the Justice Department.

The unarguable failure of the NRA completely discredited the planning approach. Arnold's tenure with the Antitrust Division, however, was just as clearly a success. Thus, Arnold's leadership was not the cause of antitrust's decline in influence, but it marked the end of its major impact just the same. The fact that antitrust did not return after the war ended suggested a larger problem for its advocates. As Brinkley has pointed out, liberals simply could not construct a compelling narrative of political economy out of the raw materials that antitrust had to offer: a regime of lawsuits against specific companies for particular actions.[79] In essence, the antitrusters got everything that they could have asked for, but an aggressive, well-funded, politically supported antitrust program was not able to get along with the business community or to sufficiently captivate the public. Antitrust had to make way for the third approach, the one that ultimately become synonymous with New Deal liberalism.

Keynes and Keynesianism

The philosophy that came to define the term *New Deal liberalism* is associated with the British economist John Maynard Keynes. The Englishman had visited the White House once in 1934, a meeting that left both Keynes and Roosevelt unimpressed.[80] Nonetheless, many New Deal policies had been moving in directions similar to those Keynes had recommended, even if he was not their architect. The widespread understanding of the New Deal as a fundamentally Keynesian enterprise does not quite capture the more nuanced relationship between economic theory and government policy that characterized the period. It is certainly true, however, that many of Roosevelt's younger staffers were quite impressed with what they knew of Keynes and that, as time went by, his approach steadily gained influence.[81]

Keynes had first made a name for himself as a member of the British delegation to the peace negotiations that concluded World War I. Disgusted with the vindictive attitudes that the Allies took toward the defeated Central powers, he resigned and published a book criticizing the negotiations. *The Economic Consequences of the Peace* (1919) proved to be prescient in its claim that reparations would only serve to destroy the German economy. Several books followed on other subjects, earning Keynes a reputation, particularly among liberals, as an important and insightful thinker. His influence began to grow significantly with the 1936 publication of his *General Theory of Employment, Interest, and Money*. In contrast to Keynes's earlier works on specific topics, *The General Theory* aimed to "contrast" its writer's views "with those of the classical theory . . . which dominates the economic thought . . . of this generation."[82] Here, Keynes referred to the body of thought dating back to Adam Smith (1723–1790), whose proponents included David Ricardo (1772–1823), James Mill (1773–1836), and his son John Stuart Mill (1806–1873), as well as Keynes's more immediate predecessor Alfred Marshall (1842–1924) and contemporary Arthur Cecil Pigou (1877–1959). Though the lives of these thinkers span two centuries and their political commitments and policy prescriptions varied markedly, what they held in common was the belief that the market mechanism of supply and demand would eventually return all markets, including the market for labor, to an equilibrium state in which everyone who wanted to work could do so. Keynes, whose "ultimate object" was "to discover what determines the volume of employment," found such an assumption unsatisfactory and, indeed, incorrect.[83]

Keynes's analysis differed with classical economics at so many points that he felt the need to initiate an entirely new school of thought. Characterizing the classical school as a self-referential system of great intellectual elegance, he nonetheless argued that it failed to correspond to experience. Keynes likened its advocates to "Euclidean geometers in a non-Euclidean world."[84] Though he agreed that the pricing mechanism would allow the forces of supply and demand to reach equilibrium, he did not think that such a state would necessarily be one in which everyone was working. Thus, the economy could remain in a depressed condition for an unacceptably long time, and the only way to remedy this situation would be for the government to insert itself prominently into the economy.

Keynes's objections to classical economics centered on three of its tenets, each of which reinforced the others. Historian Robert Collins described the first as the "conventional belief that unemployment resulted primarily from . . . the unwillingness of workers to accept lower wages[,] and the concomitant suggestion that depression be combated by means of a general wage reduction."[85] According to this theory, the market responded to the surplus of workers by lowering wages, and those workers who adjusted their expectations to accept less pay would find no shortage of available jobs. "A classical economist," wrote Keynes, "may sympathise [*sic*] with labour [*sic*] in refusing to accept a cut in its money-wage . . . but scientific integrity forces him to declare that this refusal is, nevertheless, at the bottom of the trouble."[86]

This classical interpretation of unemployment turned on the premise that the number of workers would always equal the number of jobs. This belief was founded on a second tenet of classical economics, to which Keynes also objected. Attributed to French economist Jean-Baptiste Say (1767–1832), this maxim held that money was merely a stand-in for economic products, and therefore goods were effectively paid for with other goods. In manufacturing a product, an entrepreneur was effectively declaring a desire to sell it. Since goods were (effectively) exchanged only for other goods, then that producer could only sell his or her wares to others who had also manufactured goods of their own. Thus, Say's Law held that over- or underproduction could not continue for any significant length of time. It was certainly possible for a manufacturer to produce more of a particular good than people were willing or able to purchase. But if this were the case, then the price of that good, relative to other products, would fall until all economic output had found an appropriate home. As a result, the various markets would reach equilibrium only at the point at which all available labor and raw materials were being put to use. Nothing of economic value would go unused.

The third tenet of classical economics with which Keynes took issue involved savings and investment. When considering all the income in an economy, only that portion that was not used to purchase goods—that is, the money that individuals and firms saved—could be used to invest in a new or growing business. Moreover, *all* the money that was saved would ultimately be invested. Once those who possessed money decided not to spend it, some would invest it directly, by starting a business or loaning money to someone else who was doing so. But even the money that was saved in a financial institution would still be invested because banks would pool their customers' assets and use them to make loans or purchase other assets.[87] Thus, across the economy as a whole, market forces would constantly push and pull the levels of investment and savings toward one another. If the amount of savings available for investment was smaller than that required by entrepreneurs to start or grow their businesses, then banks would pay higher interest rates in order to attract savings. This increase would encourage people to save their money rather than spend it, which in turn would provide more capital to businesspeople who would use that money to increase production. In the opposite case—if people had more money than entrepreneurs needed—the interest rate would fall, removing the incentive to save. The interest rate would continually seesaw up and down, always gravitating toward the rate that would generate the amount of money needed by the economy overall for investment.

Thus, the third major point with which Keynes took issue was the prescription that resulted from this analysis. Since economic forces would ensure that savings would always equal investment, then the solution to low investment (such as that seen in the Great Depression) would be to encourage consumers to save. More of their money would wind up in the hands of entrepreneurs, who would then use that money to put people back to work. Keynes disagreed with each of these points. To begin with perhaps the simplest of them, he did not believe that the fundamental cause of unemployment was the unwillingness of workers to accept less pay. The idea that unemployed workers could find work if they were willing to accept lower wages, he argued, was based on the assumption that potential employers needed workers but had a limited ability to pay them. According to that interpretation, such employers were offering jobs, albeit at lower wages. This scenario turned on a model of employment, perfectly reasonable under the classical paradigm, in which workers who were contemplating new employment would simply choose between their desire for, say, an hour of leisure and the enjoyment they would expect to receive from the amount of money they could earn in sixty minutes. Keynes argued that this understanding did not accurately predict a worker's behavior. If it did, then workers would quit their jobs en masse when the cost of living rose but wages did not.[88] Such a scenario represented a decline in real purchasing power identical to a cut in wages, but workers in those situations appeared to value their jobs just as much as they did before, if not more so. The only situation, Keynes argued, in which a worker could actually balance the desire to earn an hour's wages against the utility of sleeping an extra hour in the morning would be one in which the latter choice did not lead to the permanent loss of a job. This condition would be met only if the firm was unable to replace that worker by hiring someone else. If there were no surplus workers available, then even if the firm did terminate the employee, he or she would have little trouble finding a new position somewhere else. Consequently, the only time in which workers actually behaved in the fashion predicted by classical economics was under conditions of full employment. Classical economists, in Keynes's view, incorrectly and unwittingly presupposed this state of affairs in positing that "labour [sic] is always in a position to determine its own real wage."[89] Keynes concluded, therefore, that periods of unemployment were created not by workers unwilling to accept low-wage jobs but by firms unable to offer employment at any wage at all. Thus, the solution to high unemployment seen in the Great Depression was not to lower workers' wages but to address whatever issue was keeping firms from hiring.

Keynes believed that demand played a significant role in hiring decisions. This position also violated the tenets of classical economics. Say's Law, for example, held that all available work hours would always be used, which suggested that the amount of demand in the economy was irrelevant to the level of employment. Indeed, Keynes summarized this postulate (unfairly, some say) as the position that "supply creates its own demand."[90] According to the classical understanding, if employers cut wages in the face of low demand, consumers would increase their purchases as products got less expensive. Firms would ramp up production to meet the higher demand and bring people back to work. Keynes did not find this position compelling, arguing that the classical account presupposed the answer to "the precise question at issue," which was "whether the reduction in money-wages will or will not be accompanied by the same aggregate effective demand as before."[91] It seemed implausible to him that a decline in wages or employment would lead to an increase in demand. If wages were to be cut, then workers would have less money to spend. They would be able to purchase fewer goods, which was a different way of saying that aggregate effective demand would *decrease*. Facing an inability to sell their products, employers would not hire new workers. Indeed, they would be more likely to begin letting go of the ones they had.

As a consequence, Keynes argued, "when effective demand is deficient, there is under-employment of labour [*sic*] in the sense that there are men unemployed who would be willing to work at less than the existing real wage."[92] Contrary to the dictates of Say's Law, unemployment could lead to a decline in demand, which itself could cause further unemployment. This phenomenon might then create a spiral of joblessness, leading to a long period of economic misery. When demand was inadequate to keep the population employed, wrote Keynes, "not only is the public scandal of wasted resources intolerable, but the individual enterpriser who seeks to bring these resources into action is operating with the odds loaded against him."[93] Facing a collapse in demand, something had to be done to revive it; otherwise, employment would be unlikely to recover.

Keynes's analysis of investment led him to similar conclusions. Since the rise and fall of the interest rate would tend to bring the level of total investment in the economy into balance with the aggregate level of savings, classical economists urged that the key to increasing investment was to encourage saving. But investment capital requires something in which to invest, and if demand was inadequate, there would be few attractive investment opportunities. "Capital is brought into existence," Keynes wrote, "not by the propensity to save but in response to the demand resulting from actual and prospective consumption." If the entire nation's savings rate went up and income did not change, the rate of consumption would necessarily go down. Those who saved their money rather than spending it were not helping the economy by providing investment capital; they were hurting it by creating a "net diminution" of "present consumption-demand."[94] The classical prescription to save money in order to increase employment, Keynes concluded, missed the point that the need for greater investment in a depressed economy resolved itself into the need for an increase in the effective demand.

Keynes therefore believed that without an expansion of demand, an economy characterized by high unemployment was likely to remain in that state for quite some time. But since unemployment itself was the primary cause of the low demand, patiently waiting for the expected demand increase was an unwise course of action. Instead, he concluded that the "state will have to exercise a guiding influence on the propensity to consume partly through its scheme of taxation, partly by fixing the rate of interest, and partly, perhaps, in other ways." Lowering taxes and interest rates during economic downturns would free up income that could be used for consumption. The "other ways" to which Keynes referred invoked the specter of government spending, social welfare programs, public works, and budget deficits. The purpose of government spending was to put people to work in order to increase demand, so that the economy could become self-sustaining.[95]

Keynes recognized that his program would entail a massive expansion of government's role in the economy: "The central controls necessary to ensure full employment will, of course, involve a large extension of the traditional functions of government." Yet he believed that his recommendations were necessary to save capitalism itself. Immiserated by the business cycle, Americans of the 1930s were inclined to see virtue in both the command economies of socialism and the corporatist approach of fascism. Keynes was aware that his system might be attacked on the grounds that it encroached too far into the zone of individual liberty. Nonetheless, he wrote, "I defend it . . . both as the only practicable means of avoiding the destruction of existing economic forms in their entirety and as the condition of the successful functioning of individual initiative."[96]

Today, the Keynesian approach is essentially synonymous with New Deal liberalism. Such ideas were not the only ones that characterized the New Deal approach to government economic intervention, but they gradually became dominant among New Dealers, liberals, and eventually the political and intellectual class of the United States more broadly. Having government "stimulate" the economy through the tax code and targeted federal spending was far less intrusive than the corporatist and antitrust approaches. Despite having earned the enmity of conservatives in the United States almost immediately, this philosophy was actually the least invasive approach of the three that competed for primacy during the New Deal. Keynesianism offered to liberals the possibility that, in Brinkley's words, the "state could manage the economy without managing the institutions of the economy."[97] But even the broad management of the economy that would not require intrusive regulation or control over the behavior of specific firms could meet with political resistance. So, in planning for the postwar economy, liberals themselves often shied away from a commitment to the central goal of the Keynesian agenda: full employment.

Sixty Million Jobs

In the late 1930s and early 1940s, Roosevelt grew more and more concerned about the war in Europe and Asia. As much as possible, he sought to aid England as it tried to hold out against the German advance. If he had had his way, the United States would have already entered the war, but a powerful current of isolationism ran through the public at large, promoted by several prominent Republican senators. FDR's 1941 State of the Union message, delivered nearly one year before Pearl Harbor, focused on impressing upon his countrymen and -women (and their elected representatives) his concern that "at no previous time has American security been as seriously threatened as it is today." Given this state of affairs, the president said, "the immediate need is a swift and driving increase in our armament production" in order to help America's warring allies. Still, Roosevelt did not abandon New Deal themes. "Certainly," he continued, "this is no time for us to stop thinking about . . . social and economic problems," as these were the "root cause" of the "unrest" that had led to dictatorship and war. With that segue, he delivered the highlight of the speech, an articulation of the "four essential human freedoms" that should guide the world after it was made secure—freedom of speech, freedom of worship, freedom from want, and freedom from fear. The first two of these were already embodied in the Bill of Rights, and with the final freedom, Roosevelt referred to a "worldwide reduction in armaments" that would mitigate the possibility of war. His mention of freedom from want, however, seemed to suggest an entirely new set of rights. Though the New Deal was certainly aimed at minimizing want, it would be a stretch to say that the federal government was bringing its resources to bear on eliminating it entirely, much less that such a commitment was to form the basis of the nation's foreign policy. What was clear was that Roosevelt viewed poverty and unemployment as linked to the war against dictatorship and fascism and consequently as important components of democracy itself. What remained murky was the extent to which he would embody this rhetorical gesture in specific governmental commitments.[98]

Three years later, in his 1944 State of the Union address, Roosevelt returned to this theme. Now the president of a nation at war, he called on the American people to continue their great sacrifices in the name of "one supreme objective for the future." That goal, he stated, "can be summed up in one word: security." By this, he said, he meant not only "physical security" but also "economic security, social security, [and] moral security."[99]

Thus, the Allied nations recognized that they not only had to win the war but also had to create a "just and durable system of peace." Essential to that peace, he argued, would be a "decent standard of living for all individual men and women and children in all nations. Freedom from fear is eternally linked with freedom from want."[100] In his country's own case, he said, "we cannot be content . . . if some fraction of our people . . . is ill-fed, ill-clothed, ill-housed, and insecure." Roosevelt then echoed the familiar liberal theme that changes in technology and commerce had necessitated a new understanding of the political tradition. "As our industrial economy expanded," he said, the "political rights" that characterized the nation's founding "proved inadequate to assure us equality in the pursuit of happiness." That is why Americans had "accepted as self-evident" what Roosevelt called "the second Bill of Rights." These economic guarantees included the right to, among other things, a "useful and remunerative job," "adequate food and clothing and recreation," "a decent home," "adequate medical care," and "a good education."[101]

Roosevelt's assertion that many in the United States took for granted a state guarantee of a job was remarkable. The scourge of the Great Depression had largely been lifted by the economic growth generated by government spending on military preparedness and then war. With the end of World War II on the horizon, many Americans feared that once the conflict ended, production would decline and the nation would find itself right back in economic depression. Thus, in the 1945 State of the Union address, the last of Roosevelt's life, the president recommitted himself to the prospect of guaranteeing work for all Americans. The speech began with a lengthy and detailed summary of the progress in the war. Though Roosevelt emphasized that things were going well and that there was "no question of the ultimate victory," he impressed upon the people the importance of sustaining the war effort and, in particular, of continuing to work at defense industry jobs. Near the end of the speech, however, he reiterated his commitment to the economic bill of rights. "Of these rights," he added, "the most fundamental . . . is 'the right to a useful and remunerative job.'"

From there, he expressed a particularly Keynesian understanding of the economy, depicting it as being dependent on consumer demand to meet employment goals. Roosevelt noted that full employment had been attained during the war but only "because [g]overnment has been ready to buy all the materials of war which the country could produce." Stating that this amount represented approximately half of the nation's GDP, he declared that America's biggest postwar challenge would be "maintaining full employment with [g]overnment performing its peacetime functions." To meet this goal, he added, "we must achieve a level of demand and purchasing power by private consumers . . . which is sufficiently high to replace wartime [g]overnment demands." Though the administration's policy was "to rely as much as possible on private enterprise to provide jobs," he stressed that the task would not be easy. Echoing a campaign pledge that he had earlier made at Soldier Field in Chicago, Roosevelt said that meant "close to 60,000,000 jobs."[102]

The president offered no comprehensive plan in the 1945 State of the Union address that would generate the demand to support 60 million jobs. His proposals for what the government could do were scattered and varied: the guarantee of special risk to finance capital, the development of natural resources, the construction of airports and highways, the expansion of Social Security, the establishment of a federal health care system, and the revamping of federal taxes. Roosevelt did not mention what would or should happen if, despite these efforts, the unemployment rate remained stubbornly high. Some twelve weeks later, less than a month before the Allied victory in Europe and four months before the Japanese surrender, the president died of a cerebral hemorrhage caused by long-term heart disease.

Franklin Roosevelt, the most visible symbol of the New Deal, never explicitly stated what he believed the responsibility of the government toward the unemployed should be under normal conditions. That task fell to others, in particular Roosevelt's former secretary of agriculture, vice president, and secretary of commerce Henry Wallace. Called in 1955 "the most articulate and reflective of the New Dealers" by Louis Hartz and more recently described as "brilliant" by Sean Wilentz, Wallace was from the liberal wing of the Roosevelt administration.[103] He was born in 1888 into an Iowa family with interests in agriculture and politics. His father and grandfather had both edited *Wallaces' Farmer*, a newspaper that played a major role in the lives of American agriculturalists, and the former had served as secretary of agriculture in the Republican cabinets of Harding and Coolidge. Henry was a talented agriculturalist who had studied with family friend George Washington Carver as a boy; as an adult, he became wealthy selling hybrid corn that he had bred himself. Complementing his enthusiasm for farming was the interest he had inherited from his father in the economic and political implications of agricultural policy.

In 1920, Wallace published *Agricultural Prices*, the first of his many books. His biographers called it "a highly technical examination of farm commodity markets and pricing influences." The book criticized the mar-

The Works Progress Administration (WPA) employed not only construction workers but also writers, artists, and actors. The Federal Art Project, an arm of the WPA, commissioned many posters like the one here. (Courtesy Library of Congress)

ket system itself, arguing that it did not meet the needs of the nation's farmers. He asserted that since people tended to consistently want roughly the
same amount of food, agricultural prices would not be driven by changes in
demand. At the same time, however, individual farmers had little control
over the total supply of foodstuffs. As a group, then, cultivators were not
served well by traditional economic laws of supply and demand. From this
observation, Wallace began developing the attitude toward government economic intervention that he would continue to advocate for the rest of his life:
"The law of supply and demand has never been repealed and never will be
repealed. Instead of trying to repeal it, we should try to secure the best type
of price-fixing machinery thru [sic] which this law may work." Like the later
Keynesians, the Wallace of 1920 believed that government could set conditions within which markets could remain free but still also bring about
desired results. This theme would later become a common one among New
Dealers, who insisted adamantly, despite conservative contentions to the
contrary, that they were *fixing* the broken free market system rather than
trying to eliminate or replace it. Wallace made this point with an interesting
analogy. "Man has not repealed the laws of gravitation," he said, "but has
devised such machines as automobiles, airplanes, etc. thru [sic] which he
accomplishes his purposes notwithstanding."[104]

Henry took over the family newspaper when his father went to Washington, and after the older man died, he broke with his family's party by
casting his vote in the 1924 presidential election for Progressive third-party
insurgent Robert La Follette. Wallace completed his political migration in
1928 when *Wallaces' Farmer* reluctantly urged agriculturalists to vote for
Democrat Al Smith in the presidential election. In 1932, the campaigning
Roosevelt was cultivating farm support. He sent his adviser Henry Mor-
genthau to visit Wallace to request the editor's endorsement, which Wallace
gave. After winning the presidency, Roosevelt appointed Wallace to the
position his father had occupied, secretary of agriculture.

During his tenure in that post, Wallace nearly tripled the size of his
department and established its presence in every county in the nation. He
championed the interests not only of farmers but also of the rural poor and
migrant workers. Conservatives expressed concern about the new intrusion
of government into agriculture, but Wallace continued to sound the themes
that he had introduced in *Agricultural Prices*. In the words of his biographers,
he stood for the principle that "the country could no longer afford the luxury
of laissez-faire capitalism and an inactive government." In speech after
speech and in all of his many writings, he reiterated the point that the pur-

pose of the AAA was not to collectivize farming but to preserve constitutional democracy.[105]

Ever since the phenomenally popular George Washington refused to run for a third presidential term, American political tradition had frowned upon any president holding the office for more than eight years. Doing so did not violate the Constitution as it stood up to that time, and several presidents had unsuccessfully attempted to continue in the office after eight years.[106] In 1937, Vice President John Nance Garner, a conservative Texas Democrat, broke with the president over the court-packing plan and began plotting his own presidential run on the assumption that Roosevelt would not enter the race.[107] When FDR decided to run again, easily reclaiming his party's nomination on the first ballot, he preferred a new running mate. The president chose Wallace, whose name was greeted with a chorus of boos from the Democratic delegates who considered him far too liberal. A mutiny seemed likely, and Roosevelt had to threaten to drop out of the race in order to avert one.

As vice president, Wallace took on a major role within the administration. He was instrumental in mobilizing the country's economic resources for the war effort, and he even sat on the committee that advised the president on the Manhattan Project. Little by little, however, he found himself growing out of step with the administration and the president himself. His interest in liberal domestic policies did not square with a president who was ever more focused on international affairs. But even Wallace's positions on foreign policy were not in line with those of the administration.

Wallace was concerned about the shape of the postwar world and actively suggested a philosophy of peaceful collaboration with other nations, including the Soviet Union. The publisher Henry Luce had written an influential essay in 1941, titled "The American Century." He advocated the United States entering World War II by way of accepting a new international role, "to exert upon the world the full impact of our influence, for such purposes as we see fit and by such means as we see fit."[108] Wallace's response, delivered after the nation had entered the conflict, took the form of a speech (later published as a book) called "The Century of the Common Man." The main responsibility of the United States, he argued, would be to construct a new "economic peace" after the war, one that was "just, charitable, and enduring." In a world characterized by such a peace, "the citizen . . . will again have the supreme duty of sacrificing the lesser interest for . . . the general welfare." The "common man," Wallace believed, resided in every nation, not just the United States. Though both Luce and Wallace opposed isolationism, Luce's internationalism assumed that all nations would benefit from American hegemony, whereas Wallace's saw American leadership taking the form of making sacrifices for less-advantaged people around the world. "There can be no privileged peoples," he said. "We ourselves in the United States are no more a master race than the Nazis."[109]

In the end, it was Luce's view that won out among both the governing classes and the public at large. After Pearl Harbor, Wallace felt himself being slowly marginalized within the administration. By the 1944 election, the visibly ill Roosevelt replaced him on the ticket with Harry Truman, a largely undistinguished senator from Missouri. Having every reason to be bitter, Wallace nonetheless campaigned for Roosevelt and Truman, and he was rewarded after their victory with an appointment as secretary of commerce. While waiting for the Senate to convene in order to approve his renomination to the cabinet, Wallace wrote *Sixty Million Jobs*.

The book's title came from the campaign pledge that Roosevelt had delivered in Chicago's Soldier Field and then repeated in the 1945 State of the Union address. Given the population of the United States at the time, the title referenced the number of positions that would have to exist nationwide in order for everyone who wanted to work to be able to do so. Despite the ambitious nature of the goal, Wallace believed that it was "practical and attainable" and that reaching it would not require "a [p]lanned [e]conomy, ... disastrous inflation, ... [or] an unbalanced budget that will endanger our national credit."[110]

Though Wallace did not mention Keynes by name in *Sixty Million Jobs*, the program outlined in the book was obviously influenced by the economist. Wallace consistently highlighted the role of demand in fighting unemployment. "Only by thinking positively now about mass consumption instead of negatively fearing mass unemployment," he wrote, "can our free way of life survive." He presented a Keynesian conception of the interdependent nature of economic life: "To be good customers," the nation's families "must be steady customers—and to be steady customers they must have steady jobs. It is a seamless web of cause and effect—an economic one world." Additionally, Wallace argued that the government needed to have a prominent role in boosting demand when necessary. The "government domination of the economic structure" was required to win World War II, he observed, but the war was over and the United States had to eliminate such controls "as rapidly as possible." Just as important, however, was the need to "determine the areas of responsibility in providing for full employment in the transition from war to peace."[111]

Wallace usually referred to his ideas as "progressive capitalism," and he went to great pains to disavow advocacy of any form of socialism.[112] Yet in *Sixty Million Jobs*, he acknowledged that he was urging government to assume powers it had not traditionally wielded: "To put full employment on a continuing basis means that the people, through the Congress, must equip government with authority to act in immediate co-operation with private enterprise once incipient unemployment points to the danger of mass unemployment." But Wallace noted that "some people"—perhaps referencing Friedrich Hayek, whose *Road to Serfdom* had been a best seller the previous year—"tell us that we cannot have full employment without inviting or forcing government to . . . control our economy." They argued that any government intervention at all would violate the norms of capitalism, "bringing about an end to the free enterprise system." Wallace countered that argument by positing that the tradition of government economic intervention was not at all foreign to American political economy. At the very founding of the nation, this practice was represented by the influence of the ideas and policies of Alexander Hamilton. The first secretary of the Treasury believed, according to Wallace, that "our democratic government has the definite responsibility of stimulating our free-enterprise system, not just in behalf of the general welfare, but also to keep free enterprise continuously a going concern." Moreover, the Hamiltonian tradition continued to animate American political economy even after Hamilton himself had died. As evidence, Wallace pointed out that a look at American history revealed the "stimulating hand of government" in, among other actions, the Homestead Act, the "subsidizing of the railroads," the construction of roads to benefit the automobile industry, and other activities. Despite the constant presence of government economic intervention, he argued, the nation's economy had continually grown. Indeed, Wallace suggested that such growth was possible only *because* of the government economic intervention.[113]

A major point of his book was that greater government involvement in the economy would not spell the end of American capitalism. Giving the government responsibility for full employment, he argued, could take several forms. One would be a socialist solution, in which "the [f]ederal government would assign people to jobs, fix wages and prices, and control practically every other aspect of our national life." Wallace rejected that approach out of hand as not being "an American way." Also "not our way" would be a plan to issue a guaranteed income to all citizens. Wallace could not support a plan in which the government would provide a job to every person who needed one. This approach, he argued, actually would threaten the nation's free enterprise system, which would suffer from "an unhealthful climate of concern over the cost in taxes and the competition of government."[114]

The plan that Wallace believed would both guarantee full employment and preserve economic liberties in the United States would be for the "people," through Congress, to "direct the government to prepare a national budget." This document would encompass the entire economy, covering not only federal expenditures but private ones as well. When the economy was not projected to be large enough to keep the population employed, the "government should be directed to prepare a program that would promote the maximum of private expenditure and the minimum of government expenditure to produce the necessary total national production." If, by contrast, the economy was growing too quickly and inflation seemed a likely result, "the government should be directed to hold down expenditures in line with potentially available supplies of goods and services."[115] To bring about these changes, the president would be able to implement two different sorts of programs. The first would "embrace such nonspending devices as tax and credit incentives," in order to stimulate consumption so that more jobs would be created. The second type "would include the use of government funds" either as grants to states or cities for public works programs or as "actual investment directly by the [f]ederal government in development of our resources."[116]

Alvin Hansen, at the time the leading American Keynesian economist, reviewed Wallace's book in the pages of the *New Republic*. There, he waxed enthusiastic about it, writing that the volume "should be read and reread by every voter" and "studied in every high school and college in America."[117] This response should come as no surprise because the book was an attempt to implement a specifically Keynesian economic policy. Preparing a budget that would relate government expenditures and revenue to the national macroeconomic totals would institutionalize the Keynesian approach to political economy by inviting the government each year to determine the extent to which it would become involved in the economy. This would establish and legitimize government roles that had been played up to that point only on an informal and emergency basis.

By that time, liberals had embraced the notion of full employment, which Brinkley called the "central economic goal of New Deal liberals."[118] Others, however, were far less excited about this concept. Their uncertainty was manifested in the ambivalence that greeted the full employment bill introduced in 1945 by Senator James Murray (D-MT). As originally written, the proposed legislation echoed the first right enumerated in Franklin Roosevelt's second bill of rights by declaring that "every American has the right to a useful and remunerative job."[119] The mechanism that would satisfy this right would be a full-employment budget like the one championed in *Sixty Million Jobs*. Wallace had worked on the bill, and both he and President Truman endorsed it.

Though the measure easily passed the Senate on a vote of seventy-two to ten, the public reception was a bit cooler. As the Murray bill awaited consideration by the House, the *New York Times*, for example, declared in an editorial that it "could launch us upon an indefinite course of deficit financing" at a time when inflation would be "our greatest single post-war problem."[120] Business interests generally opposed the bill on the grounds that full employment would drive up wages. The US Chamber of Commerce worked with Representative Will Whittington, a conservative Democrat from Mississippi who sat on the subcommittee charged with drafting the House version of the bill, to add amendments that would water down its provisions.[121] Competing against several other versions of the bill, Whittington's iteration was approved by the committee and then the full House of Representatives. When the conference committee met, it considered a House bill that was much weaker than the Senate version. The bill that emerged reflected the conservative perspective of the larger chamber. The national budget and the language about the right to a job had been replaced by, respectively, an annual report to be prepared by the President's Council of Economic Advisers (a body created by this law) and a commitment "to create conditions" that would afford "useful employment opportunities . . . and to promote maximum employment, production and purchasing power."[122] The new law, originally conceived as a government mandate to provide a job to every American, was ultimately enacted as little more than a suggestion to provide "maximum employment." Even the word *full* had been excised from what was passed as the Employment Act of 1946.

It was during the New Deal era that Americans began to hold government accountable for employment. But even though support for a governmental full-employment policy peaked in that period, liberals were unable to wrest from the political process a true commitment to that ideal. The Keynesian approach to unemployment was the least interventionist of the three major philosophies that animated the New Deal, yet its policy implications still fell outside the acceptable options that characterized American democratic capitalism at the time. Both Keynesianism and the impulse to hold government accountable for unemployment have continued to influence policy to the present day. At the same time, however, the government has not been granted any more power or authority to deal with the problem, and unemployment has remained one of the central problems of democratic capitalism as practiced in the United States.

The Ordeal of Henry Wallace

Franklin Roosevelt died less than three months into his fourth term. Thereafter, President Truman was immediately faced with a series of difficult decisions, including those involving the use of the atomic bomb and the stance that the United States should take toward its wartime ally, the Soviet Union. The collective weight of these decisions led to the entrenchment of what soon would be known as the Cold War, an enterprise that hewed much closer to Luce's "American Century" than Wallace's "Century of the Common Man." Wallace's public statements on the matter occasionally contradicted the president's, and Truman saw little reason for the secretary of commerce to be commenting on foreign policy in the first place. Wallace was fired in September 1946.

From there, Wallace returned to journalism, taking the helm of the *New Republic* and briefly transforming that magazine into a mouthpiece for liberals who believed that Truman was abandoning the legacy of the New Deal in both domestic and foreign affairs. More and more disillusioned with the direction the county was taking, Wallace mounted a campaign for president in 1948, under the banner of the newly formed Progressive Party. At a time when the national consensus around anticommunism was hardening, Wallace oriented his campaign toward criticism of Truman's Cold War policies. He also allowed communists to work on his campaign and refused to repudiate the public endorsements that he received from their organizations. As a consequence, the reception he received from the voters was not a particularly warm one. Additionally, he was vilified in the South for his opposition to Jim Crow. Despite his relatively high profile as a former vice president, his ability to reach the public was severely compromised by the focus upon his alleged communist ties. One survey reported that 51 percent of Americans believed Wallace's party was controlled by communists. When campaigning, "the substance of his remarks," wrote his biographers, "was all but smothered by 'the communist issue.'"[123]

In the end, Truman defeated Republican Thomas Dewey in a notoriously close election. Garnering only 2.4 percent of the vote, Wallace placed fourth, behind Dixiecrat Strom Thurmond.[124] His break with the Democratic Party had left him with few political friends, and his views were wildly out of step with those of most Americans. Though his name would occasionally be bandied about by red baiters eager to establish their credentials as anticommunists, by and large Wallace descended into obscurity. He lived on his farm for the next decade and a half before dying in 1965.

The last part of Wallace's life was representative of the fate of liberalism in the New Deal. The increasing uniformity of thought on the issue of communism and the Cold War marginalized a political figure who had sat, not long before, just "a heartbeat away from the presidency." Those same ideas also reigned in the New Deal in the period after 1940 or so. Though the ambitious programs of Franklin Roosevelt established for the federal government a new responsibility of ensuring widespread employment in the United States, the reigning ideas about American political economy kept the government from getting the tools necessary to accomplish that task. This dynamic would become even more complex as the nation engaged in the Cold War with the Soviet Union. For the next three decades, liberals laboring under the constraints of the Cold War would have great difficulty defining their own priorities and strategies regarding government economic intervention.

Chapter Five

Inequality

Daniel Boorstin was one of the most prominent historians of the post-war generation. A professor at the University of Chicago for a quarter century before becoming the head of the Library of Congress, Boorstin wrote popular books celebrating a vision of the American experience that downplayed the role of conflict and political ideology. Given such a focus, it might be surprising to learn that in his youth, as a Rhodes scholar at Oxford and a young faculty member at Harvard, the historian had flirted with communism. In 1953, the House Committee on Un-American Activities (HCUA) called him to account for these indiscretions. Before the committee, Boorstin acknowledged that he had once believed the Communist Party to be "the most progressive and forward-looking of liberal groups." As an older man, however, he now agreed with his questioners that Marxist ideas were "fallacious and not good for America" and that communist organizations "should be disbanded." The historian also expressed his belief that active members of the Communist Party should not be teachers in public schools or universities. "My feeling," he explained, "is that no one should be employed to teach in a university who is not free intellectually, and, in my opinion, membership in the Communist Party would be virtually conclusive evidence that a person was not intellectually free."[1]

Perhaps wanting harder evidence of Boorstin's convictions, the members of the committee asked the witness how he had demonstrated his opposition to communism since leaving the party. The scholar responded with two examples. The first was his "religious activities" as a member of the campus Hillel Foundation, which supported his contention that religion was "a bulwark against [c]ommunism." The other was his scholarship itself. His works of history and commentary represented Boorstin's effort to express his "opposition" to communism through "an attempt to discover and explain

. . . in my teaching and in my writing, the unique virtues of American democracy."[2]

No member of the committee asked the historian what these particular virtues were, but one might infer them from Boorstin's later career. In his testimony to HCUA, the historian mentioned his book in progress, which came out later that year as *The Genius of American Politics*. In that work, Boorstin characterized his nation's political tradition as "an unspoken assumption, an axiom, so basic to our thinking that we have hardly been aware of it at all." According to this submerged consensus, "institutions are not and should not be the grand creations of men toward large ends and outspoken values; rather they are organisms which grow out of the soil in which they are rooted and out of the tradition from which they have sprung."[3] His later trilogy of narrative history, *The Americans*, was both influential and successful. Its first and third volumes were awarded the Bancroft and Pulitzer Prizes in 1958 and 1973, respectively. The series made a point similar to that in *The Genius of American Politics*, yet it did so by using demonstrative examples rather than arguments. *The Americans* was structured around hundreds of short, well-written vignettes chronicling the innovations, in many fields, of the famous and the obscure. Collectively, these stories articulated a vision of a pragmatic, problem-solving people who had little time or patience for political or ideological grandstanding. The reader of *The Americans* would have little reason to believe that the early republic was riven by factional conflict, that strife over states' rights and slavery had led the nation to a bloody Civil War, or that the Gilded Age was marked as much by labor unrest as it was by reverence for the new entrepreneurial breed.

Boorstin's take on the nation's past owed more than a little to the perspective from which he—and many Americans in the postwar period—viewed its present. This era has often been characterized as one of widespread political consensus, and the historian's testimony before HCUA is instructive in this regard. To highlight the practical character of the United States, Boorstin implied, was to contrast the country positively with the ideologically rigid Soviet Union. For many Americans at midcentury, it was the blinding commitment to principles that united the nation's great foes of the past and present: Adolf Hitler and Joseph Stalin. Ideology itself, regardless of the specific nature of particular political commitments, was the enemy.

With regard to many areas of postwar public life, neither the widespread belief in political and intellectual harmony nor the common claim that the

United States exhibited a nonideological character have held up very well to historical scrutiny. To consider only the most notable example, modern-day interpreters of the period find such a characterization difficult to square with the palpable tension surrounding racial segregation in the South. But in the realm of political economy, a rough consensus did hold from Harry Truman's administration to Richard Nixon's. The public discourse of intellectuals and policy makers during this period was largely predicated on two tenets. The first was that communism and socialism were illegitimate not only in their tendencies toward political totalitarianism but also as intellectual systems around which one might orient a national economy. The second was that the limited American welfare state represented by the programs of the New Deal was a great achievement in tempering the excesses of capitalism and ensuring a healthy body politic. As a result of these commitments, the era's liberal thinkers faced a conundrum: the principles that would support taking care of the economically less fortunate could easily come across as ideological ones. Those who sought to provide intellectual support for the welfare state, therefore, ran the risk of running afoul of the era's anticommunist consensus.

Thus, postwar intellectuals twisted and turned to explain how a government-provided safety net could be justified by something other than a specific conception of the public good. Their attempts to characterize the American welfare state as a pragmatically oriented response to the specifics of the particular situation were ultimately unsuccessful, failing to establish a stable vision of a liberal democratic capitalism that could outlast the decline in the popularity of liberal ideas. Illustrative of this phenomenon was the reception accorded the most ambitious attempt to justify this liberal vision: philosopher John Rawls's magisterial *A Theory of Justice*. Most often lauded for its contributions to the discipline of professional philosophy, the book also articulated the most compelling, rigorous, and forceful presentation of the consensus position on domestic political economy. Yet the book did not appear until 1971, well after the influence of Cold War liberalism had peaked. *A Theory of Justice* achieved a level of influence in scholarly circles unmatched by any work of philosophy in the second half of the twentieth century. Its ability to shape public political debate, however, was more limited. The fact that a work could voice a powerful argument for the welfare state but fail to bolster the liberal political project demonstrated that the American social contract had not been permanently rewritten, as some believed, to reflect the values of postwar liberalism. Instead, during the postwar years a variety of political and economic factors had created conditions that were hospitable to liberal policies and ideas. As consensus thinking unraveled, liberal support for government economic intervention on behalf of the less fortunate ceased to resonate with the American public, and the national commitment to the welfare state began to falter.

The Liberal Consensus

The February 1951 issue of *Fortune* magazine was so well received that its editors soon published it as a book. Its title borrowed from Marx and Lenin, *U.S.A.: The Permanent Revolution* was entirely devoted to a breathless celebration of "the American way of life." The understanding that it articulated was similar to that which Boorstin would soon present in *The Genius of American Politics*: the nation and its people were pragmatic, non-ideological, and anti-intellectual yet shot through with wisdom and greatness. The "essential principles" of American politics, the editors summarized, "are three: a word, a tendency and a method. The word is liberty. The tendency is equality. And the method is constitutionalism." The nation's bipartisan political system continued to work so effectively, for example, "precisely because it is *not* founded on an ideological split."[4] Stuffed with dozens of equally enthusiastic banalities, *U.S.A.: The Permanent Revolution* argued that the Gilded Age excesses of capitalism had been tamed by Progressive and New Deal reforms and that Americans had essentially determined, once and for all, a stable equilibrium between the demands of government, business, and labor.

With regard to the difficult balance between the roles of government and business, the editors asserted that the "average American . . . can hardly have escaped the conviction" that American political economy represented "the middle ground on which humanity can take its stand against totalitarianism of any kind."[5] The *Fortune* editors advocated for what already existed in the United States, which they called a "mixed economy." In America, they wrote, "ownership is predominantly private, but it is not exclusively so; and even private ownership has in many instances been highly 'socialized.'" In between the "dog-eat-dog" world of the scrap-metal industry and the complete government control of the Tennessee Valley Authority were "all shades of the economic rainbow."[6] The conservative editors of *Fortune* minimized the part played by the expanding American safety net in attacking the "social problems" of poverty, conspicuously failing to mention the role of the New Deal in this regard while emphasizing instead the growing sense of responsibility among businesses and individual Americans. Otherwise, however, this issue and the book that came from it trumpeted a tremendous confidence both in the fact that the United States was on the right track and in the belief that most Americans were as confident in this assessment as were the writers themselves.

U.S.A.: The Permanent Revolution vividly illustrated the tenor of American political and intellectual discourse during the postwar era. Through this period, many Americans confidently believed that their nation embodied a solution to perennial problems of social justice and wealth distribution, a solution that met the needs of the less fortunate without limiting the free enterprise system or ceding tyrannical powers to government or business. Moreover, they viewed this system as decidedly and essentially nonideological, embodying a moderate, consensus-oriented pragmatism. Perceiving that the totalitarianism of the old enemy—fascist Germany—and that of the new one—the communist Soviet Union—were both motivated by an emotional dedication to a systematic ideology, Americans eschewed the appearance of totalizing intellectual commitments.

The most popular political figure of the era, for instance, was Dwight Eisenhower. A hero of World War II who was courted by both major parties before launching his presidential bid, Eisenhower was hardly a divisive figure. In 1952, he was elected as the first Republican president in two decades, but Ike pointedly distanced himself from the more conservative elements of his party. His "modern Republicanism" tracked a moderate course politically, articulating (and creating) a broad-based consensus. Eisenhower ended the Korean War, shared US nuclear material with other nations, and accepted the permanence of once-radical New Deal programs.[7] His greatest domestic achievement—the building of the interstate highway system—speaks more of pragmatic problem solving than of any deep-seated ideology. His presidential campaign slogan—"I Like Ike"—communicated very little in terms of political or intellectual content, but it accurately conveyed the sentiments of millions of Americans.

Significantly, the dominant trend in the writing of history in this period was known as the "consensus" school. Undoubtedly influenced by the times in which they were writing, consensus historians saw a great continuity in the prominent ideas and practices—particularly those of entrepreneurialism and free enterprise—throughout different phases of American history. Generally considered to have been inaugurated by Richard Hofstadter's 1948 publication of *The American Political Tradition and the Men Who Made It,* the consensus school would soon include Boorstin, whose *Genius of*

American Politics appeared in 1953, and Louis Hartz, who argued in *The Liberal Tradition in America* that Americans of all historical periods had been uniquely influenced by Liberalism. Other intellectuals, however, were concerned that the consensus of the age looked less like wisdom than conformity. In 1950, sociologists David Reisman, Nathan Glazer, and Reuel Denny argued, in *The Lonely Crowd*, that contemporary Americans had exchanged their autonomy for a fundamentally "other-directed" outlook, and William H. Whyte's *Organization Man* (1956) influentially decried the decline of individualism in the modern corporation.

Indeed, one of the definitive works of the period had at its center the idea that divisive political commitments had essentially ceased. In his influential collection of essays, *The End of Ideology*, first published in 1960, Daniel Bell argued that the sweeping certainties of self-contained systems of thought such as fascism and Marxism had lost their capacity to inspire politically significant thinking. According to Bell, in the new intellectual order—which he generally welcomed—"few 'classic' liberals insist that the [s]tate should play no role in the economy." He noted a "rough consensus" politically in the "Western world" on a few central axioms: "the acceptance of a [w]elfare [s]tate; the desirability of decentralized power; a system of mixed economy and of political pluralism."[8]

For Bell, then, beyond the commitment to democracy itself, consensus thinking on domestic issues centered on the relationship between the government and the economy, and it was committed in particular to two major points: that government should be allowed to intervene in the doings of the market and that one of the purposes of such interventions should be to benefit those individuals who had not fared particularly well in the market system. Whatever issues might arise in the implementation of these commitments would be technical questions rather than clashes of competing values. The proper level and specific purpose of government economic intervention had, Bell believed, been settled once and for all.

Because of the vast influence of the New Deal, the political moderation that Americans embraced in this period had shifted decidedly to the left. Ideas and policies that midcentury thinkers perceived as pragmatic, moderate, and centrist were, in many cases, liberal ones. The renowned literary critic Lionel Trilling famously quipped in 1950 that "at this time liberalism is not only the dominant but even the sole intellectual tradition"; conservative patterns of thought, he wrote, were not "in general circulation" and could not "express themselves in ideas, but only in action or in irritable mental gestures which seek to resemble ideas."[9] Later, historian Rick Perlstein summarized the attitude of many Americans in the latter part of the consensus years: the liberal approach "was not ideology. This was *reality*. One did not argue with people who denied reality."[10]

Of course, liberals did face obstacles and opponents in attempting to institute their vision. In his history of postwar liberalism, Kevin Mattson criticized the tendency of period figures toward the "overestimation of a liberal consensus." Noting as examples the defeat of organized labor signified by the Taft-Hartley Act of 1947 and the tremendous support for Senator Joseph McCarthy's anticommunist crusade, he called the idea "little more than a myth."[11] Historians of conservatism have made similar challenges, contesting the older view that the modern-day movement originated in the backlash against civil rights and the social activism of the 1960s. They have pointed out, for example, that Ayn Rand's libertarian novel *The Fountainhead* became a best seller when it appeared in 1943. George Nash has dated the beginning of an "articulate, self-consciously conservative intellectual force" to the period after 1945, and Kim Phillips-Fein has argued that with regard to economic issues (as opposed to cultural ones), "the origin of modern conservative politics and ideology . . . begins . . . in the reaction against the New Deal."[12]

Liberals, in short, occupied a dominant position in the nation's political culture but simultaneously faced attacks on all sides. Vilified on the right as communist appeasers whose slide toward statism on economic issues threatened basic American liberties, they were at the same time charged by radicals on the left with paying insufficient attention to civil rights and advocating a belligerent international brinkmanship that threatened a nuclear conflagration. When considering their various modes of expression, Mattson argued that midcentury liberal intellectuals were "at their best . . . when they spoke less of their ideas as part of a 'consensus' . . . and more as a 'fighting faith' that had to do battles [*sic*] for the hearts and minds of their fellow citizens."[13] It was unfortunate for these thinkers, though, that many of their most influential works fell into the former category. As a result, American liberals failed to develop a rigorous public defense of the welfare state, one that would become more necessary when the country later turned in a more conservative direction.

One of the most prominent expressions of liberal thinking appeared in 1949. That year, Arthur Schlesinger, Jr., the historian, activist, and future member of the Kennedy administration, issued a manifesto of sorts. His

Vital Center became, in Mattson's words, "one of the most important books in the history of American liberal thought"[14] and the essential statement of Cold War liberalism. The overall purpose of the book was not only to promote the liberal political program but also to distinguish that platform from a radical, socialist-oriented leftism.

Schlesinger began the book with a point that would be familiar to generations of liberals since the Progressive Era, declaring that the Industrial Revolution had permanently altered the variables that set the terms for social organization. Though unleashing a great deal of creative energy, this development had decoupled economic relationships from older social ties, such as the family or the extended clan. As a result, "no one had to feel a direct responsibility for the obvious and terrible costs in human suffering." Science and technology had led to the rise of institutions—the corporation and the bureaucratic state—that maximized efficiency while doing little for human needs. Therefore, those who lived in the mid-twentieth century found themselves in what was called, by Schlesinger and many other contemporary commentators, an "age of anxiety." The primary task of modern political thinking was to respond to this shift. Industrialism led to both capitalism and communism, with their attendant excesses, and it could not be undone. When viewed in that light, choosing between these two ideologies might seem like having to select an unsatisfactory, second-best option, but Schlesinger asserted strongly that it was a choice of the utmost significance: "Even if capitalism and [c]ommunism are both the children of the Industrial Revolution, there remains a crucial difference between the USA and the USSR . . . between free society and totalitarianism."[15]

One possible response to this vexing problem, conceded Schlesinger, was ideological. The adoption of a rigid, totalizing intellectual worldview could exchange anxiety for certainty, but it did so, he argued, at too high a cost. "The liberal state acknowledged many limitations in its demands upon men," he wrote. "The total state acknowledges none." Thus, an ideological approach to politics would inexorably lead to totalitarianism, whether of the left, as in Soviet communism, or of the right, as in German fascism, which had only recently been deposed. Under such an interpretation, Schlesinger was able to view liberalism as, by definition, the rejection of ideology. Yet he recognized that ideologies filled a real need, and so he stated that liberalism "has been and will continue to be under attack from the far right and the far left."[16] Schlesinger's concern was primarily with the latter, focusing particularly on the attraction that various forms of socialism held for American liberals. He viewed ideology as an immature but dangerous utopianism and saw a liberal who tolerated, indulged, or supported such ideologues as someone who privileged his or her emotional need to avoid the era's characteristic anxiety over the much more important duty to limit the suffering of others. Clearly distinguishing between Schlesinger's own liberalism and a more radical view is perhaps the central goal of *The Vital Center*.

Schlesinger dedicated much of the book to attacking his enemies on the left, including not only the USSR and the Communist Party of the United States of America but also the figure who received the bulk of his wrath—the progressive "doughface."[17] Originally, this term applied to antebellum northern politicians who favored southern positions, but in Schlesinger's updated usage, it referred to American liberals (or, as he often called them derisively, "progressives") who were tolerant of and, in his view, naive about the intentions of communists. This doughface was, he wrote, "the fellow traveler or the fellow traveler of the fellow traveler," whose "sentimentality has softened up the progressive for [c]ommunist permeation and conquest." Schlesinger's most venomous barbs were aimed at the "well-intentioned, wooly-minded" Henry Wallace, whose third-party presidential run in 1948 "represented the most considerable undertaking ever attempted by the [c]ommunists in the United States."[18]

Yet *The Vital Center* had its own form of wooly-mindedness. The great certainty with which Schlesinger offered his pronouncements and dismissals was seldom justified by the presentation of solid evidence. The sections of the book that touched on political economy generally offered slogans rather than arguments. Schlesinger asserted without support or clarification, for example, that "we are changing from a market society to an administrative society." Given the need for such administration, he rather broadly concluded that "big government, for all its dangers, remains democracy's only effective response to big business." At the same time, however, he warned against taking this argument too far in any one direction, without explaining with any specificity what principles would define the appropriate level of intervention. Schlesinger suggested that "pinpoint" economic planning was too extreme and wrote that "the lesson of the experiments with democratic socialism is that the state should aim at establishing conditions, not making all the decisions itself." But he seemed unconcerned by the fact that one person's establishment of conditions was another's tyrannical overregulation. The argument he advanced was so imprecise that its conclusion took the form of a sports metaphor: government should allow "the free market to carry the ball as far as it can." To those readers seeking more specific direction, Schlesinger offered clarification by reference to a different sports metaphor: "The function of the state, in other words, is to define the ground rules of the game; not to pitch, catch, hit homers or (just as likely) pop up or throw to the wrong base."[19]

Though he devoted much less time to the right, Schlesinger was equally disdainful of conservative market ideology. In his view, "The modern American capitalist"—a figure whom Schlesinger invoked rather casually, alongside the "conservative" and the "businessman"—"has come to share many values with the American liberal: beliefs in personal integrity, personal freedom and equality of opportunity." Yet this figure, argued Schlesinger, was politically tethered to the then-emerging libertarian right. Consequently, he or she was quite useless to the liberal project of fighting against a dangerous communist ideology. The emerging libertarian movement, Schlesinger suggested, was more ridiculous than threatening, made up as it was of "[N]eanderthals . . . shambling around, supporting the Un-American Activities Committee, campaigning against Keynesian textbooks in the colleges, conspiring against the trade-union movement, inveighing against free milk for schoolchildren, and smearing all non-conformists as [c]ommunists."[20]

The Vital Center underscored Schlesinger's disdain for extremes of both left and right, and he offered little succor for those who supported either government ownership of the means of production or laissez-faire economics. Having rejected the twin extremes of statist economic planning and libertarian absence of regulation, however, he wrote little that could aid in defining the appropriate level of economic stewardship or explaining what exactly was "vital" about the middle course he advocated. In this, Schlesinger's book reflected the prejudices and concerns of the period in which it was written, and it highlighted its intellectual weaknesses. In advocating his own position as merely a sensible one that avoided the extremes of the left and right, Schlesinger offered few reasons why one not inclined to do so actually *should* support the welfare state. To the extent that such complacency represented the liberal worldview, a firm national commitment to the welfare state was unlikely to outlast the liberal consensus itself. In its neglect of a rigorous presentation of a program of political economy, *The Vital Center* shared the intellectual limitations of the postwar period in which it was written.

The Political Economy of Cold War Liberalism

Yet political economy should have been indispensable to the consensus project. Two of its central propositions—the rejection of socialism and the championing of the welfare state—took explicit positions on the subject. Such commitments required strong arguments for their support; moreover, they were not entirely in sync with one another. As Schlesinger recognized, liberal intellectuals needed to be able to justify their support of capitalism against the far left while simultaneously defending the welfare and regulatory state against the libertarian right. This was no mean trick. Grounding the capitalist system on a Liberal conception of inviolable property rights would have made it difficult to justify redistributive policies, whereas emphasizing the human costs of the capitalist system would have undermined the Liberal commitment to free enterprise itself. But the question did not get as much attention as it might have because the liberal consensus was as consensual as it was liberal. Since the core tenets of the liberal ideology went relatively unchallenged, few felt the need to mount a rigorous defense of them.

Even in this environment, however, such defenses did exist. The originator of the phrase *liberal consensus* was British journalist Godfrey Hodgson, who in 1976 wrote of a set of "interrelated maxims" that characterized midcentury thinking and upended the political and intellectual assumptions of the postwar era. The new worldview, Hodgson argued, had held that "the American free-enterprise system . . . has a revolutionary potential for social justice." Thus, consensus thinkers believed that capitalism was something that should be accepted not *despite* its human effects but *because* of them. The "key to this potential," wrote Hodgson, "is production: specifically, increased production, or economic growth."[21] Unlike premodern forms of economic organization, consumer capitalism could significantly increase the overall supply of goods. Government policies that enabled private industry to grow, liberals argued, could actually reduce human misery by giving each person more goods. So, the concept of economic growth could provide intellectual support for the liberal capitalist response to the socialist challenge: in terms of the overused but unavoidably compelling metaphor, if the whole pie grows in size, then even those individuals with a smaller proportional slice could wind up with an equal, or perhaps greater, total amount of dessert.

Such an attitude was easy to adopt during that period because the postwar era saw unprecedented economic expansion. Between 1947 and 1960, the gross national product of the United States rose by 56 percent, and consumer spending rose by 52.4 percent. Many contemporary observers had feared that the Great Depression, which had been interrupted by the massive government spending of World War II, would simply resume upon the conflict's end. Instead, the termination of the war unleashed the consumer demand that had been pent up by rationing and price controls. This desire for goods stimulated the need for manufacturing, which in turn kept much of the population employed. A strong labor movement ensured good wages and benefits for the assembly-line worker, and the disposable income of the working class kept consumer demand at unprecedented levels. Moreover, the Cold War prompted high levels of government defense spending, which provided stable employment in the public sector. This "virtuous circle" of postwar prosperity lasted until the early 1970s, and the maintenance of economic growth consequently occupied a central place in the political landscape of postwar America.[22]

Liberal thinking during this period reflected a preoccupation with economic growth. Some liberals, in fact, were concerned that Americans had placed too much emphasis on the phenomenon. John Kenneth Galbraith was, like Schlesinger, one of the better-known intellectual apologists for midcentury liberalism. A Harvard economist who had worked in the Department of Agriculture during the New Deal and at the Office of Price Administration during World War II, Galbraith later served as the US ambassador to India under John F. Kennedy. In his work in the 1950s, he sought to expose the economic theories under which the contemporary American economy operated, often for the purposes of urging that they be updated to reflect the reality of the postwar situation.

In 1958, Galbraith issued what would become his best-known book. In *The Affluent Society,* he claimed to be working against the grain of what he called the "conventional wisdom." This now-shopworn phrase was new when Galbraith coined it to refer to "the structure of ideas that is based on acceptability," rather than wisdom or truthfulness.[23] The particular piece of conventional wisdom that he targeted in *The Affluent Society* regarded production. Economists, in his view, had adopted increases in production, or economic growth, as the primary instrument with which to measure the nation's health. This metric had once served an important purpose in economic thought, he asserted, but it no longer did so. The primacy of such a wrongheaded belief had resulted—and continued to result—in a significant misallocation of the nation's resources.

For most of human history, Galbraith observed, people lived in a state of privation. This situation imposed upon the earliest economic thinkers three primary concerns: productivity, inequality, and insecurity.[24] As economies grew, however, productivity displaced the other two, until economic and political thinkers were concerned with little else. The economies of the wealthy nations had grown so much that "few things are more evident in modern social history than the decline of interest in equality as an economic issue."[25] Economic growth, he noted, had come to be viewed as "an alternative to redistribution" and had consequently served as "the great solvent of the tensions associated with inequality."[26] Security had met a similar fate. In a large, integrated economy, Galbraith argued, the largest threats to security—the loss of a job, failure of a business, or decline in the value of assets—were all intimately related to a decline in production.[27] Thus, the modern conventional wisdom held that all the traditional concerns could be addressed through the maximization of productivity, to the point where the other issues would be largely forgotten.

Moreover, Galbraith argued, contemporary thinking irrationally discriminated in regard to which kinds of production were esteemed and which were not. In particular, it valued private goods more than public ones, regardless of whatever social benefits each might provide. This prioritization, Galbraith claimed, was also the result of the historical origins of economics. The classical thinkers saw that the market served as an effective tool for producing and distributing food, clothing, and shelter, but they also noted that the primary good provided by government—social order—was delivered only sporadically and at great cost. A suspicion of government consequently became intertwined with the presumptions of economics, continuing to motivate opinions in the contemporary United States even as social order proved quite durable. As a result of such prejudices, Galbraith stated, "alcohol, comic books and mouth wash [*sic*] all bask under the superior reputation of the market. Schools, judges, patrolmen and municipal swimming pools lie under the evil reputation of bad kings."[28]

The collective result of all these developments was a deficit in what Galbraith called "social balance." There are relationships between the different sorts of products that a society chooses to produce as well as between those it chooses to consume. The desire for automobiles, for instance, creates the need for gasoline, roads, and insurance, whereas the appetite for tobacco and luxurious food increases demand for medical care.[29] Often, privately produced goods are not correlated with those provided publicly, which allows private decisions to create demand on public institutions. The benefits of education, for example, accrue primarily to the private interests of the student and his or her future employer, but much of its costs are borne by the public.[30] "By failing to exploit the opportunity to expand public production," Galbraith observed, "we are missing opportunities for enjoyment which otherwise we might have had." A town's citizens might enjoy having better schools or parks as much as they would like having larger cars, but "by concentrating on the latter rather than the former," they would be "failing to maximize [their] satisfactions." The conventional wisdom maintains that markets maximize the satisfaction of wants, but the fact that public goods are systematically excluded from their purview clearly demonstrates the inadequacy of such a position. "It is scarcely sensible that we should satisfy our wants in private goods with reckless abundance, while in the case of public goods . . . practice extreme self-denial."[31]

Galbraith argued that the purpose of *The Affluent Society* was largely negative: to challenge the primacy of the conventional wisdom and suggest that the presumptions of political economy should change when production was not the highest priority. Though he de-emphasized any positive program in his book, he did offer a few suggestions about how the reintroduction of the three initial concerns of economics might affect public policy. In a society characterized by consistent economic growth, economic security could be separated from production by recognizing that the specter of the voluntarily idle worker no longer had to inspire fears of a shrinking economy. Unemployment compensation therefore did not need to bear the burden of forcing people to work, and much closer attention could be paid to the average weekly wage. (Galbraith actually voiced support for providing a minimum basic income for all citizens, but he set that idea aside as a political impossibility.)[32] The issue of equality, he argued, could also be disentangled from that of production. Any private citizen who had the money could make any extravagant purchase that he or she wished, but public expenditures had to surmount a much higher bar set by the voters, who traditionally held their governments to the rather high standard of "need." Thus, the private economy was likely to take up a much larger share of the available resources than the public economy. Since public resources were more likely to be devoted to the needs of the poor, Galbraith concluded that "the economy is geared to the least urgent set of human wants."[33] To correct social imbalance, taxes would need to be higher: "A poor society rightly adjusts its policy to the poor. An affluent society may properly inquire whether, instead, it shouldn't remove the poverty."[34]

Galbraith's historical and intellectual analysis culminated in a prescription to increase aid to the unemployed and poor. But in claiming that the errors of the conventional wisdom were responsible for social imbalance, he appeared to tacitly assume that no one who was aware of the actual situation would actually believe the nation's priorities were "balanced." *The Affluent Society* did not provide any evidence that the American people would have preferred, were they given the clear choice, to use some of their great productive capacity in providing more economic security to their fellow citizens or reducing overall economic inequality. (Indeed, a primary component of the later conservative backlash against the liberal consensus would be a rejection of this very assumption.) The possibility exists that a voter who understood the implications of the conventional wisdom *really would* prefer a new car to better parks or schools.

Mattson summarized the "politics that Galbraith hoped for" as those that "would emphasize nonutilitarian and aesthetic principles over profit-driven capitalism." This vision was compellingly presented in *The Affluent Society*, but such a "a value-laden critique" would always be open to the rejoinder that Galbraith was not diagnosing injustice or inefficiency in the nation's economic system as much as he was simply registering disapproval of the judgments and decisions of others. *The Affluent Society* implied that social balance could be restored once the public understood the choices it was making. Such a conclusion turned on the belief in a fairly wide distribution of liberal values. Though perhaps presumptuous, it was nonetheless revealing of the attitude toward political economy in the postwar years.[35]

Though economic growth was at the center of consensus thinking, domestic issues were only one aspect of its attraction. Increases in production also were an important intellectual front in the battle against international communism. The Soviet Five-Year Plans and the Chinese Great Leap Forward were attempts to use the communist system to stimulate increases in production and modernization in technology.[36] One of the major intellectual fronts in the Cold War battle for "hearts and minds" around the globe was the question of whether capitalism or communism would be able to more efficiently deliver to developing nations a high-producing economy. The year after *The Affluent Society* was published, Vice President Richard Nixon and Premier Nikita Khrushchev of the USSR had argued about just these issues in a model home located in an exhibition of American consumer goods in Moscow. Amid their contentious discussion about nuclear arms, the locations of foreign bases, and the tension in Berlin, Khrushchev and Nixon still managed to focus much of their conversation on the production and consumption generated by their respective economies. In the "kitchen debate," as it has come to be known, Nixon bragged that the average American steelworker could afford a home, to which his Soviet adversary countered with the allegation that homes in the United States would only last twenty years. After being shown an American washing machine and television set, Khrushchev offered, somewhat implausibly, that the Soviet counterparts of these goods were of equal quality. He assured the assembled reporters that, though the Americans expected the Russians to be "dumbfounded" by these consumer products, they were commonplace in the Soviet Union.

Despite the somewhat immature, "tit-for-tat" tone of the Moscow debate, the discussion showcased an interesting development, as Khrushchev soon offered another rejoinder that completely contradicted his earlier point. Immediately after defending the high quality of Soviet appliances, he argued—and Galbraith might have agreed with him—that the objects on display were unnecessary bourgeois pleasures that demonstrated the capitalist misallocation of resources. "Don't you have a machine," he asked Nixon belligerently, "that puts food in your mouth and pushes it down?" Such goods were "interesting," Khrushchev admitted, but they were "merely gadgets" that were "not needed in life." Nixon's response was that the American economy was not centrally directed, and so people and firms were able to make whatever they wished. This did not mollify the premier, who pointed out that a worker who lived in the Soviet Union would be allowed to live in a house simply by the fact of his or her citizenship. In the United States, by contrast, "if you don't have a dollar, you [don't] have the right to choose between sleeping in a house or sleeping on the pavement."[37]

The kitchen debate demonstrated that the conflict between the United States and the Soviet Union was not only strategic and geopolitical but also intellectual and cultural. One American thinker who connected economic growth to the values of a society was Walt Whitman Rostow. An economic historian who became an informal adviser to Senator John F. Kennedy in 1958, Rostow served in the White House and the State Department upon Kennedy's ascension to the presidency. Rostow was an anticommunist hawk who was advising the president to commit the American military to rolling back communism in Vietnam as early as 1961. He later became Lyndon Johnson's special assistant for national security affairs (a post known today as national security adviser), and he continued his advocacy of an aggressive Vietnam policy. He was a prime advocate of bombing in that country and never stopped believing in the war, even as it became unpopular and, in the eyes of many, unwinnable.

Rostow's earlier life as an academic had also been characterized by anticommunism, albeit of a more intellectual variety. His 1960 book, *The Stages of Economic Growth: A Non-Communist Manifesto,* directly challenged communist ideas. In opposition to the Marxist notion of economic determinism, which claimed that social forces could best be understood as manifestations of more fundamental economic processes, Rostow observed that similar levels of economic development had been accompanied by a wide variety of governmental systems. Consequently, economic growth did not, he asserted, necessarily lead to any specific form of government, much less demand the totalitarian communism characteristic of Soviet Russia.

He believed that societies that reached a high level of production tended to follow a fairly consistent pattern, characterized by five stages. All such societies began as traditional, agricultural ones, with little production beyond subsistence and, consequently, no room to increase the level of output. These communities typically exhibited hierarchal social and political structures, "with relatively little scope . . . for social mobility."[38] As a result, members of these groups had little incentive to produce more than they needed, so economic growth was unlikely. What distinguished the groups that increased their economic output from those that did not, argued Rostow, was a shift in cultural values. These new motivations might include "national dignity, private profit, the general welfare, or a better life for the children," but one way or another, they had to sanction some new goal for individuals, one that had the side effect of bringing about a rise in production. Politically, this stage had often heralded the development of the nation-state, which was typically instrumental in overcoming the traditional power of "landed regional interests" or "colonial powers." In the next stage, which Rostow called the "take-off," production would begin to grow at a hitherto unprecedented rate. "Old blocks of resistance are finally overcome," and "the forces making for economic progress . . . expand and come to dominate the society."[39] New industries prospered, old ones such as agriculture incorporated more modern technologies, and investment climbed to an annual high of 10 percent of national income. Growth became a typical, rather than an inconsistent, feature of the economy.

The next phase, Rostow argued, was characterized by a steady growth in productivity and investment, which, rising as high as 20 percent per year, significantly outstripped the increase in population. In this stage, which Rostow called "the drive to maturity," the society would begin the process of spreading its technological advances out over the entire economy. Maturity itself, which Rostow identified with mass consumption, was the stage in which the society "demonstrate[d] the capacity to move beyond the original industries which powered its take-off." By this stage, technological advances would have been fully incorporated into the economy, and income would have risen to the point that most citizens could take for granted that their fundamental needs would be met. As a result of greater diversification and the ability to devote a smaller sector of the economy to subsistence, a much larger proportion of the population would live in urban areas and work in offices or factories.[40]

Despite the emphasis on historical development, Rostow aimed much of his analysis at the present. He noted that economies that had reached the "mature" stage now had options about what they could do with their surplus resources. Typically, he argued, they would put these resources into some combination of three overall projects: the "national pursuit of external power and influence," the development of the welfare state, and the "expansion of consumption levels beyond basic, food, shelter and clothing."[41] The United States flirted with the first possibility around the period of the Spanish-American War but, according to Rostow, largely abandoned its imperialist project. Consumerism took hold in the 1920s, but when the Great Depression intervened, the New Deal put into place the rudiments of a welfare state. Consumption picked up in the postwar era, but Rostow did not believe that the nation would long be able to support the same economic growth rate. Most Americans, in his view, were beginning to have all of the consumer products they could possibly need.

Rostow disagreed with Galbraith about the availability of increased leisure as a possible choice for the American economic "surplus," arguing that "it is too soon for a 4-day week and for tolerance of substantial levels of unemployment," as the "problem of choice and allocation—the problem of scarcity—has not yet been lifted."[42] If the affluent society had not quite arrived, however, Rostow believed that it soon would. Whenever that day came, he indicated that he saw the potential problems, if not their solutions, in terms similar to Galbraith's. What would Americans—and, soon enough, those from the majority of nations that would reach the "post mature" stage—do when economic necessity no longer structured their priorities? Americans might, he said, "fall into secular spiritual stagnation"; artificially reimpose economic necessity on themselves by having more children; "conduct wars with just enough violence to be good sport—and to accelerate capital depreciation—without blowing up the planet"; explore outer space; or convert themselves into "suburban version[s] of an eighteenth-century country gentleman," leisurely seeking out the modern equivalents of hunting, building estates, and pursuing "the life of the mind."[43] Rostow expressed anxiety about the available options, finding all of them either destructive or implausible.

The concept of social or national choice was central to Rostow's analysis. Indeed, it marked the major distinction between his view of economic development and the Marxist analysis with which, he pointed out, his account shared many similarities.[44] In contrast to the emphasis on economic determinism that characterized the Marxist system, however, Rostow's analysis viewed the individual as "a more complex unit," who desired, in addition to economic advantages, "also power, leisure, adventure . . . and security" and who cared for his or her family and the values of the community. As a result, national policies and the direction of societies over time "represent[ed] acts of balance rather than a simple maximization procedure."[45] What mattered in considering the progression of developing societies and nations, therefore, was not only the economy but also the "total procedure by which choices are made." Those societies that Marxists would call "capitalist" had never, Rostow said, "made all their major decisions simply in terms of the free-market mechanism and private advantage."[46] Consequently, capitalism alone did not account for the development of the United States and other societies in the "post mature" stage. A communist government could also seize power at an early stage in a nation's development and steer it toward take-off; indeed, Rostow argued that this was exactly what had happened in the Soviet Union and China.[47] But all such mechanisms were not equal, and the human costs associated with that particular method of stimulating economic growth were quite high. Since economic development was a process of balancing competing interests, Rostow recommended democracy as a political system. This endorsement did not turn on the claim that this system of government was necessarily more likely to bring about economic development. Instead, it was based on a conviction that democracy was the most able to incorporate society-wide values into economic decisions.

The anticommunism of *The Stages of Economic Growth* took the form of an intellectual assault on some of the premises of Marxist theory. Rostow shared with Galbraith certain concerns about the American system of political economy, but these doubts were clearly peripheral to his main concerns. Indeed, expressing the principles of American political economy was not central to Rostow's analysis. His project was fundamentally negative in character, its goal to refute certain aspects of communist theory rather than to support, articulate, or justify the nature of American political economy. Thus, *The Stages of Economic Growth* provided a contrast with communist theory but did little to express positive principles around which the mid-century liberal consensus project might be defined. In this, it was typical of the intellectual work of the postwar period, which generally failed to offer a rigorous or compelling argument in favor of the particular pattern of government economic intervention that enjoyed widespread support during the middle decades of the twentieth century.

The War on Poverty

The slow but steady unraveling of the liberal consensus might be said to have begun in 1962, with the publication of Michael Harrington's *The Other America: Poverty in the United States.* The book argued directly and forcefully for two interrelated theses: that there were many poor people in the United States and that the federal government should do something to reduce their numbers. The first point rubbed against the grain of consensus understandings of American society. Confident that the New Deal and postwar economic growth had bequeathed a high standard of living to essentially everyone, most Americans simply assumed that poverty no longer existed. But Harrington claimed that there were between 40 and 50 million poor people in the United States,[48] living right under the noses of those who were unaware of their existence. There were reasons, Harrington argued, for this invisibility of the poor. They tended to live "off the beaten track," in rural areas or urban ghettos. They also were hidden by romantic myths: the "traveler" who comes into contact with "a run-down mountain house" in the Appalachians decides that its residents "are truly fortunate to be living the way they are . . . and to be exempt from the strains and tensions of the middle class." Many of the impoverished were children or senior citizens, what Harrington called "the wrong age to be seen." A good number were sick. And they were "atomized," unable to form civic groups to represent their interests. With no possibility of organization, he asserted, "there is not even a cynical political motive for caring about the poor."[49]

Harrington brought to the book a surprisingly compelling combination of objective statistical evidence and moral outrage, presented in a narrative voice rich with human concern. He argued that there were serious structural limitations to poor people's ability to help themselves. The poor lived in a "culture of poverty" characterized by hopelessness and "personal chaos," and the contemporary welfare state failed to address this situation. Constructed during the New Deal by and for "the middle third," the country's social service infrastructure did not serve the needs of "the desperate" but instead addressed the problems of "those who are already capable of helping themselves." As a result, "the poor get less out of the welfare state than any group in America." To be effectively helped, they required strategies specifically designed to address the problems of individuals "who are so submerged in their poverty" that the American economic rhetoric of "free choice" simply did not apply to them. Rather than "make them wards of the state," a new, redesigned welfare state had to "help them before they can help themselves."[50]

Harrington believed that the strictures of poverty were so severe that the poor had little ability to better their own situations. As a result, "the fate of the poor," he claimed, "hangs upon the decision of the better-off."[51] To truly address the problem, nothing short of a "crusade against this poverty in our midst" would be sufficient.[52] Such a commitment, argued Harrington, had to be based on the premise that poverty formed an "interdependent system," one that could not be successfully challenged by dealing with "this or that condition" but only by programs that aimed for "the political, economic and social integration of the poor with the rest of society."[53] The plans Harrington called for were ambitious: an initiative to offer "real opportunities" (that is, jobs) to the poor; an urban housing program to abolish slums; an extension of Social Security to cover all citizens; a significant hike in the minimum wage; a "comprehensive medical program, guaranteeing decent care to every American"; and a civil rights bill to mitigate the economic effects of racism. Harrington also made the point that few institutions in the country were capable of mounting a response appropriate to the scope of the problem. Cities, he argued, held a disproportionate share of the poor whereas states were "dominated by conservative rural elements," and private charities lacked the necessary resources. The federal government was the only organization both willing and able to successfully address the problem.[54]

Harrington's urgent call for a massive federal investment in poverty might have seemed quixotic. But apparently, the time was right to raise awareness of this issue. In the *New Yorker* magazine, prominent social critic Dwight Macdonald wrote a lengthy review essay on the subject and offered great praise for *The Other America*, which would eventually sell over a million copies.[55] Moreover, the president of the United States was beginning to manifest an interest in poverty. John F. Kennedy had begun speaking on this topic as the Democratic candidate in the 1960 presidential election, two years before the publication of Harrington's book. By way of criticizing the economic policies of the incumbent Eisenhower administration, Kennedy drew

In April and May 1964, Lyndon Johnson toured several states of rural Appalachia in order to learn firsthand about the problems of rural poverty. Here, he shakes the hand of one resident of the region. In August, Johnson signed the War on Poverty into law. (Courtesy Lyndon Baines Johnson Library and Museum)

attention to the 17 million Americans who went to bed hungry every night by declaring that the "war on poverty and degradation is not yet over." (Nixon, Kennedy's Republican opponent that year, characterized the raising of the issue of poverty on the campaign trail as "grist for the [c]ommunist propaganda mill.")[56]

Once attaining the presidency, Kennedy preferred to address poverty through stimulating overall economic growth rather than by instituting specific programs that targeted the poor. Partially as a result of *The Other America,* though, he became more receptive to the latter approach. Late in 1962, Kennedy asked his staff to prepare reports that would assess the viability of various types of antipoverty programs. He became increasingly interested in implementing these initiatives but had not committed to any particular program by the time of his assassination in November 1963. Lyndon Johnson, Kennedy's vice president and now successor, was eager to reassure the American public that his "accidental" presidency would not symbolize a radical break with Kennedy's. But he also wanted to demonstrate that he was his own man, a liberal in his own right who could serve as more than a water carrier for a beloved martyr. Because the antipoverty plan was not publicly associated with the previous president, adopting it provided Johnson with the perfect opportunity to make both points at once.[57] On March 16, 1964, not quite four months after Kennedy's death, Lyndon Johnson gave a major address in which he declared "a national war on poverty."[58]

In his speech, which echoed points from his State of the Union address two months earlier, Johnson echoed Harrington's themes by using words such as *hopelessness, trapped,* and *despair* to describe the lives of those who lived in poverty. But he also stressed that the purpose of the war on poverty would not be to make the poor "dependent on the generosity of others." Instead, it would be a continuation of the American tradition—exemplified historically by "public education," "land grant colleges," and "encouragement to industry"—of "creating a nation of full and increasing opportunities for all its citizens." From there, Johnson stressed the extent to which the war on poverty would be a boon to those who were *not* impoverished. One of the central themes in this regard was, unsurprisingly, economic growth. Johnson imagined for his listeners a world in which the earnings of the poor would raise the national income, reduce government expenditures, and spur economic and technical innovation. "Giving the opportunity to those who have little," claimed the president, "will enrich the lives of all the rest."[59]

At the end of the speech, Johnson announced that he would submit to Congress a proposal for what would become the Economic Opportunity Act of 1964, which he signed into law five months later. Along with the Civil Rights Act of 1964 and the Voting Rights Act of 1965, the War on Poverty served as the centerpiece of Johnson's domestic reform agenda, which he had named the Great Society. Most of its programs were run through the Office of Economic Opportunity (OEO), which had been created by the Economic Opportunity Act to administer the antipoverty initiatives. Johnson appointed as the director of the OEO Sargent Shriver, the Kennedy in-law who was also serving as the first head of the Peace Corps. The Economic Opportunity Act established the programs—many of which continue to exist today—that constituted the War on Poverty. Among these were Head Start, which provided educational and other services to economically disadvantaged children not yet old enough for formal schooling; Volunteers in Service to America (VISTA), a national service program dedicated to fighting poverty; and the Job Corps, which provided educational and vocational training to young people. Though food stamps (today called the Supplemental Nutrition Assistance Program) dated to the Depression, they were made permanent only in 1964. The Social Security Act of 1965 rounded out the major initiatives of the War on Poverty by adding the important new entitlements Medicare and Medicaid, which provided medical care for the elderly and poor, respectively.

Johnson had always seen the War on Poverty as an extension of one of the basic premises of Cold War liberalism: that economic growth was the best weapon with which to address economic privation. But he also followed the insights of Harrington in recognizing that an increasingly productive economy was of no benefit to those who were not able to participate in it. Consequently, the War on Poverty was designed to aid the poor in developing skills and obtaining resources that would enable them to become part of the economic juggernaut that was the expanding American economy. It was emphatically not supposed to be a vehicle for delivering government handouts. "You tell Shriver," Johnson told an aide in 1964, "no doles. We don't want any doles." The OEO director himself insisted that the War on Poverty "was never a handout program, and we never handed anybody anything for nothing." As historian Irwin Unger wrote in his book on the Great Society, "Most Kennedy-Johnson programs sought to encourage self-reliance. Instead of free gifts, the War on Poverty offered education and training to promote self-help. Johnson and his colleagues never did like 'welfare.'"[60]

Johnson rejected the idea that a citizen's poverty endowed that person with an inalienable right to government largesse, and supporters of the War on Poverty consistently characterized the campaign's intentions as "a hand up, not a handout." This point is not a trivial one, as the idea of a "guaranteed annual income" (or, as it was sometimes proposed, a "negative income tax") was making the rounds in the late 1960s and early 1970s. It attracted serious advocates with many different political orientations, from radical welfare activists Richard Cloward and Frances Fox-Piven to liberal John Kenneth Galbraith to libertarian economist Milton Friedman. In 1972, President Richard Nixon proposed exactly such a plan. Authored primarily by the president's politically iconoclastic aide Daniel Patrick Moynihan, it attracted little congressional support, and Nixon quietly withdrew the plan. But Johnson's message never really took hold among the public, and the War on Poverty became a point of ferocious contention.

There were two primary reasons for this ambivalence. First, many voters simply refused to buy into the distinction that Johnson was making. By the president's own admission, handouts to the poor were completely unacceptable. Why, then, were publicly funded training programs, health insurance, and food assistance not unacceptable as well? Regardless of how the

War on Poverty was defined or, indeed, how it actually operated, many could not or would not view the developing American welfare system as anything other than a government-provided dole. The second reason was endemic to the liberal consensus itself: apologists for the War on Poverty seldom articulated a powerful argument as to why working- and middle-class Americans should shoulder the tax burden required to provide support for those in poverty. Harrington's arguments and Johnson's policies presupposed that the mere existence of poverty in a society as prosperous as the United States justified the attempts to eradicate it. Yet the government could not address poverty, Johnson's protestations to the contrary, without transferring resources from the wealthier citizens to the poorer ones. When voters began to question this project, liberals had few responses available.

When the New Deal constructed the original American welfare state in the 1930s, the Great Depression had sensitized the public to the need for collective action and government assistance. But in the prosperity of the 1960s, the consensus atmosphere in which the liberal project developed became a liability. Liberals had a very difficult time explaining why, when the economy was quite healthy, some Americans should have to pay for others. Without a compelling defense of the Great Society, the War on Poverty became a focal point in a backlash against liberalism itself, altering the terms under which Americans would understand and debate political economy going forward.

The War on Poverty was also intimately intertwined with two other issues that were fracturing the previously stable liberal consensus: the civil rights movement and the war in Vietnam. These conflicts divided liberals from the young activists of the New Left, whose support was essential for Democrats if they were to maintain their hold on power. The war's burgeoning expense curtailed Johnson's ability to fund social programs to the extent he would have preferred. The resulting budgetary constraints limited the effectiveness of the antipoverty initiatives, making the triumphant showcase of the expected social transformation far less likely. In the end, the Vietnam War was the single most important factor in Johnson's growing disfavor with voters. It ultimately cost him the presidency: in 1968, he declined to run for reelection, deciding that he had become too unpopular to have a chance at victory. In retirement, Johnson later mused upon his dilemma, using a characteristically homespun metaphor.

I knew from the start . . . that I was bound to be crucified either way I moved. If I left the woman I really loved—the Great Society—in order to get involved with that bitch of a war on the other side of the world, then I would lose everything at home. All my programs. All my hopes to feed the hungry and shelter the homeless. All my dreams to provide education and medical care to the browns and the blacks and the lame and the poor. But if I left that war and let the [c]ommunists take over South Vietnam, then I would be seen as a coward and my nation would be seen as an appeaser and we would both find it impossible to accomplish anything for anybody anywhere on the entire globe.[61]

Thus, Johnson felt that he had little choice but to augment the American presence in Vietnam; at the same time, he also believed that this decision compromised his ability to bring about the social change that he desired. The two intellectual pillars of the liberal consensus—fighting communism and supporting the welfare state—had come into unavoidable conflict, and the result was the unraveling not only of a widespread political understanding but also of a governing coalition that had been in place since the days of the New Deal.

The civil rights movement was another issue that tore apart the liberal consensus. The divisions that it wrought were not terribly philosophical. Instead, they constituted a straightforward political threat to the primary vehicle for liberal ideas: the Democratic Party. Johnson had championed the Civil Rights Act of 1964 and the Voting Rights Act of 1965, which committed the federal government to ending Jim Crow. His support for these measures alienated many white southern voters, who began to reconsider their traditional antipathy, dating to the antebellum era, toward the Republican Party. Moreover, throughout the "long, hot summers" of the late 1960s, African Americans in dozens of US cities expressed their discontent with racial discrimination and the lack of economic opportunities by rioting, setting fires, and battling the police. The ideals of "black power" were taking hold among a segment of the black population. The adherents of this movement—mostly young men—rejected the goals of racial equality and the tactics of nonviolence that had characterized the civil rights movement. The Black Panthers and other groups insisted upon political self-determination and protection from police violence, and they asserted their right to satisfy these demands themselves.

Viewing all these developments, many moderate northern whites joined their southern segregationist brethren in becoming suspicious of any attempts to help African Americans. Though the categories of poor and

In the 1970s, many Americans came to oppose liberal advances on economic issues, crime, race, gender, and sexuality. Here, demonstrators in 1977 protest in front of the White House against the proposed Equal Rights Amendment (ERA), which would have added a formal commitment to gender equality to the US Constitution. The names "Amy" and "Rosalyn" [*sic*] refer to the daughter and wife, respectively, of President Jimmy Carter. (Courtesy Library of Congress)

black are, of course, distinct ones, to many whites they overlapped enough to justify a backlash against antipoverty programs. In the minds of these voters, summarized Perlstein, "the War on Poverty came out of their hard earned tax dollars—draining money . . . toward ungrateful rioters." Additionally, though Johnson had become indelibly linked with the Vietnam War, his retirement exposed a terrible split in the liberal coalition, as Cold War liberals continued to support the US presence in Vietnam and New Left activists protested the war and encouraged draftees not to enlist. Richard Nixon, the Republican presidential candidate in 1968, encouraged resentments against both African Americans and New Leftists with his pledge to restore "law and order." The implied subtext of this endlessly repeated message was that Democrats favored giving money to destructive, violent, ungrateful (black) criminals and excusing the unforgivably unpatriotic statements of (young, liberal) draft dodgers and flag burners. Nixon, however, implicitly represented the interests of the group he would later dub the "silent majority." Though his views on many issues fit rather comfortably inside the liberal consensus, he gained so much political benefit from dividing one Democratic constituency from another that his campaign of duplicity and "culture war" effectively hid these similarities.[62]

Nixon was elected to the nation's highest office in 1968, and he continued the divisive tactics that allowed him to preside over the effective decline of the liberal consensus. By the early 1970s, wrote Jefferson Cowie in his history of that decade, "the Democratic Party faced a dilemma that it could not solve: finding ways to maintain support within the white blue-collar base that came of age during the New Deal and World War II era, while at the same time servicing the pressing demands for racial and gender equity arising from the sixties."[63] One casualty of the decline of the liberal consensus was support for the War on Poverty or, indeed, for the poor themselves. Beginning in the late 1960s and continuing well into the next decade, motorists began to sport on their cars bumper stickers that read "I Fight Poverty—I *Work*!"

The Philosopher as Liberal

Thus, the most powerful and effective defense of the domestic principles of the liberal consensus, published in 1971, was released into a decidedly inhospitable environment. *A Theory of Justice,* written by philosopher John Rawls, was a 587-page, densely reasoned, meticulously constructed work that painstakingly advanced the thesis that society had to put in place institutions to attend to the needs of the economically disadvantaged. The welfare state, it argued, was neither an act of charity nor a device to ensure economic health or political stability. It was required by the demands of justice.

Since its publication, the influence of *A Theory of Justice* has been immense. It has sold 400,000 copies in English and been translated into twenty-eight languages.[64] Modern Library ranked *A Theory of Justice* 28th in its list of the top 100 nonfiction works of the twentieth century, and today, it is widely recognized as one of the most pivotal works of American philosophy.[65] Among philosophers, the book is credited with single-handedly reviving the formerly moribund discipline of political theory. Yet Rawls's ideas take on a different meaning when placed in the context of midcentury intellectual history, where they appear as very much a product of their time. To look at *A Theory of Justice* alongside its contemporaries outside professional philosophy is to see a book that overlaps significantly in its concerns and views with the works of other liberal consensus thinkers.

John Bordley Rawls was born in Baltimore in 1921 into a wealthy, politically active, liberal family. As a child, he was affected by family tragedies in which his younger brothers, in two separate incidents one year apart, caught diseases from him and died. These were the first of several incidents that impressed upon the young Rawls the extent to which blind luck played a role in determining the prospects of different individuals. Though the significance of chance was impossible to remove, he became determined not to mistake the influence of fate for entitlement. After going through prep school and graduating from Princeton in 1943, Rawls enlisted in the army to fight in World War II. Military service continued to confirm his perception that many privileges—indeed, that of life itself—were distributed on the basis of arbitrary factors. In one case, Rawls and another soldier were needed for two different missions, one of which involved donating blood. Since his blood was of the correct type, Rawls went to the hospital. In executing the second, more dangerous mission, the other soldier died. Stationed in the Pacific, Rawls was spared from having to engage in the hazardous ground invasion of Japan by President Truman's decision to drop atomic bombs on Hiroshima and Nagasaki.[66] Upon his discharge, he returned to Princeton to obtain his doctorate in philosophy.

Rawls received his Ph.D. in 1950. Throughout the fifties, he taught in various capacities at Princeton, Oxford, Cornell, and the Massachusetts Institute of Technology. In 1962, he started at Harvard, occupying the position that he would hold for the rest of his career. Throughout this period, he was considering the ideas that would later form the basis of *A Theory of Justice*. Rawls's preferred method was to work and rework small pieces of his theory, one at a time, in articles published in professional journals. The first of these appeared in 1958,[67] and Rawls was using early drafts of *A Theory of Justice* as a basis for his seminars as far back as 1960. Though the book did not appear until the very late years of the liberal consensus period, its major themes bore the stamp of the era in which they were conceived and generated.[68]

Rawls himself situated *A Theory of Justice* in the discourse of professional philosophy, with seemingly little concern for its implications on public political debate or a wider cultural conversation. In the book's preface, he presented its purpose as a challenge to the predominance of the philosophical school of utilitarianism. This view argued that the appropriate moral framework was one that tallied the level of pleasure and pain experienced by all those who were affected by a given action; the best possible course was the one that brought, in a common formulation often attributed to Jeremy Bentham, "the greatest good to the greatest number." Rawls contended that throughout "much of modern moral philosophy the predominant systematic theory has been some form of utilitarianism." The viewpoint had been interrogated and criticized, Rawls argued, but the opponents of utilitarianism had not been able "to construct a workable and systematic moral conception to oppose it." He presented his theory as such an alternative.[69]

To that end, Rawls would "generalize and carry to a higher order of abstraction the traditional theory of the social contract," in order to present "an alternative account of justice that is superior . . . to the dominant utilitarianism of the tradition."[70] The device of the social contract is most often associated with seventeenth-century English philosophers Thomas Hobbes and John Locke. It is a thought experiment in which the writer constructs a narrative of the events that might have led human beings to create the first government. An understanding of what prompted individual, autonomous beings to give up some of their rights to the collective political entity, it is thought, might illuminate the purpose of government itself, thereby allowing philosophers to determine if specific political arrangements perform that function well or poorly.

Beginning from such a lofty and abstract starting point, *A Theory of Justice* might not be expected to reach conclusions that resonated with public concerns. Yet Rawls narrowed the scope of his book to deal specifically with issues that were relevant to midcentury political economy. As a word, he pointed out, *justice* was used to refer to many different sorts of things: actions, attitudes, laws, and the like. But Rawls restricted his inquiry to what he called *social justice*, whose appropriate focus was "the basic structure of society." With this phrase, Rawls intended to invoke the nexus of institutions that defined a specific community and the various schema by which they could "distribute fundamental rights and duties and determine the division of advantages from social cooperation." Because "the institutions of society favor[ed] certain starting places over others" and consequently rewarded "especially deep inequalities . . . that cannot possibly be justified by an appeal to the notions of merit or desert," they were the point at which ideas of justice were incorporated into a society.[71] He was thus fundamentally interested in what is often called distributive justice, that is, the question of whether and to what extent it is appropriate for specific individuals to be allowed to command certain resources.

Because his readers would have so many preconceived ideas about the nature of the institutions that structured the distribution of goods— frequently submerged values regarding the notions of desert, merit, inheritance, family, property, markets, government, and other related notions— Rawls's goal was to lay bare the intuitions that his readers might have about these matters in a way that allowed them to be examined and, if necessary, revised. To this end, he used the device of the social contract, but he handled it differently than his philosophical forebears. Rather than attempting to relate the likely origins of human communities, Rawls constructed a thought experiment to ask what values people would adopt if they had the opportunity to construct a society. His approach was not an attempt to understand institutions that actually existed as much as an exploration of the characteristics that they should ideally possess.

Rawls's setup, which he called the "original position," involved a group of people pursuing the task of creating the principles of justice that would determine the basic structure of their society. The participants in the original position were all stipulated to be free, equal, and rational; their assent to the principles of justice, in other words, could come only on the basis of publicly identifiable arguments, rather than personal idiosyncrasies. The final condition, however, gave Rawls's thought experiment its most distinctive feature. Those who participated in the original position had no knowledge of their particular situation: "No one knows his place in society, his class position or social status, nor . . . his fortune in the distribution of natural assets and abilities, his intelligence, strength, and the like." These individuals did not even "know their conception of the good or their special psychological propensities."[72] Behind this "veil of ignorance," the natural tendency to game the system to one's personal advantage would be thwarted by the individual's inability to know which particular principles would be of benefit to him or her. Given the complete inability to pursue their particular interests and the possibility that members of the group could even do themselves harm by adopting the wrong principles, the participants in the original position would be left with no option other than to advocate principles of justice that they perceived to be truly fair.

Within the original position, a person who did not know, for example, his or her racial or gender characteristics would not choose to implement a society that placed people in hierarchies based on those attributes. It therefore followed that racism and sexism did not comport with the principles of justice. Such an example illustrates how the original position would justify the moral intuitions of the vast majority of modern readers, but Rawls's device pushed this conclusion much further. Just as one who does not know his or her race would not assent to principles that distributed opportunities on that basis, a person who was unaware of his or her level of, say, talent or intelligence would not agree to the fairness of a principle that allocated resources based on those qualities. The original position, in short, issued a radical challenge to the reader's intuitions about the relationship between desert, merit, and property.

Rawls's basic intuition, which he identified as "one of the fixed points of our considered judgments," was that "no one deserves his place in the distribution of native endowments, any more than one deserves one's initial starting place in society."[73] Though Liberal political thought has long held that the accidents of a person's birth have little bearing on moral issues, Rawls's formulation was new in understanding the category of "accidents of birth" in a much more expansive fashion, so that it included native talents, intelligence, physical characteristics, and the like. From the claim that a person behind the veil of ignorance would not agree to allow any of those factors to determine the distribution of social goods, Rawls inferred the conclusion that "there is no more reason to permit the distribution of income and wealth to be settled by the distribution of natural assets than by historical and social fortune." He even questioned whether the traditionally acclaimed metric of desert in American society—hard work—apportioned goods in a truly just fashion: "The extent to which natural capacities develop and reach fruition is affected by all kinds of social conditions and class attitudes. Even the willingness to make an effort, to try, and so to be deserving in the ordinary sense is itself dependent upon happy family and social circumstances."[74] A person who did not know if he or she came from such a background would likely be unwilling to apportion social goods on the basis of those characteristics.

This was not to claim, however, that the function of society was to remedy the unfairness that resulted from the vicissitudes of nature. "The natural distribution," wrote Rawls, "is neither just nor unjust; nor is it unjust that people are born into society at some particular position." Such "natural facts" were outside of the realm of justice. But "the way that society deals with these facts" was central to the issue. "Aristocratic and caste societies" allowed "the arbitrariness found in nature" to determine their basic structure. The injustice of these arrangements did not stem from nature itself but from the society's decision to use the capricious natural distribution of assets to determine the social order. Though nothing could be done about the arbitrary and amoral quality of nature, the social system was "not an unchangeable order beyond human control." It was instead "a pattern of human action" that was consequently subject to the demands—and the judgments—of justice.[75]

Rawls's extreme conception of desert might have seemed to suggest that the appropriate standard of justice was one in which all people had equal access to social goods. If justice demanded complete socioeconomic equality, then the welfare state advocated by postwar liberals would not satisfy its terms. Most likely, what would be necessary to meet such a stringent requirement would be a widespread redistribution of resources and the nationalization of private property—in other words, some form of socialism. But Rawls rejected equality as the correct principle of distributive justice, implicitly refusing to cede to socialists the moral high ground. He did not, however, reject socialism per se. Rawls advocated market mechanisms throughout *A Theory of Justice,* but he repeatedly pointed out that this arrangement neither required nor precluded the setting of prices by government bureaucracy or the government ownership of firms. The fact that he rejected equality as a political ideal and the reasons he gave for taking this position provided perhaps the best illustration of the extent to which *A Theory of Justice* served as an exemplar of the liberal consensus. The denizens of the original position would reject the principle of equality for a reason that was derived from that most central of consensus fixations: economic growth.

Rawls believed that equality would be the starting point for the discussions that would take place among the inhabitants of the original position. Since it was "not reasonable" for any inhabitant of the original position to expect a greater than equal share of social goods and since it was "not rational" for that person to accept a less-than-equal share, "the sensible thing for him to do" would be to propose the principle of a completely equal distribution of shares. "Indeed, this principle is so obvious," declared Rawls, "that we would expect it to occur to anyone immediately." Equality was the first principle that the group would consider, but it was not the last. The people in the original position were all defined as rational and self-interested individuals. Thus, in adopting the principles of justice, their concerns would be only with the amount of resources that they themselves were able to possess. They would not base their approval on the advantages allotted to others or, in what amounts to the same thing, their own share or ratio of holdings in comparison to the total. So, if given a choice between an equal share that netted a smaller amount of goods and a smaller ratio that allowed for a larger one, an individual situated in the original position would choose the latter. If "inequalities in the basic structure" could "work to make everyone better off in comparison with the benchmark of initial equality," then, Rawls argued, those in the original position would allow them.[76]

Rawls referred to this idea as the "difference principle." According to its tenets, justice did not demand economic equality, but not all inequalities were allowed. Arrangements that deviated from equality had to work to the benefit of the person who had fewer advantages. The difference principle represented the point of departure for Rawls's theory, the place where his articulation of the demands of justice introduced a completely new idea into political theory. Though novel from the standpoint of professional philosophy, it offered what amounted to a more rigorous and demanding vision of the ideas in common currency in the larger political and intellectual culture of the era. Most significantly, this idea powerfully expressed the liberal intuition that there was a relationship between economic growth and greater public care of the less fortunate.

Rawls's particular angle on this point stemmed from his commitment to the difference principle. At first glance, it might seem mathematically impossible for an inequality to leave both parties affected by it better off than they were before. But since any given inequality obviously benefited the person who profited from it, the only way that it could satisfy the difference principle—that is, that it could also work to the advantage of the person who got the worst of the deal—would be if the total stock of goods increased as the result of the inequality itself. Such an expansion in the production of goods was the very definition of economic growth. Though the difference principle legitimized other sorts of inequalities, its justification of economic stratification on the basis of economic growth represented the paradigmatic case of its application. In a specific example, Rawls considered the fact that "those starting out as members of the entrepreneurial class in [a] property-owning democracy have better prospects . . . than those who begin in the class of unskilled laborers." It seemed unlikely that those in the original position would approve of such a disparity. But the difference principle suggested that such an "inequality in expectation" could be considered just if "lowering it would make the working class even worse off." In this example, the better prospects for the entrepreneur, in increasing innovation and productivity, might very well create jobs for the working class, whose members would be better off than if those jobs did not exist. In such a scenario, the unequal privileges of the entrepreneurial class would be just.[77]

A Theory of Justice can only be described as a careful work. In his dozens of articles, Rawls had worked out the most fruitful formulations of his theory, and the book showcased his meticulous answering of objections and criticisms. Once describing his initial intuitions, Rawls clarified and justified them extensively before formally rolling them out as actual positions. Thus it is that the final version of his modestly named "two principles of justice" did not appear in *A Theory of Justice* until the book's forty-seventh section. The first of these stated that every person had an "equal right" to what Rawls called the "basic liberties," which were the sorts of freedoms that were enshrined in the US Bill of Rights: "political liberty . . . together with freedom of speech and assembly; liberty of conscience and freedom of thought; freedom of the person along with the right to hold (personal) property; and freedom from arbitrary arrest and seizure." These freedoms took precedence over the social goods covered by the second principle of justice, so that "liberty can be restricted only for the sake of liberty," not for any social or economic concerns. The second principle, despite its subordinate status, expressed the most pivotal idea of the book. Though it partook of several conditions and clauses, its central section stated that "social and economic inequalities are to be arranged so that they are . . . to the greatest benefit of the least advantaged . . . and attached to offices and positions open to all."[78] A truly just society, then, would not ban social and economic inequality. It would only allow, however, certain specifically defined inequalities: those that benefited the people on the bottom of the social hierarchy.

Though he meticulously derived, clearly stated, and vigorously defended the two principles, Rawls devoted little attention to their specific implications regarding real-world political arrangements or policy prescriptions. In this one area, an already lengthy and detailed book might have benefited from a bit more exposition. For it would seem, in general, unlikely that a tight relationship would hold between a given inequality and the disadvantaged people who might benefit from it at any specific time. To take Rawls's example of the entrepreneur and the unskilled workers, it would be unreasonable to expect that putting in place a system that rewarded successful entrepreneurialism would necessarily provide every unemployed person with a job. Yet refusing to allow an inequality that would benefit a large number—even a great majority—of people, on the grounds that it would not benefit every single person so affected, amounts to throwing the baby out with the bathwater. But there is another way to address this problem beyond simply disallowing the inequality: if economic growth did not benefit every single member of society directly, the government could install mechanisms to ensure that it did so indirectly. It could, for instance, tax the economic "winners" in order to put in place payments and programs that would benefit the "losers." Consequently, Rawls argued that justice required, among other things, a system of public schooling; some form of public health care; and a version of unemployment compensation or, perhaps as an administrative substitute for many specific plans, "a graded income supplement (a so-called negative income tax)."[79] Using this approach, many inequalities that might not otherwise satisfy the second principle could be brought into compliance with it.

As Rawls concluded, what justice demanded, in the end, was the welfare state: a more developed version of the social order implied by the programs of the New Deal and the Great Society. Though writers such as Galbraith and Harrington argued that an economically prosperous nation could afford to eliminate the poverty in its midst, Rawls took the much stronger position that failing to do so left that society guilty of injustice. Such an argument, of course, ran afoul of the long-standing American veneration of the institution of private property. One of the primary tasks of *A Theory of Justice* was to repudiate what Rawls called the "natural inclination" to believe "that those better situated deserve their greater advantages whether or not they are to the benefit of others." He vigorously contested this libertarian intuition, on the basis of a position that challenged many traditional values: that the holdings of the well-off were not, in any absolute sense, truly "theirs" in the first place.[80]

According to Rawls, property was an institution that, like any other, was mediated by social arrangements. "It is perfectly true," he noted, "that given a just system of cooperation as a scheme of public rules and the expectations set up by it, those who . . . have done what the system announces that it will reward are entitled to their advantages." Natural intelligence, for instance, only could bring a person social and economic advantages, including property, if that person lived in a society that valued this quality and had decided to distribute social and economic goods in accordance with its possession. If that society allotted such things along different axes—say, those of athletic ability or loyalty to the nation's political leaders—very different people would occupy the more advantageous positions. Therefore, once a society established the principles by which people would hold social and economic advantages, the individuals who succeeded according to these rules were entitled to the spoils of their accomplishments. But those who contested the legitimacy of the welfare state usually offered a different argument, asserting that the society was not entitled to redistribute the holdings of the more advantaged to those who were not as well off. This claim rested on an implicit premise that the holdings to which a person was entitled were *not* dependent upon the social arrangement—that this individual went out and independently claimed a certain advantage for him- or herself before the state snatched it away. Such a claim Rawls would not grant, as any "scheme of desert presupposes the existence of the cooperative scheme." Property was a social institution, and therefore, it could not exist without a society to bring it into being. Social institutions determined the principles by which advantages would be distributed and held, so the only limitations on a society's ability to define or restrict the nature of property were those imposed by justice itself. Society could—indeed, it had to, according to Rawls—define property in such a way that contributing some of it to improve the lot of the less fortunate was a condition of being allowed to possess it in the first place.[81]

A Theory of Justice and the Liberal Consensus

In the original *New York Times* review of *A Theory of Justice*, philosopher Marshall Cohen argued that the work's "deep and elegant" arguments would "earn for Rawls's book the status of a classic."[82] The same newspaper later selected the book as one of five significant books of 1972. Though published in 1971, *A Theory of Justice* was granted entrance into the category because "it was not widely reviewed" until the later year "because critics needed time to get a grip on its complexities." In their description of the work, the editors concentrated on philosophical concepts such as utilitarianism and the social contract, but they boldly anticipated that the book's "political implications may change our lives."[83] Of the predictions in the two articles—that *A Theory of Justice* would become a classic and that it would significantly affect public debate—the first has come to pass, but the second has not. The influence of *A Theory of Justice* on the academic pursuits of philosophy, political science, and jurisprudence has been and continues to be unquestionably vast. Yet the book's ability to shift the terms of popular political discourse has been far more measured.

Rawls himself was surely not surprised by these developments. Shortly after the publication of *A Theory of Justice*, he declared himself "pessimistic of philosophy's influence" and expressed doubt that "views of this kind can have an effect."[84] Part of the book's inability to cross into public political discourse can no doubt be attributed to its length, density, and preoccupation with narrowly philosophical themes. But the book was widely reviewed and has sold an incredible number of copies for an academic work; the reason for its lack of mainstream influence would appear to lie elsewhere. The most likely culprit was pointed out by British journalist Ben Rogers, who noted in 1999 the great irony that "Rawls's successful revitalization of liberalism in political theory coincided with the decline of liberalism as a political movement in America."[85]

In emphasizing the significance of economic growth for fair economic distribution, rejecting equality as the appropriate standard of justice, and arguing for the necessity of the welfare state, *A Theory of Justice* expressed the concerns of the period in which it was composed. Its strong formulations and rigorous argumentation positioned the book as, in many ways, the culmination of this tradition's approach to domestic policy. But Rawls's magnum opus did not appear until the disintegration of the liberal consensus was well under way. During the most opportune moment for consensus thinkers to have aggressively developed their ideas on political economy— the two decades immediately following World War II—they had failed to do so. By the time such a statement arrived, the nation's political and intellectual tide was turning toward conservatism.

Chapter Six

Taxes

As he prepared to accept the Republican nomination for president in 1988, George H. W. Bush faced a number of challenges. Serving at the time as vice president under Ronald Reagan, he sought to distance himself from the numerous scandals that plagued the administration in its final year; at the same time, he needed to play up his association with the president in order to court those Republicans who doubted his conservative bona fides. Additionally, many voters found that Bush's soft-spoken demeanor and preppy New England background overshadowed his leadership of the Central Intelligence Agency and his service as a fighter pilot in World War II. As a result, he fought the characterization that he was a "wimp" who was unwilling to take tough stands in foreign policy. He also suffered from a widespread perception that he lacked what Bush himself called "the vision thing": an overarching philosophy of government to which voters could relate. Finally, he harmed himself in the run-up to his acceptance speech. His first "presidential" decision, the choice of Indiana senator Dan Quayle as his running mate, had backfired badly amid questions about Quayle's maturity and intelligence.

As he stepped to the podium at the nationally televised Republican convention in New Orleans, then, Bush had to deliver a speech that would introduce him to the American people in his own right, establish for himself a strong persona, and reassure far right Republicans that he would represent their priorities. In his remarks, the nominee emphasized the Reagan economic record, reminding his audience that "economic growth is the key to our endeavors." Citing the current administration's tremendous progress in cutting inflation, interest rates, and unemployment, Bush asked the voters who were having to "change horses in midstream" whether it did not "make sense to switch to the [horse] who's going the same way?" He also reassured voters that he did, in fact, profess a philosophy: that the United States could be a "kinder, gentler nation" in which the individual, the community, and the government could "each [do] only what it does well, and no more." For Bush, the United States was "a nation of communities . . . a brilliant diversity spread like stars, like a thousand points of light in a broad and peaceful sky."

Yet the most memorable remark that night concerned what had arguably become the right-leaning voter's most important issue—taxes. No matter who was elected, Bush argued, the Democratic Congress would pressure the new president to increase taxes. It would take someone strong, he implied, to toe the line. Bush's speechwriters had crafted an applause line for him that was guaranteed to make this point. "The Congress," he predicted, "will push me to raise taxes and I'll say no. And they'll push and I'll say no. And they'll push again and I'll say to them, 'Read my lips: no new taxes!'"[1]

One of Bush's own economic advisers had feared that this part of the speech would box in the candidate once elected; he deemed the pledge "stupid and irresponsible."[2] But its rhetorical power proved impossible to resist. The phrase *read my lips* quickly became the most memorable sound bite of a very successful speech, and the promise to hold the line on taxes assumed a central role in the subsequent campaign. After winning the election and taking office, however, President Bush had a difficult time keeping his pledge. The actual events played out in a way that was remarkably similar to the scenario that Bush had described in his speech. Congress was controlled by Democrats, and many in both parties were concerned about the federal deficits that were among Reagan's less desirable legacies. At the same time, some conservative Republican legislators would not stand for any tax increases at all. After several rounds of negotiations, which included a short shutdown of the federal government when its funds ran out, the president and Congress were able to agree on a budget that included a 3.5 percent increase in the upper brackets of the income tax.

Many Americans were up in arms at Bush's violation of the most prominent of his campaign promises, and their anger played a major role in the next presidential election. Bush's opponent, Arkansas governor Bill Clinton, touted his record on lowering taxes in his home state and ran a television ad featuring the "read my lips" clip from the convention. When protest candidate Pat Buchanan garnered a surprising 34 percent of the vote against the president in the New Hampshire Republican primary, the conservative *Manchester Union Leader* ran a headline stating READ OUR LIPS.[3] The *National Review,* standard-bearer of the right, refused to endorse Bush for the Republican nomination. His conservative base having abandoned him, he lost his office in the 1992 election.

Though other factors figured in Bush's defeat, the fact that a relatively small raise in taxes could play such a significant role in unseating a president indicated that the primary ideas that animated the relationship between government and the economy had changed since the decline of the liberal consensus. Most important in this regard were two developments. The first was that by the late twentieth century, conservatism had replaced liberalism as the dominant public philosophy of American political economy. The second was that conservatism itself had taken on new priorities. Throughout much of the twentieth century, this political orientation had served as a somewhat staid traditionalism whose major economic platform was a firm and unwavering commitment to a balanced federal budget. Long before Bush's 1992 defeat, however, it had become clear that taxes occupied the central spot in the universe of economic conservatism.

This shift in conservative thinking can be traced with some specificity to the decade of the 1970s, the most economically tumultuous since the 1930s. The primary economic issue in the later period was not depression, though, but inflation. The liberal, Keynesian programs that had defined orthodoxy in political economy for some forty years were of little use against this new problem. Conservatives pressed for new policies that addressed the specific economic issues of the day, and at the forefront of their approach was an intellectual and political movement known as supply-side economics. This school of thinking called for, above all, a cut in marginal income tax rates, and its message quickly caught on with both politicians and the broader electorate. Within a short period of time, hostility to taxation had taken a place at the center of economic conservatism. Yet the economic circumstances to which supply-side economics had responded were specific to the 1970s and unlikely to repeat themselves. By generalizing the antitax message into an ideological crusade, the conservative movement transformed a specific economic prescription into an overarching theory of government.

The "Bookish" Roots of Modern Conservatism

In one form or another, American conservatism[4] is at least as old as the republic itself. In opposing the US Constitution, Patrick Henry could have spoken for many modern-day conservatives when he argued that the purpose of government was not to increase trade or to create a mighty empire. Instead, he declared, a good citizen need only "inquire . . . how your liberties can be secured; for liberty ought to be the direct end of your [g]overnment."[5] In this sense, political conservatism, like its liberal counterpart, can be described as a specific interpretation of philosophical Liberalism, one that sees the state less as a guarantor of freedom than as the most pressing threat to it.[6]

Economically speaking, the particularly modern strain of conservative thinking arose as a response to the programs of Franklin Roosevelt. Initially, businesspeople who perceived the New Deal as a threat to free enterprise itself founded several different educational and activist organizations to warn against this growing danger.[7] But even with this activism in the United States, the most influential early statement of conservative economic concerns came from England. Titled *The Road to Serfdom* and published in 1944, the book was an almost immediate success. Its author was Friedrich von Hayek, a Viennese economist who had been teaching at the London School of Economics. Concerned about the developments in Germany and his native Austria, Hayek became a British citizen in 1938. Despite its author's Austrian background and British perspective, *The Road to Serfdom* strongly resonated with Americans, particularly those with conservative leanings who may have felt out of step with the times. In a book review in the *New York Times,* conservative journalist and movement builder Henry Hazlitt called it "one of the most important books of our generation." *Reader's Digest* excerpted *The Road to Serfdom,* and the University of Chicago Press ordered a print run of 1 million copies.[8]

Hayek wrote many technical works on economics, winning the Nobel Prize in that field in 1974. But *The Road to Serfdom* was addressed to a wide audience, and its message was straightforward and accessible. The book's central argument was that the emerging intellectual presumptions of the liberal consensus threatened economic freedom. Since political liberty depended upon the economic variety, the limitations imposed by the welfare state would lead, in time, to dangerous political consequences. By the time the citizens of the liberal democracies realized that their liberties had been limited, argued Hayek, it would be too late to get them back.

The concern he expressed was that these countries had, gradually and with good intentions, abandoned their commitment to economic freedom. The Western nations, he wrote, "[had] progressively abandoned that freedom in economic affairs without which personal and political freedom has never existed in the past."⁹ What had threatened this liberty was the drive toward socialism, and with this term, Hayek meant something quite specific. In a completely free economy, there would be no way to dictate in advance what the allocation of resources would be. Jobs, money, education, subsistence goods such as food and shelter, and everything else would be distributed according to the aggregated decisions of people in the market. An attempt to shift this distribution in the name of some other goal would require what Hayek broadly referred to as "economic planning": dictating prices, setting wages, rationing goods, and so forth.

The form of organization that Hayek believed maximized freedom was competition. He defined economic Liberalism as the position that "where effective competition can be created, it is a better way of guiding individual efforts than any other." It differed, he claimed, from laissez-faire in that it did not insist that competition was always the best method. Hayek emphasized that competition was dependent upon "a carefully thought-out legal framework," and he advised that "we must resort to other methods of guiding economic activity" when conditions rendered it "impossible . . . to make competition effective." Nor did he argue that no restrictions on competition were ever legitimate.¹⁰ Those that put in place a system that was superior to competition, as in the case of regulations against monopoly, were acceptable, as were those that furthered public goals by imposing equal limitations on all competitors. Hayek therefore did not oppose regulations on such things as working hours or dangerous workplace conditions or even "an extensive system of social services." The danger to liberty arose, he argued, only when competition was "supplanted by inferior methods of coordinating individual efforts."¹¹

Despite these caveats, however, Hayek was adamant on his central points: planning compromised economic freedom, and political liberty was impossible without economic liberty. As a result, planning led inexorably to totalitarianism. In this syllogistic framework, the significant premise was the second one. Why could people not exercise their freedom to vote, assemble, petition their government, and so on if wages, for example, or prices were set by the government? Hayek's response essentially defined the modern conservative position on the issue of government involvement in the economy. He believed that those who supported planning often based that support on the idea that few, if any, economic freedoms were as central as political liberties. "Most planners," he stated, "have little doubt that a directed economy must be run on more or less dictatorial lines. . . . The consolation our planners offer us is that the authoritarian direction will apply 'only' to economic matters." Thus, the argument went, restricting the first to maximize the second would be justified, if not required, in an egalitarian society. "By giving up freedom in what are, or ought to be, the less important aspects of our lives," the "planners" argued, "we shall obtain greater freedom in the pursuit of higher values."[12] Hayek responded that the distinction between the two types of freedom was not nearly as clear-cut as supporters of planning would have it. In one powerful example, he pointed out that it was unclear how "the freedom of the press is to be safeguarded when the supply of paper and all the channels of distribution are controlled by the planning authority."[13] Since it was impossible to say in advance which products and industries could play such a significant political role, ceding control of the economy to the government was allowing it control over all potential avenues of political expression.

The Road to Serfdom came to serve as a blueprint for the economic concerns of the conservative movement. Written in an abstract, philosophical style, the book contained few references to the particular programs or policies of any specific nation (with the exception of Nazi Germany, the subject of an entire chapter), which gave it an ageless quality, seemingly relevant to the issues of any particular time or place. Additionally, it touched on most of the themes that conservatives would take up later in the century. Few major positions regarding the interplay between the government and the economy were not prefigured in The Road to Serfdom.

But there was one exception to this trend, and it was a significant one. Hayek's passionate warning against government intrusion into the personal sphere evinced little to no concern over taxes. It is difficult to imagine a more overt case of interference with economic liberty than the government confiscating its citizens' earnings. Moreover, by contemporary American standards, taxes in the wartime 1940s were incredibly high: in the year in which The Road to Serfdom was published, the top marginal US income tax rate was 94 percent.[14] Despite this, there was no significant discussion concerning a limitation on taxes in Hayek's Road to Serfdom. The perception of taxation as inherently threatening to liberty was, quite simply, not a part of the foundational conservative worldview.

After Hayek's book came out, the conservative movement continued to grow and develop. Conservative writers issued a host of important books in the forties and fifties,[15] and William F. Buckley founded the movement's flagship magazine, National Review, in 1955. Perhaps the most popular figure in conservatism during this period was the novelist Ayn Rand. Her relationship with the growing movement, however, was a difficult one. Her 1943 novel, *The Fountainhead,* had generated an intense following, but Rand never embraced a movement that she found to be compromised and insufficiently radical. At the same time, her atheism, ideological intransigence, and self-aggrandizing personal prickliness did not endear her to many establishment conservatives. The 1957 publication of *Atlas Shrugged,* Rand's magnum opus, only continued this trend, as Buckley's *National Review* took the lead in "writing out" Rand from the movement.[16]

Within a few years, another work would articulate similar themes while avoiding the personal baggage associated with Rand herself. Its author, Milton Friedman, was an academically credentialed and highly respected libertarian economist at the University of Chicago. The book bore the simple title *Capitalism and Freedom,* and it was published in 1962. It eventually sold over a half million copies and became a touchstone for the ever-growing conservative movement.[17] In time, Friedman would become the best-known economist in the country, circulating his ideas in a *Newsweek* column and winning the Nobel Prize in 1976.

The book's first two chapters were broad and philosophical in nature, along the lines of *The Road to Serfdom.* Indeed, its points mainly reiterated arguments that Hayek had offered nearly twenty years before. In the first chapter, Friedman more forcefully echoed the point that there could be no distinction between economic and political freedom. The view that the two could be distinguished from one another and that political liberty could be guaranteed in a society that lacked economic freedom was a "delusion." He argued that given the "intimate connection between economics and politics—only certain combinations of political and economic arrangements are possible." Specifically, "a society that is socialist cannot also be democratic, in the sense of guaranteeing individual freedoms."[18] In an economy that was organized around "co-ordination through voluntary co-operation"—in other words, a capitalist one—"both parties to an economic transaction benefit from it."[19] Since the essential nature of government required compulsion, a just society would minimize the public sphere and maximize that of the market.

The condition of market freedom only held, Friedman continued, if economic actors were truly free in their ability to enter (or refrain from entering) any given exchange and when they were fully and correctly informed as to the terms of the deal. Government was necessary to establish these preconditions and ensure that they continued to be met. There were a few other functions that the market could not provide, and Friedman offered a short list of the resulting legitimate functions of government. Government should function as the "rule maker and umpire" in such matters as balancing competing liberties, defining property rights, and coining money. It should take appropriate action to deal with those situations that the market system could not solve: monopoly, for example, and what Friedman called "neighborhood effects."[20] It should ensure the safety and welfare of those, such as children and the mentally ill, who were not considered responsible for their own well-being.[21]

But the bulk of *Capitalism and Freedom* differed from *The Road to Serfdom* in offering specific injunctions about what government should *not* do, and many of these examples were rooted in American history and politics. Furthermore, Friedman's positions on these points were fairly radical, urging that the government cease performing functions that many would have considered legitimate and even routine. A list at the end of the second chapter not only mentioned somewhat predictable grievances with agricultural subsidies and tariffs but also included a more radical questioning of, among other things, the minimum wage, Social Security, public housing, military conscription, medical licensing, the monopoly enjoyed by the post office, and national parks.[22]

Capitalism and Freedom was also noteworthy for a subject to which it paid little attention: taxation. Though he devoted a bit more attention to the subject than did Hayek in *The Road to Serfdom,* Friedman said little about the onerous burden of the government's confiscation of income. His main proposal in this area—to eliminate the graduated income tax in favor of a flat tax with fewer loopholes—took up only a few pages. Again, the latter-day conservative fixation on taxes as a symptom of government tyranny was not a key feature in the seminal intellectual formulations of the movement.[23]

Within a year, Friedman had written another significant book. Along with coauthor Anna Schwartz, he published a groundbreaking work of economic history entitled *A Monetary History of the United States.* Released in 1963, it became one of the foundational texts of the economic philosophy of monetarism. Though Friedman had consistently argued that the government was far too involved in economic affairs, monetarism concentrated on one of the few economic tasks for which he believed that the government *did* bear responsibility—preserving the value of the currency that it issued. The book, which essentially traced the history of "the stock of money in the United States," began with the postbellum greenback era and continued through the reestablishment of the gold standard and the 1913 establishment of the Federal Reserve. Friedman and Schwartz found a strong correlation between the ups and downs of the business cycle and the level of stability in

the money supply: when the amount of money grew steadily and pre-
dictably, they argued, prices and wages behaved in a much more manage-
able fashion.

This understanding led the authors to a strong critique of the Federal
Reserve System. "The blind, undesigned, and quasi-automatic working of
the gold standard," they wrote, "turned out to produce a greater measure
of predictability and regularity—perhaps because its discipline was impersonal and inescapable—than did deliberate and conscious control exercised
within institutional arrangements intended to promote monetary stability."[24]
The book's most influential conclusion applied this reasoning to the Great
Depression. The cause of this catastrophic and complex event had long been
a subject of debate, and most of Keynes's influential analysis had turned on
the observation that the essence of the economic problem had been a decline
in consumer demand. Friedman and Schwartz offered an alternative analysis. Consistently throughout the stock market and banking crises from 1929
to 1933, they argued, the Federal Reserve had tightened the money supply
when it should have done just the opposite. The subsequent monetary contraction was therefore a cause, rather than a result, of the Depression. Even
more important, the Depression could have been avoided with wiser government policy: "Different and feasible actions by the monetary authorities
could have prevented the decline in the stock of money." Such actions would
have "eased the banking difficulties appreciably," leading to a reduction in
"the contraction's severity and almost as certainly its duration."[25]

Despite the fact that the narrative of *A Monetary History of the United
States* ended in 1960, it would remain the foundational text of monetarism.
Though a historical work rather than a theoretical one, its policy implications were evident. From the premise that the tight money of the Fed caused
the Great Depression came the conclusion that governments and their central banks should be concentrating on the money supply and nothing else.
Providing the appropriate amount of circulating currency was the only
macroeconomic function that governments could successfully perform.
Indeed, by 1970, Friedman was summarizing his rather technical theory with
the catchy maxim that "inflation is always and everywhere a monetary phenomenon." In the end, his philosophy boiled down to, in the case of the
United States, one recommendation: establishing a "quasi-automatic monetary policy under which the quantity of money would grow at a steady rate
of 4 or 5 per cent per year, month-in, month-out."[26] Such a policy, argued
Friedman, would result in a consistent growth in the money supply under
stable and predictable conditions.

In assigning the government only one significant economic task and then limiting even that responsibility to the application of a fairly rigid formula, Friedman's monetarism was quite compatible with, though logically distinct from, his libertarianism. And since monetarism focused its prescriptions entirely on monetary policy, it took no particular stance on taxes. Hayek and Friedman were among the most significant intellectual progenitors of the late twentieth-century libertarian conservative project, yet neither of these prominent thinkers expressed a great concern for the burdens of taxation in their most influential works. For taxation to become a central theme in the modern movement, conservatism first had to move from the intellectual arena to the political one. This began to happen slowly in the 1960s.

Conservative Political Successes

Though the postwar Republican Party included politicians and voters of all stripes, its dominant voice in the postwar period was a moderate or even liberal one. Responding to the tenor of the age, many Republicans believed that the party needed to tack to the left in order to remain competitive. Additionally, most of the party's leaders were themselves moderate. The most powerful conservative Republican, Senator Robert A. Taft, died in 1953. Throughout most of the fifties and sixties, the leading Republicans were moderates such as Dwight Eisenhower, Thomas E. Dewey, and Nelson Rockefeller. They accepted the New Deal as a permanent part of the American landscape, supported the "containment" policies of the Truman Doctrine in the Cold War, and opposed (to varying degrees) racial segregation.

The conservative movement's first flirtation with electoral success at the national level came when Senator Barry Goldwater of Arizona captured the Republican nomination for president in 1964. A half-Jewish westerner who often flew himself to campaign events in his own private plane, Goldwater was not the era's typical Republican. His personal style certainly set him apart from the mainstream, but even more significant was his unapologetic conservatism. In an era of bipartisan comity, Goldwater frequently attacked both parties by criticizing his fellow Republicans for advocating a "dime store New Deal."[27] He joined the Senate in 1952 after winning the narrowest of victories in what was then solidly Democratic Arizona. Initially, Goldwater garnered little attention in Washington. But after gaining some notoriety for defending Joseph McCarthy and opposing labor unions, he began getting national notice after winning reelection in 1958. When his friends and supporters began to stealthily pave the way for a presidential run in 1960, they suggested that Goldwater write a campaign manifesto. The book that resulted, titled *The Conscience of a Conservative*, surprised everyone by debuting at number fourteen on the *New York Times* best seller list. By the time of the November presidential election (in which Goldwater was not a candidate), 500,000 copies of the book were in print.[28]

The Conscience of a Conservative made Goldwater a household name. Like *The Road to Serfdom* or *Capitalism and Freedom*, the book offered an unapologetic defense of conservative themes. Goldwater was a politician seeking votes, however, rather than an academic thinker, and his book was neither alarmist nor quixotic. Instead, it offered a passionate appeal for his idea that "America is fundamentally a [c]onservative nation," one whose "principles are derived" not from the influence of some momentarily popular political approach but "from the nature of man, and the truths that God has revealed about his creation."[29] Much of the book expressed ideas that were outside the mainstream political thought of the era. But for many Americans, Goldwater's book "domesticated," in the words of Rick Perlstein, ideas that had theretofore appeared "radical."[30]

The Conscience of a Conservative began with an appeal to individual liberty and the notion of governmental limits that would have been familiar to readers of Hayek or Friedman. "The *legitimate* functions of government," Goldwater wrote, "are actually conducive to freedom." Yet the state had to be restricted only to those specific tasks: "[m]aintaining internal order, keeping foes at bay, administering justice, [and] removing obstacles to the free interchange of goods."[31] The purpose of the US Constitution, on this interpretation, was to restrain the natural tendency of government to expand its powers. Goldwater argued that the size, scope, intrusiveness, and expense of the federal government were at unacceptably high levels.[32] As a result, he predicted, the conservative ascendance was imminent. "The turn will come," he wrote, "when we entrust the conduct of our affairs to men who understand that their first duty as public officials is to divest themselves of the power they have been given." Those politicians would proclaim on the stump that they wished to reduce the size of government; they would promise not "to promote welfare" but "to extend freedom."[33]

The rest of the book applied Goldwater's conservative principles to the specific issues of the day. On the controversial subject of racial segregation, he argued that the only role the federal government should play would be that of guaranteeing the right to vote, as there was no constitutional guarantee of education or other civil rights.[34] Consistent with his expressed principles, Senator Goldwater would later vote against the landmark Civil Rights Act when it came before Congress in 1964. With regard to the Cold War, Goldwater criticized the nation's current posture, which, he claimed, was oriented toward peaceful coexistence with the Soviet Union. "We do not want the peace of surrender," he asserted, but one "in which freedom and justice will prevail. . . . A tolerable peace, in other words, must *follow* victory over [c]ommunism."[35] Goldwater's positions on the Cold War provided the strongest example of where he was out of step with most of the country: though conservatives had yearned to hear a politician who spoke such words, the senator's policy prescriptions and analyses ran afoul of nearly every conventional belief and practice in postwar America.

The extreme conservatism of Goldwater's positions on civil rights and the Cold War were matched by his treatment of the federal presence in the economy. He consistently claimed that the government intruded inappropriately into the market. An entire chapter of *The Conscience of a Conservative,* for example, was devoted to farm policy, with Goldwater advocating "prompt and final termination of the farm subsidy program."[36] On labor issues, his statement was not quite so absolute. Goldwater did not oppose trade unionism per se, but he expressed concern that labor organizations had come to exercise power that was inconsistent with their core mission. A union, "kept within its proper and natural bounds . . . *can* be an instrument for achieving economic justice for the working man," he observed, and it could deter workers from being attracted to socialism. Yet these functions were undermined the moment that unions stepped beyond their purview by representing workers who had not joined the organization, engaging in political campaigns, or negotiating with entire industries rather than individual companies.[37] He consequently supported right-to-work laws, a ban on union (and corporate) spending on political campaigns, and the application of antitrust laws to labor unions.

The strongest attack on the economic policies of the liberal consensus involved Goldwater's attitude toward the welfare state. He viewed what he called "welfarism" as an approach used by the "collectivists," a nebulously defined group, to bring about American socialism. After the decline of Marxism in the United States and the concomitant inability of the collectivists to realize their goal of having the state take over the economy, they turned to different tactics. These were based on the realization that "the individual can be put at the mercy of the [s]tate" by means other than making that person dependent on it for a job. Just as effective was the tactic of "divesting him of the means to provide for his personal needs and . . . giving the [s]tate the responsibility of caring for those needs from cradle to grave." Moreover, this strategy of converting Americans to socialism had a big advantage over previous incarnations. "Welfarism is much more compatible with the political processes of a democratic society," Goldwater stated. Because its negatives were "veiled" and frequently "postponed," the people would only "grumble" a bit "about excessive government spending," rather than mounting the full-scale resistance that such a development merited.[38]

Goldwater's directly stated concern that the welfare state threatened core American values hinted at the distance the American conservative movement would later travel in its economic priorities. One prominent worry of latter-day conservatives—that the welfare state would require an increase in taxes on those who were not recipients of government largesse—was not paramount among Goldwater's concerns. "Fiscal conservatives then believed," summarized historian Geoffrey Kabaservice, "that while lower taxes were desirable, to cut taxes at a time when the federal government was running a deficit would spur inflation and drown the economy in red ink. The notion that taxes should never, ever be raised would have struck them as grossly irresponsible."[39] Goldwater embodied this earlier strain of conservatism. Though he passingly characterized tax rates as "high,"[40] in the chapter in *The Conscience of a Conservative* titled "Taxes and Spending" his primary argument regarding taxes was that a well-funded federal government would find it easier to assume inappropriate duties and responsibilities. Unlike conservatives in later generations, he was not as concerned with the burden of taxation on individual citizens. In fact, his plan to cut government spending did not even commit him to returning money to the taxpayers. As "a practical matter," Goldwater wrote, "spending cuts must come before tax cuts." Any other course ran the risk of "deficit spending" and its inevitable "inflationary effects."[41]

Though unsuccessful in gaining the Republican presidential nomination in 1960, Goldwater acquired new followers and was well positioned for 1964. That year, moderate Republicans had difficulty fielding a credible candidate, and Goldwater captured the nomination at a fractured party convention. In the general election, he suffered one of the worst defeats in American presidential history, losing to the Democratic incumbent Lyndon Johnson. Goldwater's criticism of the welfare state alienated many voters who had come to accept the New Deal as a welcome and permanent development, his positions on integration were out of step with a country that was slowly reaching a consensus in favor of civil rights, and his aggressive posture toward the Soviet Union simply frightened many Americans. Most commentators at the time saw Goldwater's campaign and even his nomination as a disaster for the Republican Party generally and for conservatism in particular.

This early assessment turned out to be almost entirely incorrect. After Lyndon Johnson's abrupt withdrawal from the Democratic presidential primary, Democrats found themselves in as much disarray in 1968 as the Republicans had been four years earlier. Richard Nixon captured the presidency for the GOP in the very next election. Even more important for the development of conservatism as a political force was the fact that Goldwater's campaign inspired a great many people to get involved in politics and to self-identify as conservatives. Though the candidate himself suffered an ignominious defeat, his campaign was the genesis of the movement that came to dominate American politics.

Of all the budding conservatives whose passion or vocation for politics was inspired by the Goldwater campaign, by far the most significant was Ronald Reagan. Born into a working-class Democratic family, the actor and union president had, over the years, slowly drifted to the right. In 1954, the forty-three-year-old Reagan could see that his best days as a leading man might be rapidly coming to an end, and he took a well-paying job as the host of a weekly television anthology series, *GE Theater*. Reagan absorbed the conservative corporate culture of General Electric (GE), later referring to the period of his life spent with the company as a "postgraduate course in political science." He began speaking to GE employees and then to business-oriented groups such as the National Association of Manufacturers and local chambers of commerce. As his speeches became more and more political in content and conservative in tone, Reagan became steadily more popular as a speaker.[42]

In 1962, he registered as a Republican for the first time. Two years later, Goldwater's run provided him with the first big break of what would become his political career. Reagan had been actively campaigning for Goldwater, and his stump speech had impressed a group of California businesspeople who were on the lookout for a credible gubernatorial candidate for the next election in 1966. These wealthy donors paid for a statewide and then a nationally televised airing of Reagan's talk, as a Goldwater fundraiser. The national broadcast, on October 27, 1964, was an incredible success. Though Goldwater's defeat was a foregone conclusion, the address raised more money than any political speech had up to that point, and *Time* magazine called it "the one bright spot in a dismal campaign." With Gold-water's defeat one week later, assessed Reagan biographer Lou Cannon, "the mantle of conservative political leadership had passed from Goldwater to Reagan."[43]

Reagan opened his speech by saying that he had, until recently, been a Democrat. He intended the address to come across in a bipartisan spirit, noting that the "issues confronting us cross party lines" and closing with a quotation from liberal hero Franklin Roosevelt. Yet Reagan's self-perception and genial manner could not mask the fact that the address was a passionate ideological statement, one that Cannon called "more controversial and hyperbolic in content than any which Goldwater had given for himself."[44] The speech was, in essence, a jeremiad. Reagan challenged his listeners to avoid being seduced by the appearance of postwar prosperity and to recognize the need to "ask ourselves if we still know the freedoms that were intended for us by the [f]ounding [f]athers."

The threats to this freedom had been identified by Goldwater: the Soviet menace abroad and creeping socialism at home. With regard to the former, Reagan echoed his candidate's major theme that the consensus approach to the Cold War would "trade our freedom for security" and send the United States "down to the ant heap of totalitarianism." The latter point Reagan made by reference to what by then had become well-worn conservative doctrine, dating back at least twenty years to *The Road to Serfdom*. "A government can't control the economy," he argued, "without controlling people."

Reagan brought home his points with loosely connected stories and statistics. The government spent $43, he claimed, for every bushel of corn that it required farmers *not* to grow; while the number of farms was shrinking, the number of Agriculture Department employees was growing; the amount spent on antipoverty programs averaged out to $4,600 per family, yet each family actually received only $600; a private insurance policy could guarantee a young working man $220 a month when he retired, whereas Social Security promised him only $127 at that time; American foreign aid went for "a 2 million dollar yacht for Haile Selassie[,] . . . dress suits for Greek undertakers, extra wives for Kenya[n] government officials . . . [and] a thousand TV sets for a place where they have no electricity." This barrage of observations gave the overall impression that the essence of government was buffoonery, incompetence, and waste.

"A Time for Choosing" constituted Reagan's audition, as it were, for a much larger political role. Its success cemented his place as the favored politician of conservatives, at a time in which their movement was increasingly well connected, coherent, and popular. Within two years, Reagan would be elected governor of California, which had recently become the nation's largest state. From 1968 forward, his name was perennially listed among serious Republican presidential contenders, and ultimately, he would become the nation's fortieth chief executive, in 1981. Reagan's modern-day status as an iconic hero to conservatives illustrates an important change that took place in the conservative movement between the 1960s and the 1980s. "A Time for Choosing" was a conservative broadside in support of a conservative candidate and delivered by a conservative speaker. But nowhere in the speech did Reagan mention cutting taxes as an important policy agenda. Indeed, in a thirty-minute address, he said only a few sentences on the issue. "No nation in history," he claimed, "has ever survived a tax burden that reached a third of its national income." He pointed out that even though "37 cents out of every dollar earned in this country is the tax collector's share," the government was spending $17 million more than it took in. Thus, the one time that Reagan even mentioned the issue of taxation, he linked it not to the financial burden on individuals but to his dissatisfaction over federal deficit spending.[45] The Reagan of 1964 was not the ideological opponent of taxation that he would become as president some fifteen years later.

Reagan's shift, however, was not idiosyncratic. Instead, it reflected the direction of the entire conservative movement. During the last decades of the twentieth century, the opposition to tax increases and the elimination of current taxes became increasingly central aspects of the conservative message. What happened to reshape the movement's priorities was that the poor performance of the American economy during the 1970s altered the parameters of the nation's public debate over political economy. Specifically, the unemployment and inflation that marked the decade challenged the premises of the argument that had justified the welfare state during the consensus era. Both the philosophical justification for the welfare state and the political support that kept it going turned on the assumption of prosperity: if the United States was, indeed, an "affluent society," then the redistribution of some of its wealth to the poor and disadvantaged seemed reasonable, if not required. But with economic growth stalled, many people out of work, and inflation eating away at the wages and savings of those who *had* jobs, middle- and working-class Americans were far less willing to support the impoverished lower classes. Conservative economic thinkers adapted to this dismal economic situation with an analysis whose political ramifications helped Republicans craft an attractive message, one with tax cuts at its center.

The Politics of Inflation

Because workers, employers, and consumers were also voters, twentieth-century politicians feared inflation as much as did economists and businesspeople. "From the inflationary years of the early twentieth century through the inflation of the early 1970s," wrote historian Meg Jacobs, "the 'purchasing power question' of what people could afford remained on the political agenda . . . never far from the center of American politics."[46] Even within this broader trend, however, the 1970s stood out as a period in which inflation occupied a particularly large space in the nation's political consciousness. The annual rate of inflation during the twentieth century typically measured under 3 percent, and in almost half of those 100 years the rate was under 2 percent. In just three periods in the century did the annual rate rise above 5 percent for any sustained period of time; two of these intervals were the five years starting in 1916 (during which the peak inflation rate reached nearly 18 percent) and six of the ten years beginning in 1942. Both of those periods corresponded to world wars and their aftermaths, during which prices and wages were severely distorted by wartime production needs, labor shortages, rationing, and price controls. The third incidence of high inflation occurred in the 1970s: in the fourteen-year stretch between 1969 and 1982, the annual rate of inflation only fell below 5 percent twice, and in four of those years, the inflation rate reached double digits.[47]

Richard Nixon, who became president in 1969, had little personal interest in economic issues: one of his well-known (private) exhortations on international finance was that he did not "give a shit about the lira."[48] But the economy was central to a subject about which Nixon cared a great deal—his own political ambitions. Believing that an economic downturn had played a significant role in his 1960 loss to John Kennedy, Nixon concluded that his ability to remain in office depended upon the continued success of the economy and that proper economic functioning should be measured primarily in political terms.[49] Beyond his own reelection, however, Nixon had even grander political ambitions. He believed that white southerners and blue-collar workers, who had traditionally voted Democratic, had grown dissatisfied with their party's positions on the so-called cultural issues—those relating, primarily, to racial tensions and the youth protests of the time. Nixon saw an opportunity to reach out to these conservative Democratic voters, with an eye toward turning them into Republicans and bringing about a permanent American political realignment in which his would be the majority party.

To attract these traditional Democrats without sacrificing Republican support, Nixon had to come across as neither a radical conservative nor a slick politician conspicuously courting liberal constituencies. This strategic approach necessitated minimizing the novelty of any economic programs. Nixon's economic policy, wrote historian Allen Matusow, revealed a president who "was neither a liberal nor the conservative of popular belief" but "a politician bent on preempting the center of American politics to build a new majority." His two-pronged strategy involved, on the one hand, "social conservatism, waving the flag, and playing the race card" and, on the other, an appeal to the "center ground with judicious expansion of the welfare state." His economic policies did not reflect a conservative ideology, which at that time centered on fiscal responsibility. The president "knew that spending money was more popular than pinching pennies, and he favored balancing the budget only so long as it did not cost him votes."[50] For Nixon, economic policy was merely a tool to use in furthering his political goals.

The economy, however, would not cooperate with Nixon's strategy, which turned on the assumption that postwar prosperity would continue. In 1969, the inflation rate began to creep up. Strongly influenced by the monetarism of Milton Friedman, the administration announced a policy of "gradualism," by which the Federal Reserve would slowly reduce the growth of the money supply. The administration's economic advisers hoped that this action would tamp down the inflation rate, almost imperceptibly, while avoiding the recession that could result if money was reduced with a sudden jolt. The president himself had long believed that the public's tolerance for inflation was higher than it was for unemployment, so he was somewhat reluctant to embrace a policy that aimed to slow economic growth. But he heeded the advice of his experts and issued a lukewarm commitment to gradualism, as long as it did not appear to threaten a loss of jobs.

Soon, however, the unemployment rate began to rise, and Nixon blinked. The president pressured the chairmen of the Federal Reserve, first William McChesney Martin and then Nixon's own appointee Arthur Burns, to loosen the reins on the money supply. But both bankers continued to prioritize their concerns about inflation, keeping the money supply tight. After his initial resistance to Nixon's position, though, Burns was spooked in 1970 by fears of a liquidity crisis. Accordingly, he raised the legal interest rates that banks could pay their customers. Disaster was averted, but as a result of these actions the money supply increased 5.5 percent in 1970, a much higher rate than either the 4 percent gradualist target or the historical norm. Though an expansive monetary policy was risky in a period of rising inflation, when Burns saw the short-term positive result his enthusiasm for monetarism began to wane.[51]

The economy continued to sputter in 1970. In that midterm election year, the country's gross domestic product grew only 0.18 percent. Unemployment rose a point and a half over the same period, and inflation remained above 5 percent.[52] Republicans performed poorly in that year's elections, and Nixon became focused on improving the economy before his own campaign in 1972. Additionally, the Fed's somewhat reckless expansion of the money supply was fueling inflation without helping unemployment. On August 10, a Harris poll reported that only 22 percent of Americans rated Nixon positively on the economy.[53] The president was feeling great pressure to do *something*, and gradualism offered him few opportunities for action. Three days later, he retreated to Camp David, along with his top economic and political advisers and Burns, to formulate a response to the nation's many economic problems.

Broadly speaking, the Camp David meeting addressed two sets of problems, one international and one domestic. The first of these concerned the international financial system known as Bretton Woods, which had been put in place by the Allied nations at the end of World War II. That system had worked effectively for two decades, but it was showing its age. By the early 1970s, an overvalued dollar was significantly hurting American exports. With the country slipping into recession and the presidential election just over a year away, Nixon wished to address this issue in order to stimulate domestic employment. From an international perspective, then, the most important long-term policy change to come out of the Camp David meeting was the decision to devalue the American currency by ceasing the practice of redeeming dollars for gold.

The other economic problems were domestic in nature—unemployment and inflation. Taking aim at the former, Nixon announced a series of tax cuts: credits for companies that invested in new machinery, a repeal of the excise tax on automobiles, and an early phase-in of personal tax exemptions that had been scheduled to take effect well over a year later. To address the latter, congressional Democrats had twice voted to give Nixon the ability to freeze wages and prices. The president had signed both bills under duress, claiming that he did not want that power and would not use it. In an abrupt switch, however, Nixon ordered, as an emergency measure, a ninety-day moratorium on any such increases.

At the conclusion of the Camp David weekend, on Sunday, August 15, Nixon preempted the popular television program *Gunsmoke* to make a major broadcast address to the nation. In this address, he announced, in the midst of a serious economic crisis, that "America has the best opportunity in this century to achieve . . . prosperity without war." To reach such a goal, however, three problems had be surmounted: the nation had to "create more and better jobs[,] . . . stop the rise in the cost of living[,] . . . and protect the dollar from the attacks of international money speculators." Though the first two concerns clearly referred to unemployment and inflation, the third represented Nixon's preferred, albeit somewhat duplicitous, way of explaining the need to devalue the dollar. Given these significant problems, the president declared, "the time has come for a new economic policy for the United States."[54]

The president's description of tax reductions in his televised address demonstrated that the latter-day conservative view of taxes had not yet taken hold by the early 1970s. Nixon, who had recently told a television reporter than he was "now a Keynesian in economics," explained these cuts as devices that would allow consumers to make more purchases, increasing demand for products. This, in turn, would motivate the manufacturers of these goods to hire more workers. The break on automobile taxes, he said, "will mean that more people will be able to afford new cars," which would then increase employment, as evidenced by Nixon's (dubious) claim that "every additional 100,000 cars sold means 25,000 new jobs." The personal tax credit was characterized in terms of bringing about "an increase in consumer spending power" in order to "provide a strong boost to the economy in general and to employment in particular." Nixon obviously intended his tax cut as an orthodox Keynesian economic intervention.[55]

The efficacy of the new economic policy depended, to a large degree, on the standards by which it was evaluated. It certainly paid off for Nixon politically. Inflation had already begun to lower during 1971, but then it decreased dramatically after wage-price controls began in August. In the election year of 1972, inflation clocked in at 3.2 percent, the lowest rate in five years. By the middle of the year—just in time for the election—GDP began to pick up, buoyed by Nixon's order to his cabinet secretaries to increase spending. Politically speaking, nearly everything else broke Nixon's way: Alabama's segregationist Democrat George Wallace (who would have competed with Nixon for southern votes) survived an assassination attempt but could not continue his presidential campaign, both China and the Soviet Union hosted visits from the president that year, most of the soldiers had come home from Vietnam, and Democratic challenger George McGovern proved to be a weak opponent. The economy was the one thing that could have discredited Nixon with the voters, but it held together well enough to ensure the president a landslide victory in 1972.[56]

From an economic perspective, however, Nixon's policies only exacerbated serious problems that did not become fully apparent until his second term. Initially, wage and price controls appeared to succeed because of the lowered inflation rate. Soon, though, they outlived whatever usefulness they might have possessed. The committees in charge of authorizing particular raises in wages or prices approved a surprisingly large number of hikes, and many viewed the controls as ineffective and arbitrary. Moreover, freezes were difficult to terminate once in place because of the fear that depressed wages and prices would immediately skyrocket when set free. Nixon originally announced that temporary controls would be in effect for ninety days, but they eventually lasted for two and a half years. Finally, the freezes gave officials in the administration and at the Fed an unwarranted confidence that inflation should not be a subject of concern. As a result of this attitude and the abandonment of gradualism, wrote Matusow, "two years of exuberant fiscal and monetary policies were propelling the economy out of control."[57]

As Nixon's second term began, the extraordinary spectacle of the ongoing Watergate trials, investigations, and hearings absorbed the nation's attention. Rising prices, meanwhile, vied for consideration as the most significant domestic issue of the period. What became known as the "great inflation" of the 1970s was the result of a series of shocks to an already unhealthy system. The first of these came from the agricultural sector. The United States traditionally produced much of the world's foodstuffs. In 1972, Nixon's Department of Agriculture, worried over falling prices, raised the amount of acreage for which they would pay farmers not to plant. At the same time, weather and other natural phenomena limited harvests in many other parts of the world. The result was a worldwide shortage, which bumped up the price of food.

Shoppers were particularly outraged at the prices they were forced to pay for meat, which were rising at an annual rate of 75 percent. Nixon responded by freezing prices on beef, veal, pork, mutton, and lamb, but many consumers felt that their costs had already been allowed to rise far too high and that the prices needed to be lowered rather than merely stabilized.[58] A coalition of consumer groups and labor unions organized a nationwide meat boycott to register their frustration. *Time* magazine featured the campaign on its cover, and its reporter wrote that this one action "by no means measures the full extent to which resurging inflation has become U.S. Topic A."[59] Gallup announced that 26 percent of Americans reported actively joining the boycott, and an additional 30 percent planned to cut back on meat consumption.[60] On July 18, 1973, Nixon terminated the freeze on meat prices (except for beef) and announced the timetable for the end of all wage and price controls, which would conclude in just under a year.[61]

But as the controls were coming to a close, the country was hit with another supply shock. The consumption of oil in the United States had climbed dramatically throughout the 1960s, and domestic suppliers met only a fraction of this demand. In 1973, restrictions on other fuels and new clean-air regulations, inspired by the nascent environmental movement, increased to an even greater level the nation's dependence on foreign sources of energy. Energy prices became a political issue that year, and the Nixon administration placed price controls on oil. In the second half of the year, this commodity started becoming scarce. Then, international affairs intervened to make the situation much worse. On the Jewish holy day of Yom Kippur, Egypt and Syria marched on disputed territory that was held at the time by Israel. Israel retaliated, and the United States responded by supporting its ally with supplies and munitions. (In true Cold War fashion, the Soviet Union backed the Arab countries.) On October 23, 1973, the Arab-dominated Organization of Petroleum Exporting Countries (OPEC) declared an oil embargo against the United States and the Netherlands in order to condemn those nations for their support of Israel.

A full-fledged shortage was now at hand, and the winter of 1973–1974 became the season of the gas line. The *New York Times* reported about motorists lining up for three blocks just to fill their tanks, with typical waits of two hours. Tempers grew short, and in one extreme case, a station attendant was murdered.[62] In response to the growing crisis, in February 1974 Nixon ordered that federal oil reserves be more broadly distributed, despite the concern of some advisers that such an action would leave the country with few options should the shortage continue. In January, Nixon had sent Secretary of State Henry Kissinger to mediate an agreement between the Middle Eastern belligerents. That effort was successful, and most of the Arab states canceled the embargo in March.

The oil shock was over, but the nation's economic troubles were just beginning. After the previous economic crises—the devaluation of the dollar, skyrocketing food prices, and the oil embargo and gas lines—there was yet one more. The final inflationary shock resulted from the end of wage and price controls, which expired on April 30, 1974. When the restrictions were lifted, the result was a great rise in prices. So just as the prices of food and oil had begun to level off, the price of everything else rose, keeping the inflation rate high. At the same time, the ongoing Watergate scandal continued to do damage to Nixon's credibility and political viability. As the president lost power with each passing day, inflation remained a front-page problem.

Recognizing that the accumulating damage had left him unable to function as chief executive, Nixon resigned the presidency on August 8, 1974. Vice President Gerald Ford became the new chief executive. A former minority leader in the House of Representatives, Ford had been a Republican congressman from Michigan when a bribery scandal (completely unrelated to Watergate) forced Vice President Spiro Agnew to resign. Nixon appointed Ford to the office, putting him next in line for the presidency. Consequently, when Nixon resigned, the man who assumed the presidency had less than a year's experience as vice president—and he had not even been elected to that office. Moreover, in the wake of Watergate, voters held his Republican Party in low esteem. With something less than a mandate, then, Ford had to lead the American people through the worst economic crisis since the Great Depression.

In the words of one historian, Ford "understood the intricacies of economics and economic policy better than any president of the twentieth century." Nonetheless, he had a difficult time making inroads on the nation's problems.[63] Shortly after becoming president, he convened a summit of the nation's leading economists to discuss the problem of inflation, after which he gave a major address to Congress on the subject. Noting the plethora of competing economic proposals, the president declared that the "only point on which all the advisers have agreed" is that the nation had to "whip inflation right now." His speech contained a large number of ideas, few of which struck observers as substantial or bold enough to constitute effective leadership. Ford addressed the citizenry directly and asked them to "grow more and waste less . . . drive less, heat less." One of his proposals quickly became an object of mockery. Ford's national volunteer organization, called Whip Inflation Now, encouraged its members to battle rising prices by saving money and seeking out low-priced bargains. In an effort to revive the spirit of communal sacrifice that characterized the Depression and World War II years, members would wear buttons emblazoned with the initials of the program, WIN.[64]

Commentators dismissed such notions as silly diversions in the face of a serious problem. Another of Ford's ideas, however, was met not with derision but with outright opposition. Holding to the traditional Republican view that the worst economic sin a government could commit was failing to balance the budget and believing that federal spending would push up prices and federal borrowing would increase interest rates, Ford advocated a temporary, one-year surcharge of 5 percent on the incomes of wealthy individuals and corporations. This proclamation was issued one month before the midterm elections, and Democrats were delighted to run against the party of tax increases. Additionally, in the weeks after Ford's address, his economic team slowly came to acknowledge that the country was sliding back into recession. Seeing unemployment as a growing threat, Ford dropped his tax increase proposal.

With Watergate still fresh in the voters' minds, the midterm elections returned even larger Democratic majorities to Congress. After the elections, on the night before the 1975 State of the Union address, President Ford announced his new economic plan in an address that was broadcast on radio and television. At the center of his program was a rebate of individual income tax payments and an increase in business investment credits, both at the rate of 12 percent. The new proposal represented a tremendous political turnaround, moving from a 5 percent tax increase to a 12 percent rebate in the span of three months. The impetus for this change, however, was not political pressure from conservatives. They, like Ford, were defined more by their concern for balancing the budget than by their desire to relieve citizens of their tax burden. Movement hero Ronald Reagan, for instance, criticized the president not for his original proposed tax hike but for abandoning it in favor of the tax cut.[65]

The president's radical shift on taxes was not motivated by a change in philosophy but by the economic situation itself. In his announcement of the new policy, Ford briefly acknowledged his abrupt change of heart, telling his audience that unemployment was a "new and disturbing" aspect of the nation's economic outlook. Despite the rising deficit, he said, "what we most urgently need today is more spending money in your pockets rather than in the Treasury in Washington." Indeed, Ford argued, "unless our economy revives rapidly, [f]ederal tax revenues will shrink so much that future deficits will be even larger." To deal with the problem of inflation while attempting to stimulate the economy, he proposed a moratorium on new federal spending on all programs except for those geared toward energy independence. In the end, the president had concluded simply that the situation was an economic emergency so dire that he would reluctantly have to ignore his own budget-balancing instincts.[66]

Congressional Democrats, however, attempted to take advantage of the situation by transforming the president's proposed tax cut into a much larger one. Ford was concerned about the deficit, but the original idea for the tax rebate was his, so he did not want to come out against it. The only way he could demonstrate his commitment to keeping deficits as small as possible was to veto spending bills. In his truncated, two-and-a-half-year term, Ford vetoed sixty-six bills. He was overridden twelve times, but most of his spending vetoes were sustained.[67] About one year before the 1976 presidential election, Ford and congressional Democrats negotiated a $9 billion tax cut with a commitment to spending limits. Considered a small victory for Ford because of the spending cuts, it was insufficient to counter the impression among the electorate that he was not a strong leader. This perception, combined with the lingering taint of Watergate, led to Ford's 1976 defeat to Democrat, and Washington outsider, Jimmy Carter.[68]

Both Nixon and Ford had championed tax cuts during their presidencies. But neither had done so with great enthusiasm, nor had either claimed to be embodying conservative principles. Nixon expressed his support for tax cuts in the language of liberal Keynesianism, whereas Ford endorsed them only reluctantly as a response to a crisis. Significantly, the last two Republican presidents before the so-called Reagan revolution advanced positions on taxation that, within a few short years, would not even be recognized as conservative. Yet it was during their administrations that conservative economists and journalists were formulating the ideas that would change the meaning of economic conservatism itself.

What Was Supply-Side Economics?

Even before Nixon's resignation, it had become obvious that the country was now facing simultaneous inflation and recession. In 1974, the annual rate of inflation was 11 percent; at the same time, the economy did not merely grow slowly but actually shrank slightly.[69] Up to that point, economic theory had generally held that such a situation was impossible. Since the cause of rising prices was an excess of economic activity and since unemployment was a direct result of a decrease in production, it would seem that inflation would be incompatible with recession. Economist William Phillips presented empirical justification for this relationship in 1958. His "Phillips curve," which formally posited an inverse relationship between unemployment and inflation, had become an accepted part of economic orthodoxy.

But the experience of the middle part of the 1970s appeared to refute the Phillips curve. The combination of rising inflation and a stagnant economy prompted the widespread usage of a fairly new term: *stagflation*. The underlying circumstances that created this situation, however, were exceedingly rare. As Matusow explained, unlike in previous periods of inflation "the primary force destabilizing the economy in 1974 was not demand. It was supply." The consecutive annual supply shocks regarding food and oil were followed by the decontrol of prices in the third year, which acted like a supply shock in that prices went up despite the lack of any demand increase. The American economy, in short, had reached the limit of its ability to produce. Without economic growth, supply was unable to increase to meet growing demand. The result was rising prices without any compensatory new production or employment.[70]

In such an environment, the liberal Keynesian approach offered few answers. In the spirit of searching for a new direction, *Wall Street Journal* editor Robert Bartley began inviting conservative academics, journalists, government officials, and businesspeople to gather weekly for a discussion of economic issues, at the restaurant Michael 1 in Manhattan's financial district. Over time, two economists came to exert the largest influence on this group: Robert Mundell of Columbia (who would later win the Nobel Prize) and his protégé Arthur Laffer, a professor at the University of Chicago who was working in the Nixon White House on the budget staff while finishing his Ph.D. in economics at Stanford. (He would remain on the Nixon and Ford staffs and later rejoin the faculty at Chicago.) Another regular attendee was Jude Wanniski, who worked on the editorial page at Bartley's *Journal*. In his columns, Wanniski would soon be extolling the virtues of the economists' theory, which he initially labeled the "Mundell-Laffer hypothesis" before eventually shifting to the catchier "supply-side economics."[71]

Though Mundell had not yet attracted much attention outside of academia, his arguments had been circulating for over a decade in the journals and at the conferences familiar to professional economists. At the root of his analysis lay the observation, repeated often enough that Bartley recalled it as an aphorism, that "for every policy goal, you need a policy lever."[72] This view, as explained by Mundell to his dining companions, meant that for each specific economic problem, there is one and only one government policy that would be most effective in addressing it. Up to that point, conservatives, concerned mainly about inflation, had tended to favor tight money and balanced budgets, whereas liberals, more worried about unemployment, recommended deficit spending and loose money. Both implicitly agreed, though, that fiscal and monetary policy should be moving in the same direction. But Mundell believed that if one properly focused the correct policy on a given individual problem, then it would be acceptable to employ techniques that might "work against" each other. The art of shepherding a nation's economy lay in managing the process of what Mundell called "effective market classification": using the appropriate policy and only that policy to generate the intended response.

Stagflation was, of course, the relevant example. Mundell rejected the approach of Milton Friedman and the monetarists. Their belief that the money supply determined both the level of inflation and the rate of economic growth clearly violated the principle of effective market classification. But Mundell also disagreed even with the seemingly less controversial monetarist assumption that the policies of the Federal Reserve were the primary determinants of the money supply. Instead, he saw currency exchange rates as playing a far more significant role. In real-world economies, investors could move their money from a nation with low interest rates to one with higher interest rates. The money supply could consequently increase even if central bank policies were tight, and economic policies should be oriented toward creating an attractive investment climate. As summarized by Brian Domitrovic, historian of the supply-side movement, Mundell did not subscribe to the monetarist view that appropriate monetary policy during inflationary times necessarily meant "starving the economy of money." Instead, he believed policies that encouraged foreign capital to move to the United States would boost economic activity. In such a case, the increased "demand for dollars may require the Fed to provide more money" even while pursuing a policy of tight money.[73]

Following the principle of effective market classification, Mundell advocated other solutions to address the economic problems of growth and unemployment. Yet his solution was related to his diagnosis of the inflation crisis because he saw both as issues of underinvestment. Here, he advocated a cut in taxes, specifically the lowering of the top marginal rates of the personal and income tax. Isolated from the specifics, this was hardly a novel proposal. Keynesians had long held that the most effective way to battle unemployment was to increase demand by giving people more money to spend. From this perspective, tax cuts, government handouts, and public works programs were all essentially interchangeable. Indeed, Republican and Democratic presidents had treated them as such for decades. From Mundell's position, however, such an attitude not only violated the principle of effective market classification but also completely misdiagnosed the problem. Only permanent cuts in the marginal tax rates—not onetime tax rebates, welfare programs, or government jobs—could help the American economy.

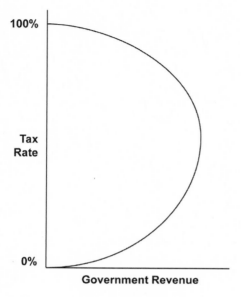

The Laffer Curve. (Courtesy Lisa Barnett)

His disagreement with the Keynesians stemmed from his belief that stimulating demand was simply the wrong economic goal. In Mundell's view, unemployment was not caused by consumers' reluctance to purchase goods (a lack of demand) but by the unwillingness of the American business class to invest in new economic opportunities (an inadequate supply). If firms lacked the desire or ability to increase production, then no amount of demand would ever motivate economic actors to behave in a way that would allow the economy to grow. And the primary reason for the lack of enthusiasm among producers, Mundell believed, was the structure of the US personal income tax. The American system has long been a progressive one: as a taxpayer's income increases, so does the tax rate on the portion of that income that is above a specified amount. Imagine, for example, a country with a progressive income tax that had two rates of 10 percent and 20 percent, with the higher rate kicking in at a $10,000 annual income. In that situation, one who made $10,000 a year would pay 10 percent of his income. Someone else in that country who earned a $15,000 annual salary would pay the same 10 percent on her first $10,000 but would pay the higher rate on all of her salary above $10,000. On the remaining $5,000, she would pay 20 percent ($1,000), for a total tax bill of $2,000. Using economic terminology, her "marginal" tax rate (the rate on the last dollar she earned) would be 20 percent, but her "effective" tax rate (the overall percentage of her entire income given over to the government) would be 13.3 percent. (Since the other taxpayer had all his income taxed at a single rate, his marginal and effective rates were both 10 percent.) Were she to consider taking on a business expansion or investment, the 13.3 percent rate would be entirely irrelevant to her calculations. What she would have to take into consideration is the fact that the next dollar she earned (the marginal dollar) would be taxed at the rate of 20 percent. Mundell reasoned that as the marginal rate went up, the incentives for people to take on such projects would decrease. Jobs, as a result, would become scarce.

Mundell's positions differed significantly from those of economic orthodoxy. Obviously, the very notion of supply-side economics rejected the liberal Keynesian notion that recessions are the result of a lack of demand. But Mundell's recommendations to cut taxes during a recession also ran afoul of a characteristically conservative economic concern: the federal deficit. This was the point at which Laffer made his most recognized contribution to supply-side economics. In 1974, he and Wanniski were meeting with Dick Cheney, the future vice president who was then an assistant to President Ford. The two supply-siders were seeking to impress upon the administration the preferability of permanent tax cuts over the short-term rebates that the president eventually enacted. When Cheney expressed concerns about the deficit, Laffer repeatedly claimed that the increase in economic activity generated by the lower rates would actually bring in *more* federal revenue. To illustrate his point, he grabbed a cocktail napkin from the bar where the men were sitting and sketched a graph against a vertical axis of marginal tax rates and a horizontal one of government revenue. The graph looked like a backwards letter C. The left side of the graph illustrated the point that if earnings were taxed at the extreme rates of 0 percent or 100 percent, federal revenues would be zero. In the former case, no matter how much one earned, no tax would be due; in the latter, no one would bother to work at all (at least legally), since every person would have to turn over all of his or her earnings to the government. Following the graph to the right, one would notice that the government could take in each possible amount of revenue with either of two different tax rates: the one on the top, a confiscatory tax that took a great deal from a small economy, or the one on the bottom, a lower rate that took a smaller bite out of a much larger economy. Though the Laffer curve was not labeled with any specific numbers, its creator strongly believed that the United States was on the top half of the curve and that lowering taxes would consequently increase government revenue. This insight lined up perfectly with Mundell's claim that high tax rates were retarding the economy's ability to grow.[74]

The Laffer curve conceptually reconciled the new supply-side emphasis on cutting top marginal tax rates with the traditionally conservative concern over balancing the federal budget. Republican politicians and voters who heard academic economists argue that lowering taxes would increase federal revenue could now reconcile their antigovernment animus with their native fiscal conservatism.

The Growing Influence of Supply-Side Economics

Ever since supply-side economics rose to prominence in the 1980s, many conservatives have viewed its conclusions as eternal verities, urging that almost any political or economic problem can be solved by cutting upper-level marginal tax rates. Liberals, by contrast, have tended to view the doctrine as merely a fig leaf that hides a conservative bias in favor of corporations and the wealthy. Neither of these views takes into account the fact that the supply-side philosophy was a reaction to the specific economic conditions of a particular time. The inflation of the 1970s *was*, to a very large degree, caused by the expansive policies of the Federal Reserve. And it *was* true that a series of supply shocks had left the economy in a state in which Keynesian "pump priming" would be likely to cause inflation without creating jobs. Most important, however, was the fact that marginal income tax rates were, by modern American standards, exorbitant. For comparison's sake, the highest top marginal rate since 1986 has been 39.6 percent; from 1968 until 1981, it was 70 percent.[75] Additionally, inflation meant that wages had to continually rise in order to maintain the same purchasing power. But because of the progressive nature of the income tax, wages that did rise would be subject to higher taxes. Until 1985, federal tax brackets and personal exemptions were not indexed to inflation. Thus, a taxpayer could easily see his or her tax rates go up even as his or her purchasing power remained exactly the same. This phenomenon, known as bracket creep, fueled public anger with taxation and primed many voters to be receptive to an antitax message.

The most significant figure in shifting the supply-side program from the esoteric province of a few professional economists to a mainstream political phenomenon was Jude Wanniski. Impressed by the economic diagnosis of Mundell and Laffer, Wanniski also saw that the GOP could reap tremendous political benefit by presenting itself to the voters as the party of tax cuts. On December 11, 1974, he effectively announced the popular debut of supply-side economics with a column in the *Wall Street Journal* titled "It's Time to Cut Taxes." There, he summarized and implicitly advocated the ideas of Mundell and Laffer, quoting extensively from an interview with the former. In Mundell's view, he wrote, "inflation and unemployment are separable problems" that required "distinct policy instruments." The economist recommended "tight money" against inflation and "expansive fiscal policies," which would "preferably" take the form of "lower taxes," to "combat the recession in a way that also works against inflation." Noting the effects of bracket creep, Mundell stated that the "national economy is being choked by taxes—asphyxiated. Taxes have increased even while output has fallen, because of the inflation." He argued that taxes "reduce the incentive to produce," and he referenced the insights behind the Laffer curve: "If total taxes and expenditures become confiscatory, all economic activity would cease and the government tax bite would be 100% of nothing." Shortly before President Ford would be negotiating with congressional Democrats to set a $9 billion tax cut, Wanniski cited Mundell's call for a cut of $30 billion.[76]

The next year, Wanniski published a twenty-two-page article in the policy journal *Public Interest,* titled "The Mundell-Laffer Hypothesis." The vast majority of this more technical piece was devoted to expressing the supply-side approach to the intricacies of currency exchange and monetary policy. Taxes were only mentioned in the last few pages, under the heading "Dealing with 'Stagflation.'" There, Wanniski cited Mundell's dictum that "monetary and fiscal policies are totally distinct policy instruments that can be employed for separate purposes and even utilized in opposing directions." Under the conditions of stagflation, he wrote, "the proper policy mix is tight money and fiscal ease . . . preferably" in the "form of tax reductions."[77] Indeed, by February 1975, Mundell and Laffer had called for a $60 billion tax cut, twice as large as the cut Mundell had recommended in Wanniski's *Wall Street Journal* editorial.[78]

In this article, Wanniski quoted from a Laffer memo, written to Treasury Secretary William E. Simon, that nicely summarized the fundamental presumptions of supply-side economics. There, Laffer stated as a "simple truth" the contention that a person would decide to commit a resource— whether his or her time as a worker or his or her money or property as an employer—based on an assessment of "the ability to earn after-tax income." It was "likewise taken as a virtually obvious proposition" that "the more an employer has to pay his factors of production the less he will want." Given these considerations, "marginal taxes of all sorts stand as a wedge between what an employer pays his factors of production and what they ultimately receive in after-tax income." Using the example of the payroll tax, Wanniski cited an employer who paid an employee $100. If both parties had to pay 5.5 percent on that money, then the employer was paying $105.50 and the employee was receiving $94.50 for that labor. The difference between what the employer spent and the amount that the employee received was $11. This $11 "wedge" would play a role in each party's decision as to whether to contract with each other, even though neither of them would receive those funds. "Any reduction in marginal tax rates," Laffer concluded, "means that the employers will pay less and yet employees will receive more." From the perspective of both parties, "more employment will be desired and more output will be forthcoming."[79] Thus, the lowering of marginal tax rates would be the most effective tool in battling unemployment.

The support that supply-side economics offered for tax cuts was entirely distinct from any consideration that an antitax message might revitalize economic conservatism. Wanniski, however, obviously saw both possibilities as mutually reinforcing. He soon ventured forth from the strictly economic aspects of supply-side economics to tout its political advantages. In March 1976, he published an opinion piece in the *National Observer,* a well-regarded but short-lived weekly newspaper put out by Dow Jones and Company. Titled "Taxes and a Two-Santa Theory," the essay might have served as a blueprint for the future conservative approach to economic issues. Bruce Bartlett, the pundit who served in the Reagan and George H. W. Bush administrations, wrote in 2012 that the essay prefigured "virtually everything Republicans say about taxes and spending today."[80]

Wanniski's recommendations, though purportedly offered to keep "the U.S. economy healthy . . . and growing," came across more clearly as political advice to the Republican Party. Beginning with the premise that Republicans had become "hypnotized by the prospect of an imbalanced budget," the writer concluded that this fixation had hampered the party politically. Ever since the New Deal, he argued, the Democrats had been able to successfully position their party as the political Santa Claus, bestowing upon the voters the gifts of redistributive social programs. When Republicans criticized these popular initiatives because of their effects on the budget, they forgot that "the first rule of successful politics is Never Shoot Santa Claus." In offering the voters a choice between popular social programs and fiscal austerity, the party was asking them to choose between Santa Claus and Scrooge. What it needed to do instead, argued Wanniski, was offer a choice between two different types of Santa Clauses. Rather than "carping against increased spending," Republicans could respond to Democratic promises of increased funding for Great Society–style social programs by offering voters the opportunity to keep some of their own money, in the form of reduced taxes. Reclaiming its rightful place as "the party of income growth," the GOP could become "the Santa Claus of Tax Reduction."[81]

By the late 1970s, the Mundell-Laffer hypothesis was ascendant among conservative intellectuals and politicians. In 1977, Irving Kristol, the intellectual often cited as the "godfather of neoconservativism," wrote enthusiastically about supply-side economics in the *Wall Street Journal*. "For the first time in half a century," he exulted, "it is the economic philosophy of conservatives," rather than that of liberals, "that is showing signs of intellectual vigor." Quoting from an old adage that one "can't beat a horse with no horse," he rejoiced in the prospect that "conservatives . . . may be in the process of acquiring a horse."[82]

Kristol was correct: the antitax message took the country by storm in 1978. Of the several events that advanced the new conservative message, among the most significant was the publication of Wanniski's supply-side magnum opus, the immodestly titled volume *The Way the World Works*. A key touchstone for late twentieth-century economic conservatism, the book became the most successful exposition of supply-side ideas. A *National Review* panel later named it to the magazine's list of the 100 best nonfiction works of the twentieth century, and panelist George Gilder (whose 1981 *Wealth and Poverty* was another important supply-side work) declared it simply the "best book on economics."[83]

The Way the World Works was as ambitious as its title suggested. In the early chapters, Wanniski articulated a "political model" that purported to explain nearly all social phenomena. His philosophy turned on the claim that large groups of people generally know what the best course of action is and are capable of clearly articulating that understanding. Individual members of such a group are particularly insightful only on one particular subject: "Each voter is superior to the consensus in making choices that suit his or her own perceived interest." The inverse of this claim, however, was that "no individual can possibly be as wise as the electorate . . . in discerning the preferred tastes of all the individuals who compose [it]."[84] As a result, "the electorate itself . . . is wiser than any of its component parts."[85] It could not fail to know its own will, nor could it inaccurately transmit that will to its leaders. Societies prosper when officials successfully hear and implement the policies that the voters tell them they prefer, and they decline when their leaders prove unable or unwilling to understand or follow the message of the electorate.

From the fact that the electorate was wiser than any of its particular members followed the conclusion that the community itself understood economics better than any experts. Wanniski listed several everyday examples to demonstrate that economic concepts were merely formalized applications of common wisdom, as when a mother and her child "trade" a clean plate for the chance to eat ice cream after dinner.[86] In the same sense, people understood, naturally and intuitively, Laffer's concept of the wedge that Wanniski had previously introduced in his article for *Public Interest*. In *The Way the World Works*, Wanniski argued that the homespun economic understanding of the people incorporated this idea. Under certain circumstances, laboring "off the books," getting paid "under the table," bartering between friends or neighbors, or engaging in black market or criminal activity might be more economically efficient than performing work that was subject to taxation. Wanniski cited the example of Smith, a carpenter, and Jones, a plumber. If these craftsmen "each want to trade sixteen hours of their skills with each other" but face a government wedge (in the form of taxes or costly regulations) of two hours, then "the two must do thirty-six hours [of] work to transact thirty-two."[87] As that wedge increases, Smith and Jones confront the possibility that they will have to work for more hours in order to achieve the same results. Under these conditions, they might decide to perform the transaction outside legal channels or forego it entirely. In this sense, an excessive tax burden can retard economic growth: "The market system becomes grossly inefficient . . . when the expanding government wedge crushes out incentives and underemploys an entire economy."[88]

Of course, the government needs revenue, and it cannot reduce taxes to some arbitrarily low point in order to encourage economic growth. Here, Wanniski enlisted the Laffer curve in service of his broader philosophy. The central insight behind the economist's observation was that "there are always two tax rates that yield the same revenues."[89] This generalization summarized the point well, but, as Laffer and Wanniski both knew, it was technically untrue. A quick glance at the Laffer curve itself would show that there was one level of government revenue that could be reached with only one tax rate. Given the backward letter C shape of the curve, this point would occur at the far right and would represent the largest possible amount of government revenue.

The Laffer curve was sketched on a napkin to prove a theoretical point. It was not derived from empirical research, and therefore, it did not advocate specific tax rates or corresponding amounts of government revenue. The curve itself, then, really only enabled two observations: a maximal level of government revenue was theoretically attainable, and the tax rate that would generate such an amount had to be somewhere between 0 and 100 percent. Given his model for political organization, however, this information was enough for Wanniski to conclude that maximal government revenue was obtained at "the point at which the electorate desires to be taxed."[90] If a point on the curve did not represent maximal government revenue, then taxes were either too high or too low. If the wedge was too great, then workers were choosing to perform work in the barter or black-market economy and the government was foregoing the proceeds that it could reap from their labor. But if tax rates were too low, then taxpayers would be willing to pay higher taxes on the work they were already doing in exchange for government services. In either case, argued Wanniski, the government was not realizing its maximum possible revenue. There was no eternally appropriate tax rate that would apply to all circumstances, as the amount of taxes a populace was willing to pay would vary tremendously based on the contingent social and historical factors in play at a given place and time. To take an extreme case, during the World War II siege of Leningrad, its citizens "produced for 900 days at tax rates approaching 100 percent." Had they "not wished to be taxed at that high rate in order to hold off the Nazi army, the city would have fallen."[91] Political leadership in the area of tax policy consisted of, again, the ability to adjust rates to the specifics of the particular situation and the will of the people. The Laffer curve, in Wanniski's telling, was a versatile instrument that should inform the perspective of policy makers.

The Way the World Works exerted a tremendous influence on conservative thinking, playing a pivotal role in bringing supply-side economics into popular political discourse. "By the end of 1978," observed Domitrovic, "Wanniski's book had made the Laffer curve virtually a household term."[92] As it brought supply-side economics into the mainstream, however, it also shifted the doctrine's message slightly. Once a technical response to the specific economic situation of the 1970s, it became in Wanniski's hands a broader philosophical and political statement. *The Way the World Works* was not a series of specific policy recommendations regarding a present-day economic crisis but a wide-ranging theoretical and historical manifesto. Chapters in the book covered the flaws in Keynesianism and monetarism, the causes of the Great Depression, an interpretation of world history since the ancient Greeks, a detailed exposition of the Bretton Woods system, and other disparate topics. The many historical examples, from ancient Japan to

Napoleonic France, all highlighted the repressive results of taxation or the liberating of economic energies that would result from lowering rates. Unmoored from the crisis of stagflation, the message that emerged from the book was that tax rates were nearly always too high. The American electorate—economically beleaguered, suffering from stagflation and bracket creep, and not terribly interested in the subtleties of economic theory—was increasingly receptive to this message, no matter what its justification.

The Rage against Taxes

The year 1978 was a watershed in the conservative embrace of the antitax idea. Wanniski's book brought a lot of attention to the issue, and it also began the process of transforming the idea of lowering taxes from a technocratic response to a specific set of economic problems to a genuine ideological crusade. Moreover, 1978 was the year that the nation's politics seemed to provide evidence for Wanniski's "two Santas" theory, as politicians realized that there were real votes in calling for tax relief. A populist crusade against taxes swept the country that year. Frequently referred to as a tax revolt, the effort was motivated by homeowners' ire at the property tax. Since these were levied on the basis of the assessed value of a given home, rather than any measurement of the owner's earning, they could rise even without any change in the owner's income. Thus, elderly or retired homeowners, for example, who might not wish to sell their lifelong residences, could find themselves owing the largest property taxes of their lives at exactly the point when their earning power was weakest. Since both inflation and rising home prices boosted the nominal value of a home without enhancing the owner's income, it should come as no surprise that the place and time that kicked off the taxpayer revolt was California in the 1970s—a land of ever-increasing real estate prices in a period of unmanageable inflation.

The leader of the California movement was Howard Jarvis, a retired Los Angeles businessman who took up political activism soon after he stopped working. Taking advantage of California's liberal initiative process, Jarvis and his organization collected hundreds of thousands of signatures to meet the threshold for getting their antitax proposals on the ballot. After several failed attempts over a fifteen-year span, he and his followers succeeded in gathering over a million signatures on a petition to place the initiative before the voters in 1978. Known as Proposition 13, the proposal allowed for a plan to amend the state constitution to limit local and county property taxes to 1 percent of the assessed value of the property. Moreover, the baseline property value would revert to the amount assessed in 1975 and would be revised only when the property was sold. From that baseline, the tax would only be allowed to increase 2 percent per year. Given rampant inflation and the California real estate market, homeowners who did not sell their houses would see, in real terms, a property tax reduction each year. Perhaps even more important, Proposition 13 required that the state legislature obtain a two-thirds supermajority in order to pass any tax increase.[93]

Arthur Laffer, who had become a state resident after accepting a faculty position at the University of Southern California (USC), called Proposition 13 "excellent" and argued that "there should be a limit on all taxes."[94] He endorsed the initiative and campaigned on its behalf. The state's political establishment, however, overwhelmingly opposed the measure. Nearly every newspaper and many of the business interests in the state came out against the initiative. California's Republican Party declined to endorse it, and the Democratic governor, Jerry Brown, opposed it, abruptly changing his position only when it became obvious that the initiative would pass. Nonetheless, the electorate strongly affirmed Proposition 13. Turnout for the June election was 69 percent, and the initiative passed with 65 percent of the vote, a nearly two-to-one margin.

Almost immediately thereafter, antitax fever swept the entire country. Within the next year, the citizens of eleven states approved initiatives to grant some form of tax relief; two of these were explicitly modeled on the California proposal.[95] Howard Jarvis himself became a national celebrity. In the week immediately after the vote, he was featured on the cover of *Time*, under the heading "Tax Revolt!" Later, he was a finalist for that magazine's "Man of the Year" award, along with President Jimmy Carter, Pope John Paul II, and Jim Jones.

The tax revolt spawned by Proposition 13 demonstrated to politicians that tax reduction could be a vote-getter. It also marked the issue as a decidedly conservative one. This was not necessarily preordained: the traditional Republican fixation on the deficit had meant that politicians who expressed concerns over tax burdens were likely to be liberal. Historian Simon Hall has pointed out that many who organized tax-relief protests both before and after Proposition 13 had been active in the New Left a decade earlier, and their protests were often based on the premise that poor citizens had difficulty paying those taxes.[96] But this argument was not the focus of the Proposition 13 campaign. Political scientist Daniel A. Smith characterized the movement as "a well-orchestrated, top-down ballot initiative campaign engineered principally by Howard Jarvis," who "successfully detected the widespread, albeit diffuse, public mood and crafted a ballot initiative enabling citizens to vent their collective anger."[97] As such, the movement took on many of Jarvis's own views, which were of a decidedly conservative, antigovernment cast. He summarized his own campaign, for example, as one whose goal was "to put a fence between the hogs and the swill bucket."[98] Additionally, Jarvis characterized his opposition to taxes in terms that invoked the backlash against liberal social welfare policies. "Property taxes," he wrote, "have been used to pay for the special interests that grew up with the government, such as social workers, food-stamp recipients, [and] aid to dependent children programs. . . . *They* are the ones who want more services—not the people who pay the bills."[99] Jarvis's own attitudes often suggested he was less a beleaguered homeowner needing relief from the ravages of inflation than an individual with a deep-seated hostility to taxes themselves, which he held to be "the number-one evil in the United States."[100]

As the tax revolt swept the nation, Washington also took notice of the antitax message. In the wake of Proposition 13, one Republican congressman from North Carolina observed that many of his fellow representatives, "who've traditionally voted for everything, no matter what it costs," were now "trying to look like fiscal conservatives."[101] President Carter, significantly misreading the political and popular mood, announced a new initiative to alter the tax code. His plan's focus was on disallowing write-offs and loopholes that benefited the wealthy, and at its center was a proposal to increase the capital gains tax by 40 percent. In the House Ways and Means Committee, William Steiger, a Republican congressman from Wisconsin, offered an amendment to the bill that would instead cut the tax on capital gains from 49 percent to 25 percent. The so-called Steiger Amendment surprisingly attracted wide bipartisan support in Congress. Meanwhile, Sam Nunn, a Democratic senator from Carter's home state of Georgia, proposed an even more radical adjustment that was based upon the previously proposed bills of Congressman Jack Kemp of New York and Senator William Roth of Delaware, both Republicans. Kemp-Roth, as the bill was known, would have cut marginal tax rates by 10 percent a year for three consecutive years. It had been proposed and voted down in the House several times before, albeit by increasingly narrow margins. The fact that a new version would be proposed by a Democrat suggested that tax cutting had arrived on the national political stage. The Nunn amendment passed in the Senate by a wide majority, but Carter sent word that he would veto any bill that contained it. Negotiations between the president and Congress yielded a final version of the bill, known as the Revenue Act of 1978, that did not contain the Kemp-Roth provision but did substantially reduce the capital gains tax.[102]

The development with the most significant long-term ramifications came about when Ronald Reagan converted to supply-side economics. Among conservatives, the former governor of California was the most popular politician in the country, and he was favored to win the Republican presidential nomination in 1980. Laffer and Wanniski had joined the orbit of Jack Kemp, and Laffer had been introduced to the Reagan camp through a connection at USC. In October 1977, Reagan endorsed Kemp-Roth. When speaking in support of this massive tax cut, both Reagan and Kemp claimed that it would increase government revenue, implicitly invoking the Laffer curve. After witnessing the Proposition 13 movement in his home state of California, Reagan became convinced that tax reform could be a winning populist issue in a presidential campaign.[103] Kemp declined to mount his own run at the Republican nomination in order to stump for Reagan, and Reagan made Kemp-Roth a focus of his 1980 campaign. He locked up the Republican nomination early, taking the lead after the New Hampshire primary. In February 1980, *New York Times* economic columnist Leonard Silk noted, "It seems clear" that candidate Reagan had "bought the line of 'supply-side economics' forcibly argued by such supporters of his as Representative Jack Kemp of New York, Prof. Arthur Laffer of the University of Southern California and Jude Wanniski, former associate editor of *The Wall Street Journal*." Remarking that these three had recently spent twenty hours over a three-day span briefing Reagan on economic issues, he concluded that "the great debate of 1980 could turn out to be demand-side versus supply-side economics."[104]

If so, then supply-side won, for Reagan routed Jimmy Carter in a landslide. In 1981, the Reagan-backed Economic Recovery Tax Act cut rates by 23 percent over three years and provided that tax brackets would be indexed to inflation beginning in 1985. Within a relatively short period, the tax cut, combined with Reagan's fervent dedication to increasing the size of the military, led to large deficits. The president, seeing the need for revenue, began to look at eliminating loopholes, much as Carter had done only a few years before. Many observers believed that such "tax expenditures" had gotten far too lenient, and Reagan again pushed for a major overhaul of the tax code, this time crusading as a tax reformer. Although the Tax Reform Act of 1986 eliminated many tax expenditures, it also lowered rates across the board: the

President Ronald Reagan on television in 1981, speaking in support of the Economic Recovery Tax Act. The chart next to him notes the Republican efforts to combat bracket creep by indexing marginal tax rates to inflation. (Courtesy Ronald Reagan Library)

top corporate rate dropped from 48 percent to 34 percent, and the highest marginal individual rate fell from 50 percent to 28 percent.[105]

Prior to the economic upheavals of the 1970s, the idea of lowering the top marginal income tax rates did not occupy a significant place in conservative thinking. The runaway inflation and high tax rates of the stagflation era, however, made cutting taxes a high priority, as evidenced by the development of supply-side economic theory, the Proposition 13 campaign, and the Reagan tax policies. In the wake of these developments, conservative economic thinking came to dominate policy and theory debates. Thus, the approach to government economic intervention that characterized the late twentieth- and early twenty-first centuries emphasized the return of government funds to citizens themselves. As memories of the 1970s began to fade, however, the initial motivation for this priority was largely forgotten, and conservatives began to view tax cutting less as an economic tool to be deployed under specific circumstances and more as something that was, in itself, inherently positive.

These are the intellectual and political assumptions that, as of this writing, define current political assumptions. It is not clear how long this particular moment will last. American intellectual and political history has been characterized by a succession of ideological frameworks within which partisans have engaged in vigorous debates over the appropriate nature and function of government intervention in the economy. If the duration of previous periods is any guide to the future, the intellectual hegemony of conservative antitax assumptions might be winding down. A new era, with its own animating ideas regarding the proper role of government in the economy, could well be on the horizon. What its concerns are likely to be, however, is not for the historian to say.

Conclusion

Democratic Capitalism in the United States

When viewed from the perspective of public political ideas about economic policy, the early twenty-first century still appears to fit comfortably within the conservative period described in this book's final chapter. The most broadly resonant idea regarding government intervention in the economy is that of returning money to the citizens in the form of tax cuts, and appeals to the intrusive nature of government spending and regulation still move broad swaths of the population. Of course, some developments suggest otherwise. The two major political parties exhibit a rough parity, trading control of various offices from time to time. Each has its own geographic and political centers of power. And the growing tolerance and even celebration of minority groups, the environment, homosexuality, and counterculturalism writ large suggest a certain social liberalism. On economic issues, however, conservative presumptions circumscribe the universe of perceptions and choices. The contemporary Republican Party grounds support for its policies, at least rhetorically, on the position that taxation and regulation are the enemies of innovation and entrepreneurialism. Liberalism, in either its New Deal articulation as the belief that a meaningful individualism is impossible without government support or in its midcentury incarnation in the principle that American values require the wide sharing of the nation's prosperity, no longer strikes a chord with the public. Democrats have been retreating on their commitment to the welfare state for two generations; today, they favor free trade and, by historical standards, low taxes. The Reagan revolution, in short, has succeeded in pushing mainstream economic discourse firmly to the right.

But the modern-day celebration of a self-sufficient people resentful of an intrusive and imposing federal bureaucracy signifies an aspiration rather than a description. It represents neither the Americans of today nor those of the past. Government actions have always affected the fates of individual economic players. Today, the federal income tax deduction on a home mortgage rewards those who buy and sell houses, thereby altering the market incentives that might otherwise have led some to develop or lease rental properties. When the military chooses one state over another for the location of a new base or when a highway is constructed near one town rather than a different one, those who live in the favored region receive an economic windfall that is denied to residents of the unlucky locale. Both immigration policies and public schooling significantly alter the carrots and sticks that shape the market for labor. Food and Drug Administration regulations affect the cost of agricultural products and medicine, altering the conditions under which individuals make their decisions. And the criminal code's outright ban on some goods and services—such as prostitution and many recreational drugs—impedes the efficiency of markets in those items while boosting demand for the construction of prisons. The list of similar examples is literally endless. In the process of carrying out its legitimate functions, the American government cannot help but alter market outcomes, often significantly.

Those who object to these actions on the grounds that they tamper with otherwise impersonal market forces neglect the important fact that such policies frequently arise in response to the demands of particular constituencies. In other words, the actions that clearly thwart the ideals of capitalism are justified by another intellectual tradition that is equally central to the American self-image: democracy. Government intervention in private markets has consistently characterized American political economy since at least as far back as Hamilton's *Report on Manufactures,* but this characteristic is not so much a violation of sacred capitalist principles as it is an indication of the fact that these values continually and inevitably collide with democratic ones.

Liberalism, Democracy, and Capitalism

That both democracy and capitalism are significant touchstones in the United States makes choosing between them difficult, yet the need to make public policy means that such decisions will always be necessary. Additionally, democracy and capitalism are both the intellectual progeny of Liberalism. To challenge their compatibility is therefore to raise questions about the influence, integrity, and robustness of that philosophical approach throughout the history of the United States.

The quest for an appropriate application of Liberalism has animated much of the nation's intellectual and political history. Americans have consistently turned to Liberal themes to articulate the nation's highest ideals, just as many of the country's most heated conflicts have been fought by groups who subscribed to competing interpretations of that same orientation. This is because the values at the heart of Liberalism—liberty and equality—are themselves in conflict. Capitalism is oriented around the first of those poles, democracy the second. The conflict between them is not an inexplicable anomaly within Liberalism but an embodiment of that tradition's central tension.

Today, it is only a small exaggeration to claim that everyone in the United States is a Liberal. Despite leftist academics' infatuation with early twentieth-century socialism, that tradition has never threatened mainstream American Liberalism. To cite one example, the high-water mark of Socialist presidential fortunes came in 1912, when Eugene V. Debs won 6 percent of the popular vote. And American conservatism, when compared to its Burkean cousin, reveals itself to be merely an intramural squabble within the country's Liberal tradition. The European strain of conservatism developed specifically to elevate the role of tradition in order to balance liberty against other concerns, but its American offshoot is essentially a defense of freedom over competing values. If, as is often argued, Barry Goldwater's 1964 presidential campaign marked the seminal moment in defining contemporary conservatism, the candidate's famous remark that "extremism in the defense of liberty is no vice"[1] should clearly mark the Liberal twang that conservatism had acquired in its migration across the pond.

Yet Liberalism has taken different forms as Americans have adapted their chief political philosophy to the challenges of a given day. Freedom is very much the watchword in the contemporary political climate, whereas equality takes a distant second; furthermore, the illiberal interest in security since September 11, 2011, might yet derail the Liberal emphasis entirely. This devotion to freedom, though, is only the most frequently cited criterion of Liberalism, not the only one. The rejection of feudal hierarchies was a central impetus in the founding of Liberalism, and libertarianism alone is not sufficient to that task. A more direct refutation of this idea is found in the egalitarian notion that no human being is superior to any other. This notion is as central to Liberalism as is the respect for individual liberty. Political philosopher Amy Gutmann argued that Liberalism can be distinguished from older political traditions specifically by its emphasis on egalitarianism. "It is only modern *[L]iberal* theorists," she wrote, "who overwhelmingly deny previous claims of a natural hierarchy, while contending that a just state must be conceived on the basis of an assumption of human equality."[2]

In the United States, Liberalism has meant a commitment to equality as much as to freedom. The most treasured words of the Declaration of Independence cede no prominence to egalitarianism for the sake of liberty: "We hold these truths to be self evident, that all men are created equal, that they are endowed by their Creator with certain inalienable [r]ights, that among these are [l]ife, [l]iberty and the pursuit of [h]appiness."[3] The ideal of equality has played a significant role in many important American political movements; revolution, abolition, suffrage, civil rights, and feminism are perhaps only the most prominent. In short, American Liberalism inherits from its classical forebear not only an emphasis on liberty but also an equally strong commitment to equality.

But by far the most significant application of Liberal equality in the United States is the country's democratic form of government. Rhetorically, democracy is often celebrated as the application of liberty, but this common trope is mistaken. The business of government is as often to restrict freedom as to expand it. The animating principle of democracy is not freedom but equality. Political scientist Robert Dahl has noted that democracy would be "little more than a philosophical fantasy were it not for the persistent and widespread influence of the belief that human beings are intrinsically equal in a fundamental way."[4] Capitalism, by contrast, is "a system of economic freedom and a necessary condition for political freedom,"[5] according to Milton Friedman. As such, it represents the purest application of the Liberal emphasis on individual liberty, leading Friedman to erroneously locate the drive for equality outside the Liberal tradition: "One must choose. One cannot be both an egalitarian . . . and a [L]iberal."[6]

The Nature of Government Economic Intervention

The fact that Liberalism contains impulses toward both freedom and equality does not mean that it has incorporated them successfully or well. The tradition itself offers few answers about how to balance these competing priorities. "Unfortunately, liberty and equality often conflict," wrote legal and political philosopher Ronald Dworkin; "sometimes the only effective means to promote equality require some limitation of liberty, and sometimes the consequences of promoting liberty are detrimental to equality."[7] This conflict lies at the root of any number of the issues that perennially dog Liberal societies. Does freedom of religion require that the state treat every spiritual practice the same, including those that impose on individuals who do not belong to the given faith? Should the ideal of racial equality justify a ban on hate speech? At what point, if any, does the equal right to communal goods such as clean air and water supersede the liberty to engage in activity that causes environmental damage? Among the most direct conflicts between these principles, however, is the clash between political and economic mandates. If for no other reason than that government activity limits economic liberty through the process of taxation, all state actions inevitably restrict freedom in some way, even while expanding equality (or other, different freedoms). Public schools increase the equality of opportunity when governments reduce liberty by requiring children to attend them. The racial equality that affirmative action programs promote also limits the opportunities of the members of the majority group. Government economic subsidies aim to create jobs in the private sector, but they also limit the success of competitor firms and industries.

Squaring this circle appears to present an intractable problem. Indeed, a philosophically elegant solution is unlikely to present itself. Yet the intellectual history of the most influential approaches to government economic intervention in the United States reveals a set of implicit guidelines regarding the nation's political economy. The system that these ideas have animated, notwithstanding its faults, has sustained an impressive level of public commitment, stability, and growth. This history is consequently a crucial one, and it reveals three major points. The first of these is that laissez-faire is neither theoretically neutral nor historically primary. The idea that the economy can and should function with little or no government stewardship is not, as its advocates frequently imply, the purest, most natural approach to political economy. Instead, it is but one orientation among several that have enjoyed primacy at different periods in the nation's history. The second major conclusion to draw from this history is that the country's intellectuals and elected officials have always been willing and able to use the political process to impose a specific vision on the economy. Those who object to economic intervention on the grounds that the government should not "pick winners and losers," by implying that such actions are foreign to the nation's experience, invoke a tradition that simply does not exist.

The fact that political victors have had a wide latitude to shape the purpose of the economy suggests that, in some sense, the country has committed to democracy more strongly than to capitalism. But the concepts of private property and the market have played a prominent historical role in the nation's production, consumption, and distribution of goods, not to mention its self-understanding. The third and final major point, then, concerns the method by which this economic guidance has taken place. Even within a structure imposed by the broad popularity of capitalist ideas and institutions, politics can play a significant role in defining the purpose of what that economy is supposed to achieve. The history of the United States has seen federal policies that have been designed, among many other goals, to provide economic stability and military security, limit the reach of the powerful, promote property rights, guarantee employment, increase economic opportunity for the poor, and lower taxes. Because pursuing one of these ideals often imposes difficulties in realizing the others, the particular goal in play at any given moment represents an expression of priorities rather than some neutral technocratic abstention from economic policy.

To garner support for their particular priorities, intellectuals and politicians offer arguments and images to make their economic vision look attractive. Every so often, the voters pass judgment on these perspectives by selecting candidates whose vision of the economy meshes most neatly with their own. Thus, political economy in the United States is indeed characterized by a system in which the policies that determine the broad purpose of the economy are subject to democratic forces. Despite the tension between liberty and equality, it is a system of democratic capitalism.

Today, some on the left argue that democratic capitalism is impossible as long as money plays as significant a role as it currently does in the political process. Conservatives, however, hold that without safeguards against the incursion of politics into the realm of economic activity, socialism is the likely result. Both sets of critics are mistaken. The American electorate has consistently proven itself capable, when roused to do so, of reining in the power of wealth; that it often resists this course of action attests less to its impotence than to its conservatism. At the same time, the free enterprise system is far more malleable than its most passionate advocates appear to believe. The impossibility of an economically neutral policy does not suggest that government should restrain itself from influencing the economy. Instead, it means that the influence it will inevitably wield should be subject to some check by the people. Throughout the history of the United States, hegemonic ideas of the economy's overall purpose have consistently shaped, sometimes substantially, the conditions under which individuals and firms compete. Yet the institutions of private property, economic liberty, and the market have invariably enjoyed wide and robust support. It is the specific nature of government economic intervention, rather than its mere existence, that defines the character of American democratic capitalism.

Notes

Introduction: The Idea of Government
Economic Intervention

1. Roger Lowenstein, *The End of Wall Street* (New York: Penguin Press, 2010), 37–38.

2. Paul Krugman, "Making Things in America," *New York Times,* May 20, 2011, A34.

3. For detailed accounts of the events of September 2008, see Andrew Ross Sorkin, *Too Big to Fail* (New York: Viking Press, 2009), and Lowenstein, *End of Wall Street.*

4. "Santelli's Tea Party," CNBC, accessed on September 2, 2011, http://video .cnbc.com/gallery/?video=1039849853#eyJ2aWQiOiIxMDM5ODQ5ODUzIi wiZW5jVmlkIjoiUkZ5Zi9qTi9yUVUoeU13djlURoRhZzo9IiwidlRhYiI6InRyY5 zY3JpcHQiLCJ2UGFnZSI6MSwiZo5hdiI6WyLCoExhdGVzdCBWaWRlbyJd LCJnU2VjdCI6IkFMTCIsImdQYWdlIjoiMSIsInN5bSI6IiIsInNlYXJjaCI6IiJ9.

5. Tea Party Patriots, "Mission Statement and Core Values," accessed on September 2, 2011, http://www.teapartypatriots.org/Mission.aspx.

6. William F. Buckley, Jr., "Our Mission Statement," National Review Online, accessed on September 4, 2011, http://www.nationalreview.com/articles/223549/ our-mission-statement/william-f-buckley-jr; Ronàld Reagan, "Letter to the Speaker of the House of Representatives and the President of the Senate Transmitting the Annual Economic Report of the President," January 10, 1989, in *Papers of the Presidents: Reagan* (Washington, DC: US Government Printing Office, 1991), 1988–1989:1709; Amity Shlaes, *The Forgotten Man: A New History of the Great Depression* (New York: HarperCollins, 2007), 6.

7. The use of the term *libertarian* throughout this book should be understood to refer to persons, texts, and arguments that are primarily concerned with promoting and/or preserving economic freedom as expressed through unimpeded markets. The intent of using it is to disentangle this particular strain of modern American conservatism from others with different primary concerns, e.g., national security, religious expression, or social issues. The purpose is most definitely *not* to

take any position on the movement that specifically refers to itself as "libertarian" and that usually eschews the "conservative" label.

Chapter 1: Stewardship

1. Kevin Baker, "The Magic Reagan: More Misguided Arguments for His Greatness," *Harper's Magazine*, May 2002, 73.

2. James Madison, "Federalist Number Fifty-One," in *The Federalist*, ed. J. R. Pole (Indianapolis, IN: Hackett Publishing, 2005), 281.

3. Thomas Jefferson, "Letter to George Washington," in *Jefferson: Writings*, ed. Merrill D. Peterson (New York: Library of America, 1984), 994.

4. Hamilton submitted other reports to Congress, for example, a *Report on the Mint* in early 1791, which inspired some legislation, and a few follow-ups to the *Report on the Public Credit*. (Indeed, the *Report on a National Bank* was technically one such addendum.) But the three mentioned here are the most significant.

5. Alexander Hamilton, "Report on the Public Credit," in *Hamilton: Writings*, ed. Joanne B. Freeman (New York: Library of America, 2001), 534.

6. Cathy D. Matson and Peter S. Onuf, *A Union of Interests: Political and Economic Thought in Revolutionary America*, ed. Wilson Carey McWilliams and Lance Banning (Lawrence: University Press of Kansas, 1990), 31–49.

7. Hamilton, "Report on the Public Credit," 534–535.

8. Ibid., 535.

9. Ron Chernow, *Alexander Hamilton* (New York: Penguin Press, 2004), 305.

10. Hamilton, "Report on the Public Credit," 540. Emphases in original.

11. Ibid., 543.

12. Ibid.

13. Joseph J. Ellis, *Founding Brothers: The Revolutionary Generation* (New York: Alfred A. Knopf, 2000), 57.

14. For more on this dinner and its broader context, see ibid., 48–80.

15. Hamilton, "Letter to James Duane," in *Hamilton: Writings*, ed. Joanne B. Freeman (New York: Library of America, 2001), 83–84.

16. The idea of the "common" person that predominated in the early national American political classes bears little relation to that concept as deployed today. This understanding excluded not only blacks, Indians, and women but also a large number of white men, for those who did not own property could not even vote. Though the idea of positioning a slaveholding plantation owner as a common person might seem somewhat ludicrous to modern readers, the framework that gave rise to such an understanding was both sincerely held and tremendously important to those who believed it.

17. Quoted in Chernow, *Alexander Hamilton*, 351–352.

18. Ibid., 347.

19. Hamilton, "Report on a National Bank," in *Hamilton: Writings,* ed. Joanne B. Freeman (New York: Library of America, 2001), 576–577.

20. Ibid., 580.

21. Frederic C. Lane, "At the Roots of Republicanism," *American Historical Review* 71, no. 2 (1966): 580.

22. Hamilton, "Report on a National Bank," 584.

23. James Madison, "Speech in Congress Opposing the National Bank," in *Madison: Writings,* ed. Jack Rakove (New York: Library of America, 1999), 484.

24. Ibid., 485. Emphases in original.

25. Thomas Jefferson, "Opinion on the Constitutionality of a National Bank," in *Jefferson: Writings,* ed. Merrill D. Peterson (New York: Library of America, 1984), 418. Emphases in original.

26. Ibid., 420. Emphasis in original.

27. Hamilton, "Opinion on the Constitutionality of a National Bank," 644.

28. Ibid., 613. Emphases in original.

29. Ibid., 626. Emphases in original.

30. Ibid., 619. Emphases in original.

31. Ibid., 621.

32. The president himself was not a member of either party. His thinking, however, tended to align him more often with the Federalists. Washington was held in such broad veneration and Hamilton's influence was so great within the administration that it was the secretary of the Treasury, not the president, who served as both the leader of the Federalist Party and the object of considerable Republican ire.

33. Joyce Appleby, "Liberalism and Republicanism in the Historical Imagination," in *Liberalism and Republicanism in the Historical Imagination* (Cambridge, MA: Harvard University Press, 1992), 1.

34. John Locke, *The Second Treatise on Civil Government* (Amherst, NY: Prometheus Books, 1986), sect. 6.

35. Louis Hartz, *The Liberal Tradition in America* (New York: Harcourt, Brace and World, 1955).

36. Bernard Bailyn, *The Ideological Origins of the American Revolution,* enlarged ed. (Cambridge, MA: Belknap Press of Harvard University Press, 1992); J. G. A. Pocock, *The Machiavellian Moment: Florentine Political Thought and the Atlantic Republican Tradition,* new ed. (Princeton, NJ: Princeton University Press, 2003); Gordon S. Wood, *The Creation of the American Republic, 1776–1787* (New York: W. W. Norton, 1972).

37. Linda K. Kerber, "The Republican Ideology of the Revolutionary Generation," *American Quarterly* 37, no. 4 (1985): 475.

38. Bailyn, *Ideological Origins of the American Revolution,* 23.

39. Wood, *Creation of the American Republic*, 52.

40. Ibid.

41. Gordon Wood, "Ideology and the Origins of Liberal America," *William and Mary Quarterly* 44, no. 3 (1987): 634.

42. Ibid., 184.

43. James Madison, "Fashion," in *Madison: Writings*, ed. Jack Rakove (New York: Library of America, 1999), 514. Emphasis in original.

44. Thomas Jefferson, "Letter to John Jay," in *Jefferson: Writings*, ed. Merrill D. Peterson (New York: Library of America, 1984), 818.

45. Joyce Appleby, "What Is Still American in Jefferson's Political Philosophy," in *Liberalism and Republicanism in the Historical Imagination* (Cambridge, MA: Harvard University Press, 1992), 312.

46. Joyce Appleby, "The 'Agrarian Myth' in the Early Republic," in *Liberalism and Republicanism in the Historical Imagination* (Cambridge, MA: Harvard University Press, 1992), 269.

47. Peter S. Onuf, "Making Sense of Jefferson," in *The Mind of Thomas Jefferson* (Charlottesville: University of Virginia Press, 2007), 27.

48. Herbert E. Sloan, *Principle and Interest: Thomas Jefferson and the Problem of Debt*, ed. Jan Ellen Lewis and Peter S. Onuf (Charlottesville: University of Virginia Press, 2001), 5.

49. Madison, "Fashion."

50. Thomas Jefferson, "Notes on the State of Virginia," in *Jefferson: Writings*, ed. Merrill D. Peterson (New York: Library of America, 1984), 290–291.

51. Drew R. McCoy, *The Elusive Republic: Political Economy in Jeffersonian America* (New York: W. W. Norton, 1982), 7.

52. Ibid., 19.

53. Ibid., 236–237.

54. Ibid., 70–75.

55. Thomas Jefferson, "Letter to James Madison," in *Jefferson: Writings*, ed. Merrill D. Peterson (New York: Library of America, 1984), 918.

56. McCoy, *Elusive Republic*, 85.

57. Hamilton, "Opinion on the Constitutionality of a National Bank," 132.

58. Hamilton, "Letter to Edward Carrington," in *Hamilton: Writings*, ed. Joanne B. Freeman (New York: Library of America, 2001), 738. The quoted passage is entirely italicized in the original.

59. Hamilton, "Report on the Subject of Manufactures," in *Hamilton: Writings*, ed. Joanne B. Freeman (New York: Library of America, 2001), 647.

60. Ibid., 649. Emphasis in original.

61. Jefferson, "Notes on the State of Virginia," 291.

62. Hamilton, "Report on the Subject of Manufactures," 656.

63. Ibid., 668.

64. Ibid., 668–669.

65. Ibid., 669.

66. Ibid., 671.

67. Ibid., 680.

68. Ibid., 681. Emphases in original.

69. Stanley Elkins and Eric McKitrick, *The Age of Federalism: The Early American Republic, 1788–1800* (New York: Oxford University Press, 1993), 301.

70. Edward Chancellor, *Devil Take the Hindmost: A History of Financial Speculation* (New York: Farrar, Straus and Giroux, 1999), xi.

71. Jefferson, "Letter to George Washington," 986.

72. Hamilton, "Report on the Subject of Manufactures," 699, 700.

73. Ibid., 701.

74. McCoy, *Elusive Republic*, 159.

75. Quoted in Douglas A. Irwin, "The Aftermath of Hamilton's 'Report on the Subject of Manufactures,'" *Journal of Economic History* 64, no. 3 (2004): 805n10.

76. James Madison, "Spirit of Governments," in *Madison: Writings*, ed. Jack Rakove (New York: Library of America, 1999), 511, 510.

77. This fact was then apparent even to Adam Smith. Hamilton, however, expressed little concern over it, going so far as to claim in the *Report on the Subject of Manufactures* that one advantage of manufacturing was that it could tap into the underutilized labor of women and children.

78. James Madison, "Republican Distribution of Citizens," in *Madison: Writings*, ed. Jack Rakove (New York: Library of America, 1999), 512–513.

79. James Madison, "Property," in *Madison: Writings*, ed. Jack Rakove (New York: Library of America, 1999), 516–517.

80. James Madison, "The Union: Who Are Its Real Friends?," *Madison: Writings*, ed. Jack Rakove (New York: Library of America, 1999), 517–518.

81. Irwin, "Aftermath of Hamilton's 'Report,'" 806–813.

82. Thomas Jefferson, "Letter to Benjamin Austin," in *Jefferson: Writings*, ed. Merrill D. Peterson (New York: Library of America, 1984), 1371.

Chapter 2: Divorce

1. H. W. Brands, *Andrew Jackson: His Life and Times* (New York: Anchor Books, 2006), 294.

2. James Madison, "The Federalist Number 10," in *The Federalist Papers*, ed. Garry Wills (New York: Bantam Books, 1982), 46.

3. John Quincy Adams, "First Annual Message," The American Presidency Project, accessed on March 23, 2013, http://www.presidency.ucsb.edu/ws/index.php?pid=29467.

4. James D. Richardson, ed., *Messages and Papers of the Presidents, 1789–1897* (Washington, DC: Published by Authority of Congress, 1898), 2:448.

5. Ibid., 3:296.

6. Alexander Keyssar, *The Right to Vote: The Contested History of Democracy in the United States* (New York: Basic Books, 2000), 5.

7. James Fenimore Cooper, *The American Democrat* (New York: Vintage Books, 1956), 142.

8. Quoted in Keyssar, *Right to Vote*, 27.

9. Ibid., 29. This book also features several tables in the appendix that list the various restrictions on the right to vote in effect in different states at different times. For anyone interested in this topic, these are an invaluable resource.

10. Ibid., xxi.

11. Alexis de Tocqueville, *Democracy in America,* trans. George Lawrence (New York: HarperPerennial, 1988), 50.

12. Ibid., 204.

13. Ibid., 210.

14. Ibid., 96.

15. Ibid., 237.

16. Ibid., 255.

17. Ibid., 474.

18. Ibid., 494.

19. Ibid., 452.

20. This claim might be less ludicrous than it sounds when considered against the fact that the time in which Tocqueville was writing coincided with the height of not only Jacksonianism but also transcendentalism. That doctrine's insistent paeans to nature make it about as pantheistic as a radical individualism can be.

21. Tocqueville, *Democracy in America*, 403.

22. George Rogers Taylor, *The Transportation Revolution, 1815–1860* (White Plains, NY: M. E. Sharpe, 1951).

23. Jeremy Atack and Peter Passell, *A New Economic View of American History from Colonial Times to 1940,* 2nd ed. (New York: W. W. Norton, 1994), 167.

24. Ibid., 178.

25. Charles Sellers, *The Market Revolution: Jacksonian America, 1815–1846* (Oxford: Oxford University Press, 1991).

26. John Lauritz Larson, *The Market Revolution in America: Liberty, Ambition and the Eclipse of the Common Good* (Cambridge: Cambridge University Press, 2009), 9.

27. Ibid., 9, 11.

28. Tocqueville, *Democracy in America*, 393.

29. Harry L. Watson, *Liberty and Power: The Politics of Jacksonian America* (New York: Hill and Wang, 1990), 10–11.

30. Ibid., 307.

31. Ibid., 59.

32. Ibid., 306–307.

33. Richard Hofstadter, *The American Political Tradition and the Men Who Made It* (New York: Vintage Books, 1989), 65.

34. Joseph Dorfman, "The Jackson Wage-Earner Thesis," *American Historical Review* 54, no. 2 (1949): 305–306.

35. Sean Wilentz, *The Rise of American Democracy: Jefferson to Lincoln* (New York: W. W. Norton, 2005), xix.

36. Ibid., 513.

37. Herbert Hovenkamp, *Enterprise and American Law: 1836–1937* (Cambridge, MA: Harvard University Press, 1991), 5.

38. Ibid., 2.

39. Ibid., 4.

40. "Discount" refers to what was then a common form of loan repayment in which the interest was deducted from the principal on payment of the original loan. The borrower was then responsible for repaying the original principal rather than the principal plus interest, as is more common today. The "discount function" of a bank thus refers to its capacity to loan money.

41. Arthur M. Schlesinger, *The Age of Jackson* (Boston: Little, Brown, 1953), 525.

42. The first national currency was the "United States note"—the infamous "greenback" that would cause so much trouble after the Civil War—authorized by the Legal Tender Act of 1862.

43. In fact, a modern dollar bill actually *is* a note, issued by the Federal Reserve.

44. Wilentz, *Rise of American Democracy*, 440.

45. Atack and Passell, *New Economic View*, 92–93.

46. Quoted in Ralph C. H. Catterall, *The Second Bank of the United States* (Chicago: University of Chicago Press, 1960), 19n5.

47. Wilentz, *Rise of American Democracy*, 361.

48. Bray Hammond, *Banks and Politics in America from the Revolution to the Civil War* (Princeton, NJ: Princeton University Press, 1957).

49. Though Jackson had vowed to "kill" the bank, his veto did not technically do so but only denied it a federal charter. After the federal charter expired in 1836, the bank struggled on for a few more years with a charter from Pennsylvania.

50. Catterall, *Second Bank of the United States*, 239.

51. Richardson, *Messages and Papers of the Presidents*, 2:581.

52. Ibid., 2:582–587.

53. Ibid., 2:590.

54. Ibid., 3:301.

55. Ibid.

56. Ibid., 3:302.

57. Ibid., 3:303.

58. When Jackson protested this action, the Senate refused to enter his note to that effect into its journal. A few years later, Jackson's reliable ally, Senator Thomas

Hart Benton of Missouri, succeeded in passing a motion to expunge the censure from the Senate record.

59. Quoted in Brands, *Andrew Jackson*, 500. Emphasis in original.

60. Daniel Walker Howe, *The Political Culture of the American Whigs* (Chicago: University of Chicago Press, 1979), 13.

61. Ibid., 12.

62. Ibid., 101–102.

63. Wilentz, *Rise of American Democracy*, 485–486.

64. Major L. Wilson, *The Presidency of Martin Van Buren*, ed. Donald R. McCoy, Clifford S. Griffin, and Homer E. Socolofsky (Lawrence: University Press of Kansas, 1985), 43.

65. Richardson, *Messages and Papers of the Presidents*, 3:328.

66. Ibid.

67. Ibid.

68. Ibid., 3:329.

69. Ibid., 3:330.

70. Ibid., 3:332.

71. Ibid.

72. Ibid.

73. Ibid., 3:333.

74. Ibid.

75. Ibid., 3:334.

76. Ibid., 3:344.

77. Ibid.

78. Wilson, *Presidency of Martin Van Buren*, 134.

79. *Congressional Globe* 8, no. 26 (1840): 406.

80. "Appendix to the Congressional Globe, for the First Session, Twenty-Sixth Congress: Containing Speeches and Important State Papers," *Congressional Globe* 8 (1840): 523.

81. Ibid., 557.

82. Quoted in Wilson, *Presidency of Martin Van Buren*, 203.

83. After Harrison died in office, his successor, John Tyler, proved to be even less amenable to the Whig plan to restore a national bank. The Democrats regained power in 1844, and in 1846, they passed an independent treasury act that was virtually identical to the previous one. The independent treasury system stored and managed the nation's specie until the establishment of the Federal Reserve in 1913.

Chapter 3: Property

1. "Excerpts from Two Wilson Hearings before Senate Committees on Defense Appointment," *New York Times*, January 24, 1953, 8.

2. Wilson, for the record, was confirmed after agreeing to sell his stock.

3. Charles E. Lindblom, *Politics and Markets: The World's Political-Economic Systems* (New York: Basic Books, 1977), 5.

4. Richard Hofstadter, *The American Political Tradition and the Men Who Made It* (New York: Alfred A. Knopf, 1976), 213.

5. Charles W. Calhoun, "The Political Culture: Public Life and the Conduct of Politics," in *The Gilded Age: Perspectives on the Origins of Modern America,* ed. Charles W. Calhoun (Lanham, MD: Rowman & Littlefield, 2007), 239, 251.

6. Robert G. McCloskey (revised by Sanford Levinson), *The American Supreme Court,* ed. Daniel J. Boorstin, 4th ed. (Chicago: University of Chicago Press, 2005), 69.

7. Morton J. Horwitz, "*Santa Clara* Revisited: The Development of Corporate Theory," *West Virginia Law Review* 88, no. 2 (1985): 173.

8. John Micklethwait and Adrian Wooldridge, *The Company: A Short History of a Revolutionary Idea* (New York: Modern Library, 2005), 17–18.

9. William G. Roy, *Socializing Capital: The Rise of the Large Industrial Corporation in America* (Princeton, NJ: Princeton University Press, 1997), 49.

10. Some political intrigue motivated this attempted power grab as well. New Hampshire's governor, William Plumer, was a Republican. The Dartmouth board of trustees represented one of the few remaining Federalist strongholds in the state, but the school's perpetual charter rendered it untouchable by outside political forces. Daniel Webster, the Dartmouth alumnus who eloquently presented the college's case to the Supreme Court, was also a Federalist at the time.

11. *Trustees of Dartmouth College v. Woodward,* 17 U.S. 518, 625, 27 (1819).

12. Ibid., 636–637.

13. Ibid., 638.

14. Gregory A. Mark, "The Personification of the Business Corporation in American Law," *University of Chicago Law Review* 54 (Fall 1987): 1454.

15. Hovenkamp, *Enterprise and American Law,* 33.

16. Stuart Weems Bruchey, "Corporation: Historical Development," in *The Changing Economic Order: Readings in American Business and Economic History,* ed. Alfred Dupont Chandler, Stuart Weems Bruchey, and Louis Galambos (New York: Harcourt, Brace and World, 1968), 145. The Jackson quote appears there as well.

17. Naomi R. Lamoreaux, "Table Ch392–401, Business Incorporations in New England, by Industry and Type of Incorporation Law: 1700–1875," in *Historical Statistics of the United States: Earliest Times to the Present,* Millennial Edition, ed. Susan B. Carter, Scott Sigmund Gartner, Michael R. Haines, Alan L. Olmstead, Richard Sutch, and Gavin Wright (New York: Cambridge University Press, 2006), pt. C, p. 548.

18. Alan Trachtenberg, *The Incorporation of America: Culture and Society in the Gilded Age* (New York: Hill and Wang, 1994), 83.

19. Horwitz, "*Santa Clara* Revisited," 181.

20. Locke, *Second Treatise on Civil Government*, 49.

21. *Scott v. Sandford*, 60 U.S. 393, 407 (1857).

22. Hovenkamp, *Enterprise and American Law*, 118.

23. *Slaughter-House Cases*, 83 U.S. 36, 2 (1873).

24. Ibid., 11–12.

25. Campbell also presented other arguments that were not based on the Fourteenth Amendment. One such effort was the rather preposterous claim that in denying the butchers the unfettered use of their own land and livestock, the state of Louisiana had effectively enslaved these men in violation of the Thirteenth Amendment. The majority decision paid this argument little heed.

26. McCloskey, *American Supreme Court*, 79.

27. This *is* the specific meaning of another part of the amendment, the equal protection clause. That clause, however, does not restrict the ability of states to make laws but only requires them to enforce consistently whatever laws they do make. Consequently, it was of little use to Campbell.

28. *Slaughter-House Cases*, 37.

29. At least, he does not make this point in the transcript, which makes clear that Campbell argued the case "at great length." Consequently, the court reporter could not "pretend to give more than such an abstract of the argument as may show to what the opinion of the Court was meant to be responsive." *Slaughter-House Cases*, 18.

30. Ibid., 38.

31. Ibid., 53.

32. Ibid., 66.

33. Ibid., 70.

34. Ibid., 71–72.

35. Ibid., 76–78.

36. Ibid., 109–110.

37. Ibid., 93.

38. Ibid., 94–95.

39. Ibid., 96.

40. Ibid., 97.

41. *Corfield v. Coryell*, 6 F. Cas. 546, 551–552 (1823).

42. *Slaughter-House Cases*, 112.

43. Ibid., 120.

44. Ibid., 127.

45. Robert Green McCloskey, *American Conservatism in the Age of Enterprise: 1865–1910* (New York: Harper Torchbooks, 1951), 90. Emphasis in original.

46. Ibid., 114.

47. Michael A. Ross, *Justice of Shattered Dreams: Samuel Freeman Miller and the Supreme Court during the Civil War Era* (Baton Rouge: Louisiana State University Press, 2003), 189.

48. See Ronald M. Labbé and Jonathan Lurie, *The Slaughterhouse Cases: Regulation, Reconstruction, and the Fourteenth Amendment* (Lawrence: University of Kansas Press, 2003), and Ross, *Justice of Shattered Dreams.*

49. Akhil Reed Amar, *The Bill of Rights: Creation and Reconstruction* (New Haven, CT: Yale University Press, 1998), 213.

50. *County of Santa Clara v. Southern Pacific Railroad Company*, 18 Fed Reporter 385, 390 (1883). Emphasis in original.

51. *Santa Clara County v. Southern Pacific Railroad Company*, 118 U.S. 394, 416 (1886).

52. Ibid.

53. Horwitz, "*Santa Clara* Revisited," 173.

54. U.S. Code, Title 15, Chapter 1, Section 7.

55. Connecticut General Life Insurance Company v. Johnson, Treasurer of California, 303 U.S. 77, 90 (1938).

56. Hovenkamp, *Enterprise and American Law*, 12.

57. *Santa Clara County v. Southern Pacific Railroad Company*, 411.

58. *County of Santa Clara v. Southern Pacific Railroad Company*, 391. Emphasis in original.

59. Ibid., 394–395.

60. Ibid., 395–396.

61. Ibid., 397.

62. Ibid., 403.

63. Ibid., 404. Emphases in original.

64. Ibid., 405.

65. Jeffrey Rosen, *The Most Democratic Branch: How the Courts Serve America*, ed. Kathleen Hall Jamieson and Jaroslav Pelikan (Oxford: Oxford University Press, 2006), 16–17.

66. "Supreme Court Decisions: No Jurisdiction in the Polygamy Cases/California Railway Taxes," *New York Times*, May 11, 1886, 2.

67. "The Tax Cases: The Railroads Are Not Exempt from Taxation, but—Field's and Sawyer's Decisions: The Value of the Mortgages Must Be Assessed to the Holders—the Freights and Fares Case," *San Francisco Daily Examiner*, September 19, 1883.

68. "Railroad Taxes," *San Francisco Daily Examiner*, September 18, 1883.

69. Martin J. Sklar, *The Corporate Reconstruction of American Capitalism, 1890–1916* (Cambridge: Cambridge University Press, 1988), 13.

70. Walt Whitman, "Our Real Culmination," in *Complete Prose Works* (Philadelphia: David McKay, 1892), 337.

71. Henry C. Adams, "Relation of the State to Industrial Action," *Publications of the American Economic Association* 1, no. 6 (1887): 13.

72. Sklar, *Corporate Reconstruction of American Capitalism*, 5–6.

73. Quoted in Trachtenberg, *Incorporation of America*, 84.

74. Richard T. Ely, "Social Studies I: The Nature and Significance of Corporations," *Harper's New Monthly Magazine*, May 1887, 971.

75. Ibid., 975.

76. Ibid., 975–976.

77. Richard T. Ely, "Social Studies II: The Growth of Corporations," *Harper's New Monthly Magazine*, June 1887, 78.

78. Richard T. Ely, "Social Studies III: The Future of Corporations," *Harper's New Monthly Magazine*, July 1887, 260.

79. Ibid., 261.

80. Ely, "Social Studies II," 73; *County of Santa Clara v. Southern Pacific Railroad Company*, 405.

81. McCloskey, *American Supreme Court*, 88.

82. Hovenkamp, *Enterprise and American Law*, 42–43. Emphasis in original.

Chapter 4: Employment

1. Harvey L. Schantz and Richard H. Schmidt, "The Evolution of Humphrey-Hawkins," *Policy Studies Journal* 8, no. 3 (1979): 369.

2. Helen Ginsburg, "Historical Amnesia: The Humphrey-Hawkins Act, Full Employment and Employment as a Right," *Review of Black Political Economy* 39 (2012): 130–131.

3. Schantz and Schmidt, "Evolution of Humphrey-Hawkins," 372.

4. "The Cruel Hoax of Humphrey-Hawkins," *New York Times*, February 28, 1978.

5. Ginsburg, "Historical Amnesia, 135–136.

6. Michael R. Haines, "Table Aa 716–775, Population, by Race, Sex, and Urban-Rural Residence: 1880–1990," in *Historical Statistics of the United States: Earliest Times to the Present*, Millennial Edition On Line, ed. Susan B. Carter, Scott Sigmund Gartner, Michael R. Haines, Alan L. Olmstead, Richard Sutch, and Gavin Wright (New York: Cambridge University Press, 2006), vol. 1.

7. Russell H. Conwell, *Acres of Diamonds* (New York: Harper & Brothers, 1915), 17.

8. Ibid., 18, 21.

9. Richard Hofstadter, *The Age of Reform: From Bryan to F. D. R.* (New York: Vintage Books, 1955), 132.

10. Richard Ely, "The Evolution of Industrial Society," in *The Social and Political Thought of American Progressivism*, ed. Eldon J. Eisenach (Indianapolis, IN: Hackett Publishing, 2005), 57.

11. Louis D. Brandeis, "What Publicity Can Do," *Harper's Weekly*, December 20, 1913, 10.

12. 15 U.S.C.S., § 1, July 2, 1890.

13. William J. Hausman and John L. Neufeld, "How Politics, Economics and Institutions Shaped Electric Utility Regulation in the United States: 1879–2009," *Business History* 53, no. 5 (2011): 724.

14. Michael McGerr, *A Fierce Discontent: The Rise and Fall of the Progressive Movement in America* (New York: Oxford University Press, 2003), 306.

15. Ronald D. Rotunda, *The Politics of Language: Liberalism as Word and Symbol* (Iowa City: University of Iowa Press, 1986), 22–25.

16. David W. Noble, "Herbert Croly and American Progressive Thought," *Western Political Quarterly* 7, no. 4 (1954): 537.

17. David K. Nichols, "The Promise of Progressivism: Herbert Croly and the Progressive Rejection of Individual Rights," *Publius* 17, no. 2 (1987): 27.

18. Herbert Croly, *The Promise of American Life* (Boston: Northeastern University Press, 1989), 20, 22.

19. Ibid., 39, 40.

20. Ibid., 42.

21. Ibid., 43.

22. Ibid., 88.

23. Ibid., 104.

24. Ibid., 116.

25. Ibid., 204–205.

26. Ibid., 149.

27. Ibid., 152.

28. Ibid., 371.

29. Ibid., 380.

30. Ibid., 418.

31. Ibid., 173–174.

32. An important theme of the article was the juxtaposition of nationalism and partisanship in the Wilson administration and the president's conflicting Jeffersonian and Hamiltonian aspects. These tropes suggest Croly as the piece's author.

33. "Woodrow Wilson," *New Republic*, June 24, 1916, 186.

34. Rotunda, *Politics of Language*, 39.

35. Alan Ryan, *John Dewey and the High Tide of American Liberalism* (New York: W. W. Norton, 1997), 36.

36. John Dewey, *Liberalism and Social Action* (Amherst, NY: Prometheus Books, 2000), 35.

37. Ibid.

38. Ibid., 54.

39. This calculation is based on information from Richard Sutch, "Table Ca 208–212, Gross National Product: 1869–1929 [Standard Series]," in *Historical Statistics of the United States: Earliest Times to the Present*, Millennial Edition On Line,

ed. Susan B. Carter, Scott Sigmund Gartner, Michael R. Haines, Alan L. Olmstead, Richard Sutch, and Gavin Wright (New York: Cambridge University Press, 2006), vol. 3.

40. Maury Klein, *Rainbow's End: The Crash of 1929*, ed. David Hackett Fischer and James M. McPherson (New York: Oxford University Press, 2001), 103, xvii–xix.

41. "Financial Markets: Prices of Stocks Move More Irregularly—Money Rates Unchanged, Sterling Quiet," *New York Times*, August 21, 1929.

42. David Kennedy, *Freedom from Fear: The American People in Depression and War, 1929–1945*, ed. C. Vann Woodward (New York: Oxford University Press, 1999), 38, 39.

43. Ibid., 35.

44. Ibid., 43–59; Richard Sutch, "Table Ca 74–90, Gross Domestic Product, by Major Component, 1929–2002," in *Historical Statistics of the United States: Earliest Times to the Present*, Millennial Edition, ed. Susan B. Carter, Scott Sigmund Gartner, Michael R. Haines, Alan L. Olmstead, Richard Sutch, and Gavin Wright (New York: Cambridge University Press, 2006).

45. Kennedy, *Freedom from Fear*, 65–68.

46. Ibid., 70.

47. Susan B. Carter, "Table Ba 470–477, Labor Force, Employment, and Unemployment: 1890–1990," in *Historical Statistics of the United States: Earliest Times to the Present*, Millennial Edition, ed. Susan B. Carter, Scott Sigmund Gartner, Michael R. Haines, Alan L. Olmstead, Richard Sutch, and Gavin Wright (New York: Cambridge University Press, 2006); Kennedy, *Freedom from Fear*, 70.

48. William E. Leuchtenburg, *Franklin D. Roosevelt and the New Deal* (New York: Harper Torchbooks, 1963), 13.

49. Martin L. Fausold, *The Presidency of Herbert Hoover*, ed. Donald R. McCoy, Clifford S. Griffin, and Homer E. Socolofsky (Lawrence: University Press of Kansas, 1985), 155.

50. Roy Jenkins, completed with the assistance of Richard E. Neustadt, *Franklin Delano Roosevelt*, ed. Arthur Schlesinger, Jr. (New York: Times Books, 2003), 4.

51. T. R. B., "Washington Notes," *New Republic*, November 23, 1932, 43.

52. "The Week," *New Republic*, October 5, 1932, 189.

53. Franklin Delano Roosevelt, "Commonwealth Club Campaign Speech," in *Franklin D. Roosevelt: Selected Speeches, Messages, Press Conferences, and Letters*, ed. Basil Rauch (New York: Holt, Rinehart and Winston, 1964), 77–79.

54. Ibid., 80–81.

55. Ibid., 82–83.

56. Franklin Delano Roosevelt, "First Inaugural Address," in ibid., 91–93.

57. Franklin Delano Roosevelt, "Acceptance Speech," in ibid., 74.

58. Kennedy, *Freedom from Fear*, 135–136.

59. Michael Hiltzik, *The New Deal: A Modern History* (New York: Free Press, 2011), 73.

60. Kennedy, *Freedom from Fear*, 144; Hiltzik, *New Deal*, 66–68.

61. Jason Scott Smith, *Building New Deal Liberalism: The Political Economy of Public Works, 1933–1956* (New York: Cambridge University Press, 2006), 22, 2.

62. Kennedy, *Freedom from Fear*, 252–253.

63. Franklin Delano Roosevelt, "Statement upon Signing the Social Security Act," in *Franklin D. Roosevelt: Selected Speeches, Messages, Press Conferences, and Letters*, ed. Basil Rauch (New York: Holt, Rinehart and Winston, 1964), 144.

64. Hofstadter, *Age of Reform*, 307–308.

65. Alan Brinkley, *The End of Reform: New Deal Liberalism in Recession and War* (New York: Vintage Books, 1996), 3.

66. Ellis W. Hawley, *The New Deal and the Problem of Monopoly: A Study in Economic Ambivalence* (New York: Fordham University Press, 1995), 12, 13.

67. Ira Katznelson, *Fear Itself: The New Deal and the Origins of Our Time* (New York: W. W. Norton, 2013), 64, 65.

68. Arthur Crock, "Court Is Unanimous: President Cannot Have 'Roving Commission' to Make Laws by Code," *New York Times*, May 28, 1935.

69. Hiltzik, *New Deal*, 261–284; Kennedy, *Freedom from Fear*, 177–189.

70. Hiltzik, *New Deal*, 280.

71. Brinkley, *End of Reform*, 18–19.

72. Kennedy, *Freedom from Fear*, 363.

73. Brinkley, *End of Reform*, 3.

74. Hawley, *New Deal and the Problem of Monopoly*, 149.

75. Ibid., 429–430.

76. Wilson D. Miscamble, "Thurman Arnold Goes to Washington: A Look at Antitrust Policy in the Later New Deal," *Business History Review* 56, no. 1 (1982): 5.

77. Brinkley, *End of Reform*, 111.

78. Ibid., 121.

79. Ibid., 122.

80. Steve Lohr, "F.D.R.'s Example Offers Lesson for Obama," *New York Times*, January 27, 2009.

81. Nicholas Wapshott, *Keynes Hayek: The Clash That Defined Modern Economics* (New York: W. W. Norton, 2011), 154–170.

82. John Maynard Keynes, *The General Theory of Employment, Interest, and Money* (Amherst, NY: Prometheus Books, 1997), 3.

83. Ibid., 89.

84. Ibid., 16.

85. Robert M. Collins, *The Business Response to Keynes, 1929–1964* (New York: Columbia University Press, 1981), 7.

86. Keynes, *General Theory*, 15.

87. Of course, this is not true of money that is saved under a mattress or in a private safe, rather than at a bank or investment firm. (The same pertains if banks or corporations hold excess funds in the form of cash reserves.) From the perspective of the economy, this money has simply disappeared, as surely as a shipload of bills that was lost at sea. (It will "reappear," having lost value to inflation, at some point in the future when its owners decide to spend or invest it.) Thus, economists do not consider those funds to have been saved at all, and they differentiate the two practices by referring to holding cash as "hoarding."

88. Certainly, workers would leave an employer who refused to raise wages in response to an increase in the cost of living if opportunities for better-paying jobs existed elsewhere. But Keynes was considering the entire economy. If the average cost of living rose and the typical wage remained the same, there would be nowhere else for these workers to go.

89. Keynes, *General Theory*, 274.

90. Steven Kates, "'Supply Creates Its Own Demand': A Discussion of the Origins of the Phrase and of Its Adequacy as an Interpretation of Say's Law of Markets," *History of Economics Review* 41 (Winter 2005): 49–60.

91. Keynes, *General Theory*, 274.

92. Ibid., 289.

93. Ibid., 381.

94. Ibid., 368, 210.

95. Ibid., 378.

96. Ibid., 381.

97. Brinkley, *End of Reform*, 7.

98. Franklin D. Roosevelt, "Franklin D. Roosevelt: Annual Message to Congress on the State of the Union," The American Presidency Project, accessed on June 24, 2013, http://www.presidency.ucsb.edu/ws/index.php?pid=16092; Cass Sunstein, *The Second Bill of Rights: FDR's Unfinished Revolution and Why We Need It More Than Ever* (New York: Basic Books, 2006), 82–83.

99. Roosevelt, "Franklin D. Roosevelt: Annual Message to Congress," 339.

100. Ibid., 340.

101. Ibid., 346–347.

102. Franklin D. Roosevelt, "Franklin D. Roosevelt: State of the Union Address," The American Presidency Project, accessed on June 24, 2013, http://www.presidency.ucsb.edu/ws/index.php?pid=16595&st=state+of+the+union&st1=.

103. Louis Hartz, *The Liberal Tradition in America* (New York: Harcourt, Brace and World, 1955), 271; Sean Wilentz, "Cherry-Picking Our History," *New York Review of Books*, February 21, 2012, 15.

104. John C. Culver and John Hyde, *American Dreamer: The Life and Times of Henry A. Wallace* (New York: W. W. Norton, 2000), 51–52.

105. Ibid., 158, 70, 73, 227.

106. The Twenty-Second Amendment, ratified in 1951, later disallowed any president from serving more than two complete terms.

107. Kennedy, *Freedom from Fear*, 332–333; Leuchtenburg, *Franklin D. Roosevelt and the New Deal*, 252–253.

108. Henry Luce, "The American Century," *Life*, February 17, 1941, 63.

109. Henry Agard Wallace and Russell Lord, *The Century of the Common Man* (New York: Reynal and Hitchcock, 1943), 19, 20.

110. Henry Agard Wallace, *Sixty Million Jobs* (New York: Reynal and Hitchcock, 1945), 12, 4.

111. Ibid., 14, 39, 15.

112. Culver and Hyde, *American Dreamer*, 452, 478.

113. Wallace, *Sixty Million Jobs*, 33, 69, 72.

114. Ibid., 152–153.

115. Ibid., 153.

116. Ibid.

117. Alvin Hansen, "The Wallace Goal," *New Republic*, September 17, 1945, 353.

118. Brinkley, *End of Reform*, 229.

119. Stephen Kemp Bailey, *Congress Makes a Law: The Story behind the Employment Act of 1946*, 1st ed. (New York: Vintage Books, 1950), 47 (reprinted in 1964).

120. "The 'Full Employment' Bill," *New York Times*, June 5, 1945.

121. Collins, *Business Response to Keynes*, 105.

122. Ginsburg, "Historical Amnesia," 127.

123. Culver and Hyde, *American Dreamer*, 481, 64.

124. Ibid., 501.

Chapter 5: Inequality

1. Eric Bentley, ed., *Thirty Years of Treason: Excerpts from Hearings before the House Committee on Un-American Activities, 1938–1968* (New York: Viking Press, 1971), 608, 609, 610.

2. Ibid., 604.

3. Daniel J. Boorstin, *The Genius of American Politics* (Chicago: University of Chicago Press, 1953), 6.

4. The editors of *Fortune*, in collaboration with Russell W. Davenport, *U.S.A.: The Permanent Revolution* (New York: Prentice-Hall, 1951), 41, 116. Emphasis in original.

5. Ibid., 168–169.

6. Ibid., 189.

7. Eisenhower did possess a hard edge as both a committed cold warrior and a pragmatic politician. He had the Central Intelligence Agency overthrow the dem-

ocratically elected governments of Iran and Guatemala in 1953 and 1954, respectively, out of a fear that they might be sympathetic to communism. In 1956, however, Eisenhower succumbed to a more practical fear of geopolitical consequences and did *not* intervene when the Hungarian people revolted against their Soviet-controlled government. For better or worse, these sorts of actions played little to no role in defining Eisenhower's public persona, then or now.

8. Daniel Bell, *The End of Ideology* (Cambridge, MA: Harvard University Press, 1988), 402–403.

9. Lionel Trilling, *The Liberal Imagination: Essays on Literature and Society* (Garden City, NY: Doubleday Anchor, 1953), vii.

10. Rick Perlstein, *Before the Storm: Barry Goldwater and the Unmaking of the American Consensus* (New York: Hill and Wang, 2002), xi. Emphasis in original.

11. Kevin Mattson, *When America Was Great* (New York: Routledge, 2006), 13–14.

12. George H. Nash, *The Conservative Movement in America since 1945* (New York: Basic Books, 1976), xiii; Kim Phillips-Fein, *Invisible Hands: The Businessmen's Crusade against the New Deal* (New York: W. W. Norton, 2010), xii.

13. Mattson, *When America Was Great*, 14.

14. Kevin Mattson, "Arthur Schlesinger, Jr.," *Proceedings of the American Philosophical Society* 153, no. 1 (2009): 115–126, quote on 119.

15. Arthur Schlesinger, Jr., *The Vital Center* (New Brunswick, NJ: Transaction Publishers, 2005), 4, 7–8.

16. Ibid., 9, xxi.

17. Ibid., 37–38.

18. Ibid., 36, 116.

19. Ibid., 182–183.

20. Ibid., 29, 32.

21. Godfrey Hodgson, *America in Our Time: From World War II to Nixon—What Happened and Why* (Princeton, NJ: Princeton University Press, 2005), 76.

22. See Robert M. Collins, *More: The Politics of Economic Growth in Postwar America* (New York: Oxford University Press, 2000). Statistics are from p. 41.

23. John Kenneth Galbraith, *The Affluent Society* (Boston: Houghton Mifflin, 1958), 18.

24. Ibid., 75–77.

25. Ibid., 82.

26. Ibid., 95.

27. Ibid., 115–120.

28. Ibid., 135.

29. Ibid., 253–255.

30. Ibid., 272–275.

31. Ibid., 259–260.

32. Ibid., 296–302.

33. Ibid., 309.

34. Ibid., 317.

35. Kevin Mattson, "John Kenneth Galbraith: Liberalism and the Politics of Cultural Critique," in *American Capitalism: Social Thought and Political Economy in the Twentieth Century*, ed. Nelson Lichtenstein (Philadelphia: University of Pennsylvania Press, 2006), 106.

36. Economically speaking, the Russian program was mostly a success, the Chinese experience a colossal failure. Both were characterized, however, by massive cruelty and major human rights violations. The two governments conducted these affairs with such secrecy, however, that it remained possible for others around the world to see communism as a way out of economic stagnation. Given, also, that many developing nations had borne the brunt of Western colonialism, the peoples of the developing world were often more open to communism than Americans could believe or accept.

37. "The Two Worlds: A Day Long Debate," *New York Times*, July 25, 1959, 1.

38. W. W. Rostow, *The Stages of Economic Growth: A Non-Communist Manifesto*, 3rd ed. (Cambridge: Cambridge University Press, 1999), 5.

39. Ibid., 6–7.

40. Ibid., 10.

41. Ibid., 73–74.

42. Ibid., 81.

43. Ibid., 91.

44. Ibid., 148.

45. Ibid., 149–150.

46. Ibid., 150.

47. Ibid., 159–164.

48. Michael Harrington, *The Other America: Poverty in the United States* (New York: Scribner, 2012), 1.

49. Ibid., 3, 5, 6.

50. Ibid., 164–165.

51. Ibid., 162.

52. Ibid., 170.

53. Ibid., 171.

54. Ibid., 173.

55. Dwight Macdonald, "Our Invisible Poor," *New Yorker*, January 19, 1963.

56. Carl M. Brauer, "Kennedy, Johnson and the War on Poverty," *Journal of American History* 69, no. 1 (1982): 101.

57. Ibid., 103–116.

58. "Text of President Johnson's Special Message on Poverty Presented to Congress," *New York Times*, March 17, 1964, 22.

59. Ibid.

60. Michael L. Gillette, ed., *Launching the War on Poverty: An Oral History*

(New York: Oxford University Press, 2010), xiii–xiv; Irwin Unger, *The Best of Intentions: The Triumphs and Failures of the Great Society under Kennedy, Johnson and Nixon* (New York: Doubleday, 1996), 350.

61. Doris Kearns Goodwin, *Lyndon Johnson and the American Dream* (New York: St. Martin's Griffin, 1991), 251–252.

62. See Perlstein, *Before the Storm*. The quote is from p. 198.

63. Jefferson Cowie, *Stayin' Alive: The 1970s and the Last Days of the Working Class* (New York: New Press, 2010), 6.

64. Thomas Pogge, *John Rawls: His Life and Theory of Justice*, trans. Michelle Kosch (New York: Oxford University Press, 2007), 3.

65. The Modern Library, "The Modern Library 100 Best Nonfiction," accessed on August 30, 2008, http://www.randomhouse.com/modernlibrary/100bestnonfiction.html.

66. In 1995, Rawls published an article in *Dissent* magazine on the morality of the American use of the atomic bomb. It was the only time that he ever wrote on a specific public political issue. He opposed the bombing.

67. John Rawls, "Justice as Fairness," in *John Rawls: Collected Papers*, ed. Samuel Freeman (Cambridge, MA: Harvard University Press, 1999), 47–72.

68. The biographical sketch is based on material in Pogge, *John Rawls*, 3–27, and Ben Rogers, "Behind the Veil," *Lingua Franca* 9, no. 5 (1999): 57–64.

69. John Rawls, *A Theory of Justice* (Cambridge, MA: Harvard University Press, 1971), vii–viii.

70. Ibid., viii.

71. Ibid., 7.

72. Ibid., 12.

73. Ibid., 104.

74. Ibid., 74.

75. Ibid., 102.

76. Ibid., 150–151.

77. Ibid., 78.

78. Ibid., 61, 303.

79. Ibid., 275.

80. Ibid., 103.

81. Ibid.

82. Marshall Cohen, "*A Theory of Justice*, by John Rawls," review of *A Theory of Justice*, by John Rawls, *New York Times*, July 16, 1972.

83. "Five Significant Books of 1972," *New York Times*, December 3, 1972.

84. "Rawls Is Given Two Awards for Book on Justice Theory," *Harvard Crimson*, December 7, 1972, accessed on January 18, 2014, http://www.thecrimson.com/article/1972/12/7/rawls-is-given-two-awards-for-/.

85. Rogers, "Behind the Veil," 58.

Chapter 6: Taxes

1. "The Republicans in New Orleans; Transcipt [*sic*] of Bush Speech Accepting Nomination for President," *New York Times*, August 19, 1988. The newspaper apparently printed the advance version of the speech, as the paper's copy differs slightly from Bush's remarks as delivered. The other excerpts from the speech have been taken from the newspaper account, but the "read my lips" quotation was transcribed verbatim from a video of the speech that is posted online by the Miller Center for Public Policy at the University of Virginia. "Acceptance Speech at the Republican National Convention (August 18, 1988)," Miller Center for Public Affairs at the University of Virginia, accessed on May 21, 2012, http://millercenter .org/president/speeches/detail/5526.

2. John Robert Greene, *The Presidency of George Bush*, ed. Homer E. Socolofsky (Lawrence: University Press of Kansas, 2000), 37.

3. Ibid., 187.

4. George Will characterized early American conservatism as "remarkably bookish" in his introduction to Barry Goldwater, *The Conscience of a Conservative*, ed. Sean Wilentz (Princeton, NJ: Princeton University Press, 2007), x.

5. Patrick Henry, "Speeches of Patrick Henry," in *The Anti-Federalist Papers and the Constitutional Convention Debate*, ed. Ralph Ketcham (New York: Penguin Putnam, 1986), 200.

6. Indeed, Friedrich Hayek eschewed the description "conservative" (as did Ayn Rand, for different reasons), and he expressed frustration that his preferred label, "classical Liberal," had been so tarnished by political liberalism that it was no longer available to thinkers of his ilk. The members of Hayek's Mont Pelerin Society were never able to come up with an appropriate name for their philosophy, suggesting, perhaps, that Hayek was a bit out of step with the intellectual currents of his own time. For more, see Angus Burgin, *The Great Persuasion: Reinventing Free Markets since the Great Depression* (Cambridge, MA: Harvard University Press, 2012).

7. Phillips-Fein, *Invisible Hands*, 13, 10, 26.

8. Henry Hazlitt, "An Economist's View of 'Planning,'" *New York Times*, September 24, 1944, BR1; Wapshott, *Keynes Hayek*, 202.

9. F. A. Hayek, *The Road to Serfdom* (Chicago: University of Chicago Press, 1994), 15–16.

10. For more on this point, see Burgin, *Great Persuasion*.

11. Hayek, *Road to Serfdom*, 41–43.

12. Ibid., 97.

13. Ibid., 95.

14. Internal Revenue Service, "Table 23, U.S. Individual Income Tax: Personal Exemptions and Lowest and Highest Bracket Tax Rates, and Tax Base for Regular

Tax, Tax Years 1913–2008," accessed on January 19, 2014, http://www.irs.gov/uac
/SOI-Tax-Stats-Historical-Table-23.

15. Among the conservative intellectual touchstones were William F. Buckley,
Jr., *God and Man at Yale* (Washington, DC: Gateway, 2002); Russell Kirk, *The Conservative Mind: From Burke to Eliot*, 7th rev. ed. (Washington, DC: Regnery Publishing, 2001), and Whittaker Chambers, *Witness*, rev. ed. (Washington, DC: Regnery Publishing, 1987).

16. For more on the difficult relationship between Rand and mainstream conservatism, see Jennifer Burns, *Goddess of the Market: Ayn Rand and the American Right* (New York: Oxford University Press, 2009).

17. Milton Friedman, *Capitalism and Freedom*, 40th Anniversary ed. (Chicago: University of Chicago Press, 2002). The sales figure is given on the cover.

18. Ibid., 8.

19. Ibid., 13.

20. Also referred to as "spillovers" or, more technically, "market externalities," these scenarios are among the most frequently cited in critiques of capitalism. Pollution is perhaps the most common example. In such a scenario, an economic actor may contract with suppliers, workers, landlords, and other relevant parties to manufacture a product. But if the manufacturing process pollutes the nearby environment, then the factory's neighbors are exposed to negative experiences without having agreed to them or being compensated for them. Thus, market transactions do not, in this circumstance, capture the true cost of the good.

21. Friedman, *Capitalism and Freedom*, 33–34.

22. Ibid., 35–36.

23. Ibid., 168–172.

24. Milton Friedman and Anna Jacobson Schwartz, *A Monetary History of the United States: 1867–1960* (Princeton, NJ: Princeton University Press, 1963), 10.

25. Ibid., 301.

26. Milton Friedman, *The Counter-Revolution in Monetary Theory* (London: Institute of Economic Affairs, 1970), 24, 27.

27. Perlstein, *Before the Storm*, 27.

28. Ibid., 34–42, 63.

29. Goldwater, *Conscience of a Conservative*, xxi.

30. Perlstein, *Before the Storm*, 64.

31. Goldwater, *Conscience of a Conservative*, 9.

32. Ibid., 12–13.

33. Ibid., 15. In the original, the first sentence appears entirely in italics.

34. Ibid.

35. Ibid., 85. Emphasis in original.

36. Ibid., 36, 37. In the original, both of these quotations appear entirely in italics.

37. Ibid., 40, 41.

38. Ibid., 64–65. In the original, the sentence beginning "Welfarism . . . " is entirely in italics.

39. Geoffrey Kabaservice, *Rule and Ruin: The Downfall of Moderation and the Destructon of the Republican Party, from Eisenhower to the Tea Party*, Kindle ed. (New York: Oxford University Press, 2011), location 1686.

40. Goldwater, *Conscience of a Conservative*, 12, 62, 69.

41. Ibid., 58.

42. Lou Cannon, *Reagan* (New York: G. P. Putnam's Sons, 1982), 32, 88–97; Cannon, *Ronald Reagan: The Role of a Lifetime* (New York: Simon & Schuster, 1991), 282–288; Phillips-Fein, *Invisible Hands*, 111–114.

43. Cannon, *Reagan*, 13, 98–103. The quote is on p. 98.

44. Ibid., 98.

45. Ronald Reagan, "A Time for Choosing," The Ronald Reagan Presidential Foundation and Library, accessed on May 30, 2012, http://www.reaganfoundation.org/pdf/ATimeForChoosing.pdf.

46. Meg Jacobs, *Pocketbook Politics: Economic Citizenship in Twentieth-Century America* (Princeton, NJ: Princeton University Press, 2005), 3.

47. Annual inflation rates are notoriously difficult to measure. Since it is impossible to measure the price of all goods or to isolate the decline in the value of money from the increased demand for a specific good, those wishing to track inflation generally establish a "basket" of goods that they believe is representative of typical economic purchases; then they compare the basket's price to what it would have cost the year before. Since different sources will base their calculations on different goods, they tend to publish a consumer price index (CPI), a measure that will vary depending on what goods are included in the basket and how the price of the basket is computed, rather than an actual inflation rate. All annual inflation rates cited here were obtained by dividing the difference between the CPI for a given year and for the previous year by the previous year's CPI. The CPI itself is listed in Peter H. Lindert and Richard Sutch, "Table Cc 1–2, Consumer Price Indexes, for All Items: 1774–2003," in *Historical Statistics of the United States: Earliest Times to the Present*, Millennial Edition, ed. Susan B. Carter, Scott Sigmund Gartner, Michael R. Haines, Alan L. Olmstead, Richard Sutch, and Gavin Wright (New York: Cambridge University Press, 2006).

48. Richard Nixon and H. R. Haldeman, "Transcript of a Recording of a Meeting between the President and H. R. Haldeman in the Oval Office on June 23, 1972 from 10:04 to 11:39 AM," Nixon Presidential Library and Museum, accessed on October 15, 2012, http://www.nixonlibrary.gov/forresearchers/find/tapes/watergate/wspf/741-002.pdf.

49. Allen J. Matusow, *Nixon's Economy: Booms, Busts, Dollars and Votes* (Lawrence: University Press of Kansas, 1998), 18–19.

50. Ibid., 35.

51. Ibid., 74–75.

52. Sutch, "Table Ca 74–90"; Carter, "Table Ba 470–477"; Lindert and Sutch, "Table Cc 1–2."

53. "Nixon Economic Rating Drops to 22% in Poll," *New York Times*, August 10, 1971, 21.

54. Richard Nixon, "Address to the Nation Outlining a New Economic Policy: The Challenge of Peace," The American Presidency Project, October 1, 2012, http://www.presidency.ucsb.edu/ws/?pid=3115.

55. "Nixon Reportedly Says He Is Now a Keynesian," *New York Times*, January 7, 1971, 19; Nixon, "Address to the Nation."

56. Matusow, *Nixon's Economy*, 187–192; Lindert and Sutch, "Table Cc 1–2."

57. Matusow, *Nixon's Economy*, 192–198, 220.

58. Robert D. McFadden, "Few Shoppers Are Pleased by the Meat Price Ceilings," *New York Times*, March 31, 1973, 1.

59. "The Lasting, Multiple Hassles of Topic A," *Time*, April 9, 1973, 96.

60. "Gallup Poll Finds One Third Will Eat Less Meat," *New York Times*, May 17, 1973, 20.

61. Matusow, *Nixon's Economy*, 230–234.

62. Ira D. Guberman, "3 Months on the Gasoline Lines; Lines and Wait Lengthen," *New York Times*, April 7, 1974, 11; Matusow, *Nixon's Economy*, 265–269.

63. John Robert Greene, *The Presidency of Gerald R. Ford* (Lawrence: University Press of Kansas, 1995), 68.

64. "Transcript of the President's Economic Address to a Joint Session of Congress," *New York Times*, October 9, 1974, 24.

65. Greene, *Presidency of Gerald R. Ford*, 75.

66. Gerald Ford, "Gerald R. Ford: Address to the Nation on Energy and Economic Programs," The American Presidency Project, accessed on October 18, 2012, http://www.presidency.ucsb.edu/ws/index.php?pid=4916&st=&st1=.

67. Greene, *Presidency of Gerald R. Ford*, 77.

68. Ibid., 80.

69. Lindert and Sutch, "Table Cc 1–2"; Carter, "Table Ba 470–477."

70. Matusow, *Nixon's Economy*, 284.

71. The account of the development of supply-side economics is taken from Brian Domitrovic, *Econoclasts: The Rebels Who Sparked the Supply-Side Revolution and Restored American Prosperity*, Kindle ed. (Wilmington, DE: ISI Books, 2009).

72. Quoted in ibid., location 2294.

73. Ibid., location 1851.

74. Ibid., location 2091–2099.

75. Internal Revenue Service, "2011 Tax Table," accessed on November 9, 2012, http://www.irs.gov/pub/irs-pdf/i1040tt.pdf; John Joseph Wallis, "Table Ea 773–826, Federal Income Tax Rates, by Income Group—Average and Marginal Rates: 1968–2000," in *Historical Statistics of the United States: Earliest Times to the*

Present, Millennial Edition, ed. Susan B. Carter, Scott Sigmund Gartner, Michael R. Haines, Alan L. Olmstead, Richard Sutch, and Gavin Wright (New York: Cambridge University Press, 2006).

76. Jude Wanniski, "It's Time to Cut Taxes," *Wall Street Journal*, December 11, 1974, 18.

77. Jude Wanniski, "The Mundell-Laffer Hypothesis," *Public Affairs*, no. 39 (1975): 31–52. Nearly all of the words in the original quotations were italicized.

78. Ibid., 50n.

79. Ibid., 50.

80. Bruce Bartlett, "The Origin of Modern Republican Fiscal Policy," *New York Times*, accessed on October 20, 2012, http://economix.blogs.nytimes.com/2012/03/20/the-origin-of-modern-republican-fiscal-policy/.

81. Jude Wanniski, "Taxes and a Two-Santa Theory," *National Observer*, March 6, 1976, 7–14.

82. Irving Kristol, "Toward a 'New Economics'?," *Wall Street Journal*, May 9, 1977, 20.

83. Richard Brookhiser et al., "The 100 Best Non-fiction Books of the Century," *National Review* 51, no. 8 (1999): 46–47.

84. Jude Wanniski, *The Way the World Works*, 4th ed. (Washington, DC: Regnery Publishing, 1998), 9.

85. Ibid., 13.

86. Ibid., 47–48.

87. Ibid., 84.

88. Ibid., 96.

89. Ibid., 97.

90. Ibid.

91. Ibid., 99.

92. Domitrovic, *Econoclasts*, location 2960.

93. Howard Jarvis, *I'm Mad as Hell: The Exclusive Story of the Tax Revolt and Its Leader* (New York: Times Books, 1979), 32–36, 38–41.

94. Ibid., 193.

95. Ibid., 178–179.

96. Simon Hall, *American Patriotism, American Protest: Social Movements since the Sixties* (Philadelphia: University of Pennsylvania Press, 2011), 101–105.

97. Daniel A. Smith, "Howard Jarvis, Populist Entrepreneur: Reevaluating the Causes of Proposition 13," *Social Science History* 23, no. 2 (1999): 187.

98. Jarvis, *I'm Mad as Hell*, 118.

99. Ibid., 125. Emphasis in original.

100. Ibid., 188.

101. "All Aboard the Bandwagon!," *Time* 111 (June 26, 1978): 8–11.

102. Domitrovic, *Econoclasts*, locations 2532–2806, 3216–3255.

103. W. Elliot Brownlee, *Federal Taxation in America: A Short History*, 2nd ed. (Washington, DC: Woodrow Wilson Center Press and Cambridge University Press, 2004), 140.

104. Leonard Silk, "Economic Scene: Reagan Camp's Young Bloods," *New York Times*, February 29, 1980, D2.

105. Brownlee, *Federal Taxation in America*, 150, 74.

Conclusion: Democratic Capitalism in the United States

1. Barry Goldwater, "Goldwater's 1964 Acceptance Speech," Washington Post, accessed on July 30, 2008, http://www.washingtonpost.com/wp-srv/politics/daily/may98/goldwaterspeech.htm.

2. Amy Gutmann, *Liberal Equality* (Cambridge: Cambridge University Press, 1980), 18. Emphasis in original.

3. Thomas Jefferson, "Declaration of Independence," in *The Declaration of Independence and the Constitution of the United States*, ed. Pauline Maier (New York: Bantam Classic, 1998), 53.

4. Robert Dahl, *Democracy and Its Critics* (New Haven, CT: Yale University Press, 1989), 85.

5. Friedman, *Capitalism and Freedom*, 4.

6. Ibid., 195.

7. Ronald Dworkin, "Liberalism," in *Public and Private Morality*, ed. Stuart Hampshire (Cambridge: Cambridge University Press, 1978), 123.

Index